WO CUP GLORY

Peter Jenkins and David Campese

Follow The Wallabies

Published in Australia by
SANDSTONE PUBLISHING,
Unit 1, 360 Norton Street, Leichhardt, NSW, 2040

Jenkins, Peter, 1962–

World Cup glory: Peter Jenkins and David Campese follow the Wallabies.

ISBN 1 86505 139 X.

1.Campese, David. 2. Jenkins, Peter, 1962 — 3. Wallabies (Rugby team).
4. World Cup (Rugby Union football), (1999). 5. Rugby Union football
— Australia. I. Campese, David. II. Title. III. Title: Peter Jenkins and
David Campese follow the Wallabies.

796.33365

Designed by: Corlette Design, Rushcutters Bay
Typeset by Asset Typesetting Pty Ltd, Marrickville.
Printed by Griffin Press Pty Limited, Netley.

WORLD CUP GLORY

Peter Jenkins and David Campese

Follow The Wallabies

SANDSTONE PUBLISHING

ABOUT THE AUTHORS

PETER JENKINS has been an award-winning rugby union
correspondent for *The Australian* since 1991, covering the past three
World Cups for the national newspaper and the 1987 tournament for
the Daily Telegraph in Sydney. His other major assignments for News
Limited have included the 1996 Olympic Games and 1998
Commonwealth Games. But rugby union remains his passion.
A former first-grade five-eighth with the Parramatta club in Sydney,
he has written about the game at Test level for 15 years. He won
the major print media award for coverage of the Wallabies in 1998,
and carried off the prize again for the most outstanding story of
the 1999 season — a profile of Stephen Larkham and Jannie de
Beer that is reprinted here in *World Cup Glory*. This is his third book,
after collaborating with David Campese on *My Game
Your Game*, and compiling the 100-year history of Australian Test
Rugby, *Wallaby Gold*.

DAVID CAMPESE is a legend of Australian sport and one of the
most lauded figures in the history of international rugby union.
He is the only Wallaby to have played 100 Tests and holds the world
try-scoring record with 64 from his 101 appearances. Campese made
his Australian debut as a teenager on the 1982 Wallaby tour of New
Zealand and remained part of the Test scene for 15 seasons, until
announcing his retirement at the end of a 1996 visit to the UK.
His crowning moment was the 1991 World Cup, when his attacking
brilliance was instrumental in the Wallabies winning the William
Webb Ellis trophy for the first time. Campese was later named the
player of the tournament. Holding strong views on how the game
should be played and never afraid to voice his opinion, he started
writing for *The Australian* newspaper in 1999. During the World Cup,
his columns in *The Australian* were quoted around the world, usually
under back page headlines.

ACKNOWLEDGEMENTS

The authors would like to thank Campbell Reid, editor of
The Australian newspaper, for his kind permission in allowing their
work, published during the tournament, to be reproduced in
World Cup Glory. Appreciation is also extended to Colin Gibson,
Garry Ferris, Chris Stedman and Sarah Dease from *The Australian*
sports desk, for their enthusiasm, encouragement, and support over
the seven weeks of the World Cup. To Deborah Callaghan, author
agent without peer, another heartfelt thank you for behind-the-
scenes efforts above and beyond the call of duty. To the Australian
rugby union team, whose success led to this publication, their
willingness to be available for interviews, both at home and abroad, is
gratefully acknowledged. And to skipper John Eales, the gentleman
captain and a sportsman whose demeanour away from the arenas of
battle is only matched by his on-field talent, the warmest of thanks
for writing the Foreword during a hectic time of travel and
promotional commitments. Congratulations too, on the World Cup
achievement. Champions deserve the highest rewards. Enjoy the
moment.

PETER JENKINS
DAVID CAMPESE

🔺 **THE AUSTRALIAN**

November 1999

FOREWORD
BY JOHN EALES:
captain of the Wallabies

Saturday the 6th of November 1999 will always be a special memory. For the Wallabies it was the culmination of a four-year journey that embraced every emotion.

The World Cup itself was a roller coaster ride of emotions. From the lows of seeing Brett Robinson, Patricio Noriega and Phil Kearns depart through injury to the climax where we realized our dream of being crowned the World Champions. From the nerves felt before and shown during the quarter final against Wales to the composure exhibited in the titanic extra time win over South Africa. And of course the difficulties of being away from home and the exhilaration of our extra long victory lap where players were able to share special moments with family and friends in the crowd.

These were all part of the World Cup journey and the many memories that are very strong in my mind. Unfortunately over time, (mum thinks that it will not be until after I turn at least fifty), the abilities of the human mind and its capacity to remember clearly are lessened. A book like *World Cup Glory* will forever help to fill in the blanks, not only for me but for all those who followed our progress.

This book's biggest advantage is that it is not simply written from memories long after the event but it is partly compiled through articles written as history itself unfolded. This allows the reader to get an accurate feel for the mood of a player, of the public, and of a match, at any time throughout the tournament.

Peter Jenkins is one of the most respected rugby writers the world over. Writing for Australia's major national newspaper he is also one of the most influential. It is comforting to know that the reporting of rugby on a national level is in safe hands.

Peter is also the author of the outstanding book *Wallaby Gold*. That book will always be the definitive history of the first 100 years of Australian rugby. The exhaustive amount of research and the subsequent attention to detail and accuracy observable within the pages of *Wallaby Gold* will long survive as a tribute to Peter as a journalist and as a lover of rugby.

In his day to day role with *The Australian* Peter maintains his high standards. While one may not always agree with what he writes, you can be assured that it is always meticulously thought out before it is logically presented. It is always a pleasure to deal with Peter on both a professional and a personal basis and I wish him the best with this new book, *World Cup Glory*.

David Campese is another writer whose work you may not always agree with however his contribution to Australian rugby cannot be questioned. David is the most capped and probably the most recognisable Wallaby on the international stage and his articles always make for an interesting read.

To all the readers I thank you on behalf of the team for all the support that was given to us while we were at the World Cup. It provided constant motivation for our cause. I hope that the pages of this book will bring back as many happy memories for you as they will for me.

JOHN EALES

November 1999

BILL COMES HOME

As the motorcade snaked its way slowly past the sea of well-wishers lining George Street in central Sydney, the world champion Wallabies, two or three to a car, were dressed in all-gray off-field ensembles that gave them the appearance of hired killers.

It was November 17. The tickertape parade. The heroes' homecoming for an Australian team 11 days into their reign as the kings of rugby union. Streamers fell and paper fluttered from the windows of office blocks lining the route, and beaming faces screamed the names of newfound or long-standing idols. More than 150,000 had turned out to celebrate the World Cup achievement. The success of what was now a band of smiling assassins.

Number eight Toutai Kefu was in the lead car, with his backrow teammates David Wilson and Matt Cockbain. Along with the rest of the squad — a party of playing and coaching personnel that numbered more than 40 — they had left, almost two months before, on a mission to 'Bring Back Bill'. It had been the catchcry to symbolise their campaign in Europe to claim and return with the William Webb Ellis trophy. Six games and seven weeks later, the contract was completed. France had been buried 35–12 in the World Cup final at the Millennium Stadium in Cardiff and Bill, in all his golden glory, could be booked for a flight to Australia.

'That was a magical day,' said Kefu. 'But I think it's only now, sitting at the front of the parade, with all these people out here to see us, this moment that I'll never forget, that it's really sunk in what exactly we've done. Until now, it's been something very personal. But to have people calling your name, people you'll never know, it just makes you realise the importance of it all. How much it has meant to everyone back here. Honestly, I just feel like a big kid. It's something I never thought would happen to me.'

The Sydney procession was one of four staged around the country, with crowds in Melbourne, Brisbane and Canberra also gathering in their thousands to pay tribute to a side that created history by making Australia the first nation to win the World Cup twice. There were civic receptions too, and an endless stream of welcome home functions, including a 1900-strong dinner the night of the Sydney parade, where the Wallabies climbed on stage en masse, linked arms, and sang. They had done the same after receiving the World Cup from the Queen on November 6 in Cardiff. On that occasion their song of choice was *Advance Australia Fair*. At a convention centre in Darling Harbour almost two weeks later it was the John Williamson-penned ballad *True Blue*.

'When we were up there singing, it was as if that was our last moment together,' said Kefu. 'As a team, we're losing a couple of guys to retirement, and form might mean others will come and go as well. But the words of *True Blue*, the lines about standing by your mate, it's exactly what this side has been all about. It's the camaraderie and the spirit. This team has had it in truckloads. It's a special feeling I don't think could ever be matched again.'

Prop Andrew Blades is one Wallaby who will remember the two-try win over France, a victory lap of Millennium Stadium and a guzzle of beer from the guts of Bill as the final highlights of his Test career.

'And after days like today, you just don't want these feelings to end,' he said on the night of the Sydney dinner. 'During the tickertape parade and standing on the balcony of the Town Hall, as we got to do, you want it to go on and on. At the same time, people probably don't realise just what it meant to have the support we did from home. So while we're enjoying the moment, I hope it's also our way of saying thank you to everyone here. It's all a bit mind-blowing for me. And I know I'll never be part of it again. Never be part of what was a very special group of guys.'

It was a Wallaby side that opened its campaign in Belfast on October 3, then worked its way through Dublin, Limerick, Cardiff, London, and back to Cardiff on the first Saturday in November to complete a mission that is only attempted once every four years. The following morning, just 14 hours after being crowned champions, the Wallabies flew out of Britain. And they had Romania, Ireland, USA, Wales, South Africa and France engraved on the gun belt, while the name Australia was engraved on Bill.

'Unbelievable,' said Kefu. 'But you know what the strange thing is. If you ask me for the one moment that I'll never forget from our time over there, it won't come from the playing side of things. What I'll always remember is the day we got there. The day we flew into Ireland. It was 10am when we arrived. By noon we were on the golf course at Portmarnock and, after the round, we all went to the pub for a team bonding session. That's what sticks in my mind more than anything else. It brought us all together very early on and everything seemed to flow from there.'

Kefu was not alone. Winger Joe Roff, asked for his favourite memory, told of the same occasion.

'Having a few Guinness in Ireland that first day, talking about what lies ahead, it finally dawned on us what we were about to embark on,' he said. 'We had spent the previous two years focussing on the World Cup and suddenly it was here. From then on, it was on for young and old. And to achieve what we set out to do then come home and see all those people at the tickertape parades, it was quite bizarre. Even to see a few of the highlights of the World Cup on video now gives me goose bumps. There have been guys from the past, guys from the 1991 World Cup winning side at a few of the functions, and people still say 'there goes so and so'. They're all legends those guys, and maybe in 10 years that sort of thing's going to happen to us.'

If Joe hadn't noticed, it's already happening. It started the day he and his Wallaby mates brought Bill back from Britain.

How It All Began

The seaside resort of Caloundra, an hour's drive north of Brisbane, was sleepily seeing out the final days of autumn, with holiday-makers long gone and the streets near enough to deserted.

It was here, in this tranquil setting on the Queensland Sunshine Coast, in May of 1998, that the Wallabies started a journey, a trek that carried them around the globe and finally to Cardiff for a match to decide the next rugby union world champions.

Australia and France, it had come down to this. The ultimate 80 minutes in front of 73,000 at Millennium Stadium and a billion others watching on television in more than 100 countries. Destination reached — 18 months after the elite of the game from NSW, Queensland and the ACT were brought together at a training camp and presented with a vision for the future.

The chief architect of the master plan was self-made businessman Rod Macqueen, an advertising executive from the northern beaches of Sydney, whose love of the surf rivalled his devotion to an oval ball game, which had brought him minor representative honours as a player and greater recognition in retirement. He had coached NSW in the early 1990's, served as an Australian selector, and was the inaugural coach of the ACT Brumbies when they arrived on the Super 12 scene early in 1996.

Two years later, in the twilight of the millennium, he was preparing to enter his first full season in charge as coach of the Wallabies.

Macqueen had come to the helm the previous October, at a time of turbulence for the game in Australia.

Previous coach Greg Smith had resigned — saving himself from the axe — after the Wallabies suffered their worst defeat in almost 100 years of Test match combat. The 61–22 humiliation at the hands of the Springboks in Pretoria was an historical low point. It ranked as arguably the darkest day in Australian rugby union. A loss to sit alongside the defeat by Tonga in 1973 as the most embarrassing, most disgraceful, most inept display by a Wallaby side.

No Australian side had previously conceded 50 points in a Test. Only one other had let the opposition reach 40. But on that Saturday night at Loftus Versfeld, in August 1997 — against a

Springbok side many in South Africa considered a sub-standard outfit — the Wallabies were slaughtered.

They let in 43 points in the second half, their defence crumbling quicker than a soggy tissue. Australian Rugby Union boss John O'Neill questioned the mental toughness of players in the wake of the humiliation, and slammed the performance as unacceptable for athletes on $10,000 per Test.

'It was a devastating defeat,' O'Neill said on the night. 'To be cleaned up by eight tries to three ... we've been talking about how we play great second halves but today, after the break, we just got towelled.'

The second half avalanche included six South African tries.

Perhaps most incredibly, that Australian side included 10 of the players that two years, two months and two weeks later were crowned kings of the game in Cardiff after disposing of France 35–12 in the most one-sided World Cup final on record.

A team so driven in defence they gave up just one try in six matches, in more than 500 minutes of football, on their way to the title. The turnaround, triggered by that pathetic Pretoria performance, was complete. And it had started with a change of coach. Greg Smith, later revealed to be suffering a brain tumour that clearly affected his thought processes, stood down from the post.

Within two months Macqueen was at the helm. A man more in the mould of an English soccer manager than your traditional rugby union coach. He oversees the running of the side rather than spending time as a hands-on coach. While he is undoubtedly the top man in the organisation, to him delegation is a key to success.

But back for a moment to Pretoria, and O'Neill, whose post-match blast upset many players. On November 6, 1999, they might have, in a quiet reflective moment, looked back and acknowledged they needed it to get where they were as the leaders of the game internationally.

'It's sobering, no it's devastating,' was the O'Neill reaction on that infamous night on the veldt. 'You just don't lose Test matches by this score. I mean, were we beaten by a team so much better? I don't think so. I think we saw a couple of players behave in a very undisciplined way, and for $10,000 a Test that lack of discipline was pretty unacceptable.

'You've got to say for $10,000 a Test, it's not just a question of are the players good enough, but do they have it in the head as well as physically? This is an expensive business with $13.5 million in salaries this year. You expect a level of performance.'

The night of the World Cup final, after the Queen had handed over the William Webb Ellis trophy to Wallaby skipper John Eales, there were few outside the immediate team wearing broader smiles than the ARU general manager. O'Neill had been recruited for the job after the disaster that was Australia's 1995 World Cup campaign. It was not all peaches and cream.

'I said to the team the night before the final when Rod asked me to address them to remember the highs and lows they have experienced on the way to where they are now,' he said. 'For me the low points included the six consecutive losses to the All Blacks in 1996 and 1997. It's no fun sitting in front of a bunch of All Black officials having your ear chewed off or under assault from these calls of 'come on Fitzy, come on Zinny'.'

'But the real bottom of the barrel was Pretoria. It wasn't just the score in that match. It was the way we lost. Apart from the way Stephen Larkham held his head up with a courageous performance at fullback, it was a sad, sad day for Australian rugby.

'I remember one of the South African officials, Professor Jannie Claasen, at the after match function saying there was only one team on the paddock, but then again Australia had never been any good at rugby.'

After Macqueen took over and took the team to Argentina in November of 1997, there was another stumble, a second Test loss to the Pumas in Buenos Aires.

'For Rod Macqueen, I think the baptism was very difficult, but in the longer haul perhaps that was not a bad thing. It made him realise the job was not going to be an easy job,' O'Neill said. 'We couldn't beat the All Blacks, we had the shocker in Pretoria and now we were beaten by Argentina. It made us all have a good long look at ourselves and collectively all the rugby brains in Australia realised we had to pull our fingers out.

'We had to do things a lot differently, we really had to get serious. The players also had to learn the gravy train wasn't there anymore.'

According to O'Neill the turning point was in Christchurch last year. The Wallabies, having broken through for a win over the

All Blacks in Melbourne, went to the south island of New Zealand with a chance of sealing the Bledisloe Cup. An emphatic first half ensured it and, 2–nil up, the silverware had been won.

'But even after that, and after going to South Africa, losing there and missing the chance to take the Tri-Nations trophy as well, they returned to Australia and finished the job on New Zealand, for our first clean sweep in 69 years,' said O'Neill.

'That was gutsy stuff. And as I've said to the players, you can always savour the high points to the max if you also remember the low points. And the key now is not to lose touch with reality. I think perhaps the All Blacks did, and it helped lead to their downfall. This Wallaby team will not detach itself. They won't lose touch with the people. And I've learned too. Rugby is not a product, it's rugby, and the Wallabies are not a brand, they're the Wallabies.'

Euphoria — such a long way from Pretoria.

But the two are inexorably linked in the 1999 World Cup triumph because one, in many ways, was the catalyst for the other. The real concern about the Springbok loss was that it could not be dismissed as a one-off stumble, an aberration to be casually dismissed with a 'she's right Jack' attitude.

Symptoms of decline had long been evident, and were highlighted by that four-year drought in matches against trans-Tasman rivals the All Blacks. Ultimately, results against the nearest neighbours are what counts in any barometer reading of Australian rugby union, and high-pressure systems had been in short supply.

Troughs and more troughs had been the outlook since 1994.

It was, for Australian administrators with an eye to the 1999 World Cup, time for change. And that Smith fell on his sword after Pretoria saved them from burying their own knives. When Macqueen was installed as coach, he took the Wallabies, at short notice, to Argentina, England and Scotland in the November, a tour that included that second Test loss to the Pumas, and a draw with the Poms.

But the rebuilding work was only in its infancy. A management team and specialist support staff were still being recruited to help launch the Wallaby revival, from assistant coaches with executive backgrounds to high-profile fitness gurus, defensive experts and leaders in the field of sports science.

Former Wallaby players Jeff Miller and Tim Lane were

appointed as assistant coaches to Macqueen; former rugby league international, John Muggleton, was brought on board to stiffen the Australian defence — his brief was to make it the best in the world; and another former league identity, conditioner Steve Nance, was poached from the Brisbane Broncos.

When the off-field structure was cobbled together, when Macqueen had studied the early mistakes he had made in Argentina and when he was confident about the course he was plotting, the coach turned to the playing personnel.

It was two weeks before the opening Test of the 1998 season, when Macqueen called the ground-breaking meeting at the Caloundra apartment complex the Wallabies were to make their semi-permanent base for the next two seasons.

'We talked about it as day one, as being the beginning of our journey towards the World Cup,' Macqueen recalled. 'And for our beginning to work, we had to change. We put down some structures and, I suppose, criteria for the players.

'We discussed our goals, and the World Cup was obviously the ultimate one at the end. But for us to have any chance it was clear we had to change, and there was general agreement we should.'

Strength and fitness programs were altered dramatically, Caloundra became a home away from home, and a sense of pride in the jumper, perhaps not evident when the Boks ran riot the previous year, was instilled as a non-negotiable necessity.

'We talked about this beginning, and the sort of players they needed to be,' said Macqueen. 'Part of it encompassed having a loyalty to the country and to each other, people who put the team first. We weren't just going to go out and select the best 15 players. They had to fit within our structure.

'We don't have any curfews or bans on alcohol, and we don't have a dictatorial system, but a system where we expect them to be men. And if they're going to be men you know they're going to do the right thing, be available when needed, be fresh when they need to train, and to look after their bodies.'

After dabbling in the theories of psychology, there was, for Macqueen, a more practical task to perform, in stamping a new pattern of play on the side. He wanted multi-skilled, athletic players capable of carrying the ball. Even props had to be mobile and contribute in the loose, not just hold up a scrum.

He detailed what he wanted from each position then went out looking for the men, or man, for the job. When it came to five eighth, he chose Stephen Larkham, the ACT Brumbies fullback.

It was a decision vehemently opposed — by me, for one — but a selection experiment that has significantly shaped the destiny of the Wallabies under the Macqueen regime.

Larkham made his debut against England, a fortnight after the Caloundra get together, and starred in a record breaking 76–0 demolition of a second rate side.

'I'd known Steve from when I coached at the Brumbies, and he was very good running in traffic, in highly congested areas,' said Macqueen. 'In the last game of the 1997 tour, he made several breaks against Scotland with players all around him.

'So it became very obvious he wasn't fazed by having people in his face all the time. He also had a kicking game, a very complete game, and it was then we felt he might be the answer. We sent copies of (All Black five eighth) Andrew Mehrtens and (Springbok) Henry Honiball to him and from the start the other players had a lot of confidence in him.'

The England victory sparked a season of success, where the Bledisloe Cup was won in a clean sweep of three Tests, the first whitewash since 1929. Only South Africa proved insurmountable, with the Wallabies losing both Tri-Nations Tests to the eventual series champions. By year's end, the Wallabies were vying with the All Blacks and Springboks for World Cup favouritism. But they had also suffered the first of a trio of injuries that left Macqueen wondering if World Cup aspirations might be derailed well before the tournament started.

Fullback Matt Burke needed re-constructive surgery on a shoulder. So too, when 1999 kicked off, did skipper John Eales. When Larkham also went down with a dislocated knee and ligament damage, alarm bells were ringing.

'I was concerned because we didn't have our captain, our playmaker, or our goal-kicker, and if you talk about three main elements of a side, that's what they'd be,' said Macqueen. 'It called for a bit of survival and the good thing was the other players never spoke about it, they just got on with the job.'

After beating Ireland in a two-match series, the Wallabies took on and beat England in the Centenary Test in Sydney. Surprisingly, it is a victory Macqueen places above even the Bledisloe Cup series triumphs, of both 1998 and 1999, because of the underdone nature of his team.

There was, however, another hiccup to come. In the Tri-Nations match against South Africa in Cape Town on August 14, the Wallabies lost 10–9. The one-point difference was not what gave Macqueen heartburn, rather the manner in which the Australians had played.

'For me, that was the most devastating defeat since I've been coach,' he said. 'Only because I felt we let ourselves down so badly. The only game I can recall where this team didn't play with character was Cape Town.

'It was concerning to me and it made me think whether we were on the right track. But we spoke about it, streamlined things a bit. There's a very fine line between having these guys overdone and giving them time for bodies and minds to recover.'

The right mix was found within a fortnight, as the Wallabies collected another record — a 21–point winning margin — as they retained the Bledisloe silverware in beating the All Blacks 28–7.

From there the World Cup beckoned. Six matches, six victories, and Bill, as they call the William Ellis trophy, was on his way home. But Macqueen is adamant: the best of these Wallabies, the 1999 World Cup winners, has not yet been seen.

'There's a lot more to come, and we haven't played our best football here,' he said, in an honest appraisal amid the delight of a Cardiff night he will never forget. 'We openly acknowledge that. But the players have been self-critical and that's what helps to lift our standards.

'Have we reached our potential? I don't think so.'

You can hear the rest of the world groaning already.

September 22

The Wallabies leave for the World Cup, as David Campese contemplates the likely stars of the upcoming tournament.

Big Jonah stole the show at the 1995 World Cup, becoming within a month a household name across the globe, which was fitting in a way because the guy is built like a three-storey waterfront mansion, and worth as much to boot these days. It's part of the beauty of rugby union's showpiece event.

Every four years, someone comes on the scene to light up the code, to lift it to new heights and to leave kids an icon they can emulate in backyards or dusty streets across the 150 countries that will take television coverage of the tournament.

So who will the star be in 1999, with the fourth World Cup to kick off tomorrow week in Cardiff when Wales play Argentina? Followers of the Australian side will jump to two obvious contenders — John Eales and Stephen Larkham.

Eales is the complete forward, a second-rower who can do everything his position demands and more, like kicking goals from the sideline. Larkham is the playmaker, the catalyst for the Wallabies attack, and a fearless defender. But if we move away from the pair, two others I am expecting an enormous contribution from and who could emerge as the unexpected stars of the six weeks are fullback Matt Burke and winger Ben Tune.

Burke has not shown his potential this year since coming back from a shoulder injury. He hasn't got involved as much as he should, he seems content to be a soccer goalkeeper, standing at the back to catch and kick the ball. Against the All Blacks last month it was almost as if he was concentrating only on his goalkicking, and while he did that wonderfully well, he has to realise it is

only part of his game. There are others he needs
to explore.

Burke's biggest asset is his attack. When he hits the
line down the blindside, running off halfback George
Gregan, or makes his entry through the midfield, to
create opportunities on both his inside and out, he is at
his best. It was rare to see him run the ball this season
but he has to do it if the Australian backline is to have
the options they will need to scuttle the best and take
the title.

Likewise Ben Tune. I have mentioned before I
don't like the way he has been turned into a battering
ram. Ben came on the scene in 1996, when I was still
playing, and he was a player of immense promise. He was
exceptionally quick and with terrific evasive skills.
Somewhere along the line he, or his coaches, have
turned him into a power player, and that's not his go.

At the World Cup, hopefully we will see Tune
going back to what he does best, beating players one on
one by running around them, not through them. Instead
of being the first receiver when he comes in off the
wing, he should position himself outside the first man to
get the ball and look to be sent through a hole. He is a
born finisher, not a creator. Those swallow dives of his
when scoring tries, that's what the world wants to see,
what the kids want to see and what I, as an old try-
scoring winger, want to see as well. An on-song Tune
will hold the world spellbound.

From the other nations, watch our for Christian
Cullen in his new found position in the midfield. My
mail from the Shaky Isles this week is that Cullen has
been told by coach John Hart he will be in the centres
for the World Cup. Rightly or wrongly, the world's best
fullback has been shifted to the wing and now to the
centres, and the latest move should serve as a warning to
rival teams. He is a such a gifted runner, with blistering
pace, that Cullen will cut holes in any backline defence.
And he will be in the prime position to create tries for
his outside men. This could be Cullen's tournament and,

ironically, his positional switch will allow for the return of Jonah Lomu to the starting team on the wing.

South Africa will rely heavily on halfback Joost van der Westhuizen, there's no secret there. But their key forward is flanker Andrew Venter. He is big, immensely strong, and you'll see plenty of him during the tournament.

As for England, I hope they do try to move the ball and not revert to their usual 10–man rubbish. If they opt for attacking rugby, keep an eye on young five-eighth Jonny Willkinson and fullback Matt Perry. They are two of the younger brigade destined for enormous futures.

Could their time be now?

September 27

Wallaby coach Rod Macqueen has produced his first surprise of the World Cup, dumping Queensland second rower Mark Connors for Australia's opening game against Romania in Belfast on Sunday night.

The return of skipper John Eales to the Test side for the first time this season was always a fait accompli. He will, barring injury, play every match in the Wallabies campaign. But the unfortunate player to be nudged aside for Eales to re-claim his place in the pack was expected to be his winter-long stand-in, ACT Brumbies forward David Giffin.

When the Australian captain was missing from day one of the domestic Test program, Giffin was considered the lineout specialist, best equipped to take over the ball-winning role. One of the few constants in a pack that was tinkered with and later revamped during mixed results leading into the World Cup, Giffin was partnered by Tom Bowman, John Welborn and finally Connors as the selectors searched for a suitable second-row blend. Now they have delivered another policy change, and Connors has been the unluckiest of losers.

Apart from forfeiting his Test jumper after an impressive display against the All Blacks in Sydney on August 28 — his first starting appearance for the Wallabies — he has suffered the double whammy of being overlooked for the reserves bench as well. Where the Bowmans, Welborns and Connors were wanted for grunt, or in the case of the last one, mobility, this time the plan is to play two lineout experts.

Macqueen though, would blanch at such a simplistic analogy, suggesting it sells short the contribution Giffin can make in general play, away from his lineout leaping. 'His work rate has been excellent throughout, and he has the mobility,' the coach said in making just the one change to the side that beat New Zealand by a record-breaking 28–7. Giffin has been there all the way through, but it was a close decision. And it does not rule out the possibility of Connors being there in the future.'

The decision not to include Connors among the seven

reserves is not as transparent as the head-to-head choice selectors had to make between him and Giffin for a starting position.

The bench to play Romania includes two backrowers, Owen Finegan and Tiaan Strauss, who will command game time for different reasons. Finegan has not had a lot of football since returning from shoulder surgery, while Strauss is likely to be tried at some stage as an openside flanker, the position he will be forced to fill if first-choice David Wilson is sidelined by injury during the tournament. It explains why Connors, the ideal reserve with his ability to cover two of the three backrow positions plus the second row, will be watching from the grandstand in collar, tie and blazer.

Elsewhere, the selectors stuck by the side that retained the Bledisloe Cup with their win at Stadium Australia.

Jason Little retains a spot on the wing ahead of Joe Roff, Rod Kafer continues to keep the five-eighth position warm for the imminent return of Stephen Larkham, and Matthew Burke holds down the fullback spot despite a concerted attempt by Chris Latham to dislodge the long-time incumbent.

On the reserves bench, Jeremy Paul is the back-up hooker to Phil Kearns, establishing a clear pecking order that sees Michael Foley at number three.

The Australian team: Matt Burke, Ben Tune, Daniel Herbert, Tim Horan, Jason Little, Rod Kafer, George Gregan, Toutai Kefu, David Wilson, Matt Cockbain, John Eales, David Giffin, Andrew Blades, Phil Kearns, Richard Harry. Reserves: Joe Roff, Nathan Grey, Chris Whitaker, Tiaan Strauss, Owen Finegan, Patricio Noriega, Jeremy Paul.

September 28

Former Kangaroo forward John Muggleton has debunked the myth that rugby union players are powder puff defenders, claiming the Wallabies have the strength and technique to mix it with the best of rugby league's hit men.

Muggleton, who has worked with the Australian team for the past two seasons and is in Ireland as part of the World Cup coaching staff, said the jibes of the past no longer apply.

'As far as I'm concerned, the gap that once existed between league and union defences is gone, it's closed,' he said, as the Wallabies trained in Dublin in preparation for Sunday night's campaign opener against Romania in Belfast.

'With the power these guys generate, and their physical strength, they hit as hard as any players in rugby league. I'll tell you now, you would not want to roll off the side of a maul into one of our forwards. They'll sit you straight on your backside.'

During his rugby league career, Muggleton played with one of the game's legendary tacklers, Parramatta prop Ron Hilditch, and during his post-playing days worked as a defensive consultant with the North Sydney Bears. Since being brought on board with the Wallabies by coach Rod Macqueen, he has presided over the building of a brick wall that this season has won the Australians widespread acclaim as the finest defensive unit in international rugby.

'Basically, we have a well structured pattern, where we've worked to make sure people know their job, what they have to do, and the job of the person next to them,' he said. 'It's when people are unsure that you see mistakes in defence. And I can only think of one breakdown for us this year, when Andrew Mehrtens scored for New Zealand in the Bledisloe Cup game.

'That was just a communication thing. But apart from that one problem, I think we've been pretty good all year.'

Muggleton said the technicalities of tackling — with priority on the correct positioning of the feet and the need for leg drive — have helped stiffen the Wallabies defence.

'Have a look at someone like (outside centre) Daniel Herbert,' he said. 'He's very strong in the legs as well as the upper body. That's the secret to his front-on defence. But these guys are all strong, all well-conditioned, and once you have that in place it's a matter of harnessing it so when they tackle, they can use that force on the guy with the ball.'

Herbert and reserve centre Nathan Grey spring to the minds of most rival players when asked whom they would least like to confront. Muggleton though, said the Wallaby forwards are still the hardest hitters.

'(Second rower) David Giffin and (flanker) Matt Cockbain generate a lot of force,' he said. 'And then you've got the front rowers. Their body shape, being low to the ground, mixed with good technique, makes them very powerful in the tackle. It's reached the point where at training you have to put guys of equal size on the bags they're hitting. A lot of the forwards, they'd snap me in half.'

Five-eighth Stephen Larkham, yet to play a Test this season after a winter of injury woes but planning to be back for the World Cup pool game with Ireland next week, is not renowned as a bruising tackler. Rather he is lauded for his never-miss strike rate, even in a team that prides itself on defence.

'He is a terrific defender, one of the most effective we have, a very good technique,' said Muggleton. 'Our statistics last year showed he went five Test matches without missing a tackle. And he's in an area where there's always a lot of traffic.'

Halfback George Gregan also came in for mention. Not unexpectedly, considering it was his tackle on All Black flyer Jeff Wilson in 1994 that remains one of the most talked about on-field incidents of the past decade.

'Part of his success is that he reads a game so well,' said Muggleton. 'And it helps make him a very good cover defender. He knows where to be. In open field, he's devastating.'

September 29

David Campese questions the motives of the game's leading officials as the countdown continues to the start of the tournament.

Anyone with a suspicious mind, and a knowledge of history, will sit down to watch the opening game of the World Cup and think it somehow odd that Wales are lining up against Argentina.

In 1991 a tradition was started — or so it seemed — when the organisers kicked off the second World Cup with a match between the host nation and the defending champions. England played New Zealand in a heavyweight contest at Twickenham to get the event underway, and four years later in South Africa it was the Springboks as the home union taking on the world champion Wallabies.

Logically then, the World Cup opener in Cardiff should have been Wales, the host union, against South Africa, the current holders of the William Webb Ellis trophy. But think back to when the draw for the tournament was made, and we're talking well over a year, well before the Welsh rugby revival.

Am I being too cynical in suggesting that World Cup bosses saw no value in pitting the might of South Africa, who were about to embark on a world-record equalling winning streak, against a Welsh side which had been walloped around the ears for years?

The England–New Zealand and South Africa–Australia openers were big games, crucial games, to start the two previous World Cups. The results impacted on every other contender in the tournament because it decided into which half of the draw the two combatants fell for the knockout stages.

When the 1999 World Cup draw was being worked out, there was no danger of Wales being a hope for the title. At that stage, qualification for the quarter finals would have been a triumph. A match against South Africa would have been a landslide, and buried the Welsh spirit for the remainder of the tournament. So, oddly enough, Wales ended up in a pool with Argentina, Western Samoa and Japan. Suspicious? Do we sense a not too random leg-up for the local lads?

Maybe, when three of the other four pools all had two top-tier nations in them — Australia and Ireland, New Zealand and England, South Africa and Scotland.

France also snagged a good draw in lining up in the pool stages against Canada, Fiji and Namibia. I ran into one of the World Cup heavies in Singapore recently and asked him why the 'tradition' of pitting the host nation against the defending champions in the first match of the tournament had not been retained.

His reply was: 'There's five pools this time.'

So what? Why could South Africa not have been put in a pool with Wales rather than Scotland? The way it's headed now Wales will top their pool and run into the Wallabies in the quarter finals, and there's a lot of confidence in Cardiff, and in the valleys, that they can knock off the Australians.

They're a pretty cocky mob the Welsh. Eight wins in a row they've racked up, and New Zealander Graham Henry, since his appointment as coach at the start of the year, has certainly turned things around.

But they're not as good as they think they are, and Australia will be too tall an obstacle for them to clamber over when the business end of the tournament arrives.

Jason Jones-Hughes, the Randwick and NSW centre, and one-time Wallaby, might have cracked it for a spot in their starting line-up by then. He's gone all that way, gone through all the off-field dramas as the Australian and Welsh rugby unions argued over whether he could wear the Welsh jumper, and then only makes the bench.

It just shows to me that while Jason will give Wales more depth for their World Cup challenge, he will not strengthen their top team to any great extent, if at all. If he is to be a key to their backline, Henry would have him in there straight away.

Jason has been in camp with them for a couple of weeks now, it's not as though playing him first up would have broken any code of loyalty between Henry and the players who have won eight in a row.

Still, at some stage in the second half tomorrow night, I am sure we'll see Jason Jones-Hughes running out in a jumper whose colour will make his old Welsh dad swell with pride. But if World Cup bosses had been fair dinkum, he would have been making his Test debut not against Argentina, but against the Springboks, in front of a packed Millennium Stadium.

That would have been something to treasure.

Romanian players being sent to the rugby gallows against Australia in Belfast on Sunday night will be paid like paupers at the World Cup — $25 a day in wages — while English stars are poised to pocket $250,000 per man if they win the final on November 6.

The chasm between the fulltime professionals of the heavyweight nations and the have-nots left to make up the numbers in this tournament's 20–team field is mirrored most notably in the plight of Romania.

When the Wallabies face them at Ravenhill Park, the eastern Europeans will have but the shell of the side they were hoping to bring to the UK and Ireland. And at the heart of their troubles is money. Nineteen of their finest players, unable to make a living from the game at home and contracted to French clubs for the current northern hemisphere season, declared themselves unavailable for the World Cup. Not that they wanted to bypass the code's showpiece event.

But with metaphorical guns aimed at their heads — the French clubs were going to dock their weekly payments if they joined the Romanian campaign — the list of non-starters grew embarrassingly long. Six other French-based players did agree to make the trip and can expect, by the time they exit the tournament at the end of the round robin matches, to fly out of Heathrow having earned in total around $500 a head. Compare that to the Wallabies' $9000 a game, and an incentive payment of $20,000 if they win the final, or the breathtaking potential collect for England players.

'Of the guys who pulled out, 10 or 11 of them would have come straight into our side,' said New Zealander John Phillips, who has worked with the Romanians for the past two and a half months as their technical director. It would have made a huge difference and it annoys the crap out of me. The International Rugby Board should have clauses put in contracts that if a player is called up for national duty, then the clubs like those in France who have the Romanian players should have to continue paying these guys.

'In the case of Romania, the Rugby Federation does not have

the money to pay them what they're making at the clubs, so someone has to step in and fix the situation.'

Phillips says the game in Romania is on its knees financially, and has been struggling to find cash since the overthrow of the hated Ceaucescu regime in the December 1989 revolution. The communists had bankrolled the game, as they did most sports in Romania, and the majority of players were placed in the police force or army.

'They trained every day, it was all there for them on a platter,' said Phillips.

Before the bloody uprising, in which several Romanian players were killed, including the captain of the time, Florica Murariu, the Romanians had beaten Wales in Cardiff, and there had been wins over France as well.

But the past decade has been barren.

'The lack of equipment is mind-boggling,' said Phillips. 'There's one scrum machine in the whole of Romania, there are no tackle bags. Romania has been left there in a pile of dung. If the IRB make 50 million pounds profit from this World Cup, they should help out these sort of countries. It's a real Catch 22 for Romania.

'They produce players good enough for the French clubs to sign then don't have them for national duty. And, when the results are not good, they struggle to find sponsorship.

'There is talent in Romania. They have very good youth players, the equivalent of any under 19 sides in England. But it falls off after that because of this lack of equipment and expertise. I asked one coach about sprint programs and he just looked at me.'

What has struck Phillips is the spirit of the Romanians.

'They never grizzle, they just make do,' he said. 'Before we left, a local club held a farewell for them and gave each of the players a bag of toiletries. They were so proud of that.'

As for Sunday and the clash with the Wallabies, Phillips said a good result for Romania would be scoring 10 to 15 points, even if they lost by 40. In their only two Tests this year, they have gone down 62–8 to France and 60–19 to Scotland.

'What they are happy about is that Australia are fielding their best side,' he added. 'They look at it that Australia have honoured us. They're excited about the chance to play against people like John Eales and Phil Kearns. They see it as a huge occasion.'

They call him the King, or the Great Redeemer. At a Welsh training session three weeks ago, the crowd applauded as he took the field to oversee his team's preparation.

New Zealander Graham Henry — coach of the host nation that kicks off the World Cup tomorrow with a match against Argentina at the new 73,000–capacity Millennium Stadium in Cardiff — is as you might have gathered a popular import.

That he has been at the helm of a Welsh side now unbeaten in their past eight matches has won him the hype and status Tom Jones would envy. Women might not throw their knickers at him, but Henry is making the whole place swoon. And his image will only be enhanced if the Welsh take the first step towards a quarter final showdown with the Wallabies by disposing of the Pumas.

Wallaby coach Rod Macqueen, whose own side was beaten by Argentina less than two years ago, does not believe an upset is on the cards. Wales, he predicts, will be too strong.

'It's difficult for any side to win eight games in a row, and beating South Africa as they did is no mean feat,' he said.

As for the theory that the Welsh form may be false, that leading sides have under-estimated them during the revival, Macqueen sniffs. 'I think it's false to assume they're not a good team in good form,' he said.

Henry though, is playing down the Welsh chances of taking the high road all the way to the tournament final.

'Can Wales beat the world on their day?' he's been quoted as saying. 'Yes, if everything goes right for us and everything goes wrong for them.'

October 1

POOL MATCHES

WALES 23 ARGENTINA 18

FIJI 67 NAMIBIA 18

The Wallabies have joined fellow World Cup heavyweights in a revolution against tournament bosses who lost the plot on lineout laws as the sport's showpiece event opened in Cardiff today. In an edict that has floored the leading nations — and the 16 referees who will control World Cup matches — organisers handed down a last-minute ruling that players cannot be lifted or supported in lineouts below the level of their shorts.

Flying in the face of common practice, where teammates hold players aloft by their thighs, the order has caused chaos among the 20 competing teams. So too will the admission of IRB chairman Vernon Pugh, who has said he expects penalty counts to soar in the early matches of the tournament as referees officiate to the strict letter of the law, as commanded.

'I'm not a worrier,' he said. 'I think referees will whistle up certain offences early and yes, it could be penalty ridden early. But once coaches and players understand where the referees are coming from I'm sure we'll see some spectacular games.'

Australia, England, South Africa and New Zealand are among several countries who have banded together to lodge a protest with International Rugby Board boffins about the 'lineout lunacy'.

The Wallabies have also sent a written submission of their own to IRB headquarters. Australian captain John Eales said he could not understand the IRB argument that lifting or supporting players below the waist was dangerous.

'It's more dangerous this way,' he said. 'What if we have a tall guy like David Giffin lifting a jumper from behind and a shorter player like Dan Crowley supporting from the front. If Giffin was at full stretch, Crowley would be lucky to reach the jumper's knees.'

The inference from Eales is that the lifted player could tumble face first into the ground, and from some height. Wallaby coach Rod Macqueen was incensed by the decision, and by the late notice. When the Australians left home last week, there was no mention of the change in interpretations. Only two days ago were the Australians made aware of the decision.

'We even thought about wearing extra long shorts,' said Macqueen, whose side opens its campaign against Romania in Belfast on Sunday.

According to Eales, there is every chance penalty counts will increase and the standard of football will slip — all because officials took a puzzling decision on the eve of a tournament that will be beamed into more than 150 countries.

'It can only affect the quality of rugby,' he warned. 'People lifting or supporting on the legs over the last couple of years has been a clean aspect of the game.'

Equally concerning for the powerhouse nations from the southern hemisphere is Pugh's expectation that penalty counts will be high, bringing a stop start nature to the game early in the piece. Australia, New Zealand and South Africa all want to play the game at pace, with endless continuity, believing that is where they have the edge on European sides.

Pugh said: 'We don't want the referees to be the main men on the field. But if in the early games it means they blow the whistle to set the ground rules, then I don't think it matters. If a pattern is set by consistent refereeing that's the key to it. Players these days are good enough to adjust. I think we all understand too that no coach coaches within the laws. Every coach sees what advantage he can gain, they test the referees to the limit.'

Wallaby coach Rod Macqueen has revealed he is still uncertain whether to rush back Stephen Larkham, his World Cup linchpin, for Australia's crucial pool match with Ireland in Dublin on October 10. Larkham has yet to play a Test this season after major knee surgery and still has a broken thumb in a mini-cast, with the fibreglass protection to be stripped off today.

But while the Irish match has long been the target in the Larkham comeback plans, and there have been no further setbacks during his daily training to prompt a revision, Macqueen is reluctant to risk any premature return. Larkham, quite clearly, is too important.

'It's not a fait accompli Steve will be in the side to play Ireland,' said the coach, as the Australians prepared for their World Cup opener against Romania in Belfast. It's an important game, it would be his first game back, and we'll have to weigh up the importance of his getting time on the field with the question of whether he might be too underdone.

'He looks pretty good and we'll see how he goes in contact work when the plaster comes off. You'll tell in training how confident he is. At this stage he's been doing virtually everything with the team, and we have done a fair bit of opposed work.

'The plaster is only small and it won't be that much different to the strapping he'll have on the hand. But we'll wait and see.'

Considering Australia will have only one other pool match after the Irish game — against the United States in Limerick on October 14 — before the knockout stages, there is a pressing need for Larkham to get match hardness into both body and mind.

Macqueen acknowledges the importance of his number one pivot re-acquainting himself with game conditions, and all but confirmed if Larkham does not start against Ireland, he will be one of the seven reserves.

'We can bring him off the bench,' he said.

When Larkham fractured the knuckle at the base of his thumb during the interstate challenge series early last month, the frustration was obvious as his World Cup build-up hit another snag.

'I was thinking 'who's got the voodoo dolls out',' he said. 'It had been a terrible season. A hernia operation, the knee operation, I suppose it all works in threes.'

In his absence against Romania, and possibly against Ireland, fellow ACT Brumbies backline playmaker, Rod Kafer, will handle the five-eighth role. As for those voodoo dolls, Kafer laughed: 'Steve must have had one of me a few years ago, and I've got it now. I just pulled the head off and changed the face.'

The chunky inside back — he refers to himself as short and fat — impressed against New Zealand when the Bledisloe Cup was retained on August 28. But he is only too happy to step aside, in Australia's best interests, when Larkham is ready to resume.

'In my opinion, he is the best five-eighth in the world,' said
Kafer. 'And he's crucial to Australia's success at the World Cup.
If I was picking the team, I'd pick him ahead of me in the No.10
every time. That's the reality. I have an enormous amount of respect
for Steve as a footballer.'

Another five-eighth, England's now retired Rob Andrew, the
man whose dropped goal sank Australia in the quarter finals of the
1995 World Cup, has ignored the Wallabies in making his predictions
for the 1999 tournament.

'When it comes to identifying the winner, there's no need to
look beyond England (and) New Zealand,' he wrote in a London
newspaper column.

He also claimed Wales had 'a real chance' of beating Australia
if, as expected, the two sides meet in a quarter final in Cardiff.

Australian team doctor John Best believes World Cup organisers have
wasted an ideal public relations opportunity by not drug testing
every player before the tournament kicked off.

Half the personnel in each of the 20 national squads, 300
players in total, were tested on arrival for the five-week event, with
All Black hooker Anton Oliver returning the only positive.

Oliver received a reprimand over the levels of
pseudoephedrine in his sample, caused by taking a medication for an
ear infection.

'Imagine if they had tested all 600 players, and having just one
positive for pseudoephedrine,' said Best. 'That would be quite
exceptional, especially when compared to other professional sports.'

The Oliver finding was minor. Pseudoephedrine can act as a
stimulant but is usually only tested for on game days. In effect, Oliver
could take the same medication on match eve and not risk failing a
doping test the following afternoon.

But it was of little solace to the All Black, who now carries the
stigma of being the first player to return a positive sample in four
World Cups.

Wallaby halfback George Gregan has indicated the current World Cup will be his last. While still only 27, Gregan expects to be retired when the next tournament heads down under, to Australia and New Zealand, in 2003.

'Another World Cup? I don't think so,' he said on the eve of Australia's opening game against Romania in Belfast. 'I'll be 31 then, too old.'

It was pointed out Wallaby flanker David Wilson, who captained the side during the absence of John Eales earlier this year, was 32.

'That makes him a machine,' smiled Gregan.

———

Lawrence Dallaglio, stripped of the England captaincy over a sex and drugs scandal earlier this year, claims he is faster and sharper thanks to the wife of a former Olympic sprint champion. Margot Wells, who coached her husband Allan to the 100 metres title at the Moscow Games, was hired by Dallaglio as his personal trainer during the months when his future hung in the balance.

As he waited for English authorities to hand down a decision on whether he could play in the World Cup — in the end he received a $35,000 fine for bringing the game into disrepute — Dallaglio trained under Wells and claims the move was one of his better decisions.

POOL MATCHES

FRANCE 33 CANADA 20

URUGUAY 27 SPAIN 15

ENGLAND 67 ITALY 7

IRELAND 53 USA 8

Easily the most impressive of the big guns on the opening two days of competition, England sent a shiver through their main rivals, and set the scene for a classic showdown with the All Blacks next weekend, by crushing Italy with a superb mix of forward power and backline precision.

Flanker Lawrence Dallaglio caused havoc running wide, winger Dan Lugar proved he has the size and speed to be a finisher to fear in the weeks ahead, fullback Matt Perry joined the line with the exact timing of Big Ben chiming on the hour, and halfback Matt Dawson mixed his game well at the scrumbase.

After a disappointing Five Nations, coach Clive Woodward asked to be judged on the performances of his team at the World Cup. Woodward had set his side to peak at the tournament and, while the opposition was second rate, the variety in the English display was eye-catching. They probed the blindside well and their backrow was outstanding.

As for the French, former Test five-eighth Thierry Lacroix was far from impressed with his countrymen's opening effort against a Canadian side with plenty of brawn but restricted footballing brains.

'It was a big mess,' groaned Lacroix. 'I am scared about the future. If we play like that against Fiji we might not go through (on top of the group). After watching that we don't know what the French team want to do.'

Canada led 10–8 with four minutes left in the first half before centre Richard Dourthe regained the lead with a penalty goal. Five-eighth Tomas Castaignede, the attacking spearhead for France, drifted between dynamic and disinterested. He was eventually shuffled to fullback.

Star of the show was French second rower Abdel Benazzi, remembered for being sent off against Australia in his Test debut in Sydney in 1990. Benazzi was a tower of strength in attack. Canadian five-eighth Gareth Rees, the only player to play in all four World Cups, showed his age. He limped off with a knee injury before half time.

POOL MATCHES

AUSTRALIA 57 ROMANIA 9

NEW ZEALAND 45 TONGA 9

SOUTH AFRICA 46 SCOTLAND 29

SAMOA 43 JAPAN 9

The Wallabies have launched their opening salvo on the World Cup campaign trail only to have their assault upstaged by strippers on a bizarre and bawdy night in Belfast. Flanker Matt Cockbain was the first to shed his gear, in a private pre-game trauma, after being injured in a mishap just minutes before kickoff against tournament minnows Romania.

'It's shattering, one of the hardest things I've had to do,' he said of peeling off his Test jumper.

But a female streaker, with the Australian flag proudly painted across her rump, was far less reluctant to discard her clothes for a late in the game and very public dash across a floodlit Ravenhill Park. Suspending play as well as belief — considering the temperature had fallen to five degrees — she brazenly cartwheeled and slapped the flag in a bottoms-up salute to the victorious Wallabies.

Even ground security were spellbound until an elderly steward, the aptly-named Jack Moon, hustled the intruder from centre stage for Australia to complete a nine-try romp 57–9. It was light relief for the Australians, Cockbain in particular, after he strained a thigh muscle just above the left knee when tangling with fellow backrower David Wilson in the final seconds of the Wallabies pre-match warm-up.

When the medical staff stood him down, Owen Finegan was rushed into the starting team and Mark Connors, preparing for a guest commentary stint on ABC radio, had to be hurriedly called to the dressing rooms as a late addition to the reserves bench. But after being overlooked for the original squad, Connors arrived at the ground only in blazer and tie and was forced to borrow Cockbain's full match kit jersey, shorts, socks and boots while a mouthguard was hastily boiled and moulded.

He later added to his Test match appearances with a cameo in the final 15 minutes.

'It all happened literally minutes before we ran out,' said Wallaby coach Rod Macqueen. 'Connors was still changing when the teams took the field.'

The pre-game distraction had little effect on the Wallabies. After 93 seconds, centre Tim Horan speared on to a pass from five-eighth Rod Kafer to score. He also netted, in the process, $25,000 to be donated to charity for having beaten a target set by tournament sponsor Guinness, for the first try scored in the opening two minutes of a match. Number eight Toutai Kefu crossed for the first of his three tries five minutes later and the signs for Romania were ominous. But this band of $25 a day footballers, mounted a worthwhile resistance.

They forced the Australians into handling errors at times with a bustling defence, and were only put to the sword when the Wallaby backline dusted off rust to string together several pace-laden movements.

Skipper John Eales, in his first Test for almost 12 months after being sidelined by shoulder surgery, admitted there was improvement to be made.

'But there were a lot of really positive aspects,' he said. 'It was a good physical workout for us and they exposed a few areas we need to work on before playing Ireland next Sunday.'

Macqueen was also satisfied. It was not a performance to win a World Cup, but it was a sound enough starting point.

'We haven't played for five weeks and it showed,' he said. 'But the scrum was good, some of the backline play was promising, even though we put down some ball, and we were certainly a lot better at the breakdown than we have been.'

Horan was one of Australia's best, while hookers Phil Kearns and Jeremy Paul were both heavily involved in their 40 minutes apiece. Winger Joe Roff, a second half replacement, also served notice he wants a return to the starting line-up.

Wallaby coach Rod Macqueen has been left with a delightful dilemma as he contemplates how to squeeze three world-class wingers into two positions for the rest of the tournament.

Joe Roff, dropped from the side for the Bledisloe Cup decider back in August, was given a 40–minute shot at redemption against the robust Romanians and virtually demanded a return to the team with his two-try performance. Roff drifted in from the blind wing with a well-timed run for his first score and, with the other, left two defenders hopelessly beaten on the outside after a subtle body swerve carried him past them in a confined space close to the sideline.

Jason Little, who shifted from the left wing to the right to make way for Roff's entrance when Ben Tune was replaced at half time, also snared one of nine tries.

'It's something we're going to have to sort out,' said Macqueen. 'Joe did play well. He injected himself into the game and you can't ignore performance. But we will be looking to use all three of those guys during our games. Players still want to be in the starting 15, but the reality is it's a 22–man squad. Joe came off the bench tonight. Whether we do the same thing next time, we have to decide.'

While Roff was celebrating a try double, number eight Toutai Kefu opened the tournament with a hat-trick, leaving him second on the World Cup standing behind Ireland's four-try hooker Keith Wood.

'It would have been nice if I'd actually done something for them,' he laughed. 'It was more a case of being in the right place at the right time. Have I done it before? Yeah, once at club level I think. Oh, and in the under 7's, for Souths against the Kenmore Bears.'

Has Justin Marshall played himself out of the All Blacks side during a skittish World Cup opener for the pre-tournament title favourites? Replaced with 16 minutes left by Otago livewire Byron Kelleher, Marshall was soundly upstaged. Where his service lacked zip, Kelleher was slick. Where Marshall played the predictable provider, Kelleher mixed his game with blindside raids, and had the acceleration to burn off defenders.

The question for coach John Hart is: does he persist with the Marshall–Merhtens combination, so important this season to both Canterbury and New Zealand, or does he punt on the prince, the heir to the throne at the scrumbase? In Marshall's defence, he was the link between backs and forwards when Tongan torpedoes were short-circuiting the All Blacks attack. By the time Kelleher hit the ground running, the sting had gone out of the islanders' defence, except for the occasional head-high shots which fullback Siua Taumalolo has practiced to perfection.

If he continues with the coat hangers, he can expect an early tournament departure. It was a rusty All Blacks performance, one that will have English players strutting, chests puffed like peripatetic pigeons.

As for the return of Jonah Lomu, it was fitting that the king of the 1995 World Cup should return wearing a black tiara. Or was that a strategically placed patch of hair left upon his shaven head?

Coach John Hart was upbeat later: 'The Tongans were very physical. They're a good hard side. We had a lacklustre first half (leading only 16–9 at the break). But once we got the go forward and drive, we were far more effective.'

Hart, however, must be concerned. His experiment with Christian Cullen in the centres was far from a resounding success.

So much for the voice of the masses.

Despite the call from leading nations for the International Rugby Board to do away with its lame new lineout regulation banning teams from listing or supporting jumpers below the level of their shorts, the game's bosses have been too busy mixing it with the rich and famous in Cardiff to listen.

While the opening ceremony on Friday night was a chance for boffins to don their blazers and look important, the people who matter in the game — the players and coaches who bring in the crowds — were being shunned.

And the lunacy of a lineout law that Wallaby skipper John Eales has blasted as dangerous and which teams knew nothing of until two days before the tournament kicked off was evident on day one of play. In the Wales–Argentina match, Welsh second rower Mark

Wyatt was clearly lifted by his legs in the opening minutes, and referee Paddy O'Brien did nought.

Later in the game, Wales were penalised for the same offence. Argentina this time bagged three points. The Namibians also felt the wrath of the referee in their match with Fiji, being penalised for lifting on legs while trailing hopelessly at 29–6.

Why the decision-makers would have contemplated bringing in a regulation that would increase the number of penalties is confusing enough. But to have not told teams until tournament eve of the change in interpretation is dereliction of duty. Are these officials aware the game is now professional, not muddled amateur exercise?

I doubt it. Even now they are probably too busy discussing their 15 seconds of fame when they rubbed shoulders with Shirley Bassey, Tom Jones, Prince Charles and co. to worry about the concerns of the best teams in the world.

An Australian flavour has been thoroughly stirred through this World Cup, with five of the first six matches having a taste of Oz — and that was before the Wallabies opened their campaign against Romania today.

When Wales played Argentina, NSW centre Jason Jones–Hughes came on as a second half replacement. In the Fijian side that thrashed Namibia, born and bred Queenslander Jacob Rauluni, the Reds halfback, scored one of nine tries. The Canadian side that went down 33–20 to France had Australian David Clarke watching from the grandstand as their technical director. Italy fielded former Wallaby fullback Matt Pini against England while another Australian raised player, Mark Giacheri, packed into the second row.

And at Lansdowne Road, Ireland had former NSW Waratah Matt Mostyn on the wing, while the USA brought on ex-Sydney club player and one-time St George rugby league signing David Niu as a replacement five-eighth. The Americans have also recruited former Wallaby fullback Roger Gould to act as assistant coach.

A World Cup first was created today when the Bachop brothers, Stephen and Graeme, lined up on opposite teams for the Samoa–Japan pool match at Wrexham. Even more bizarre is that the Bachop siblings are both former All Blacks.

Five-eighth Stephen has played 15 Tests for Samoa and five for New Zealand while halfback Graeme, after 31 caps for the All Blacks, has now settled in Japan and made six international appearances in the red and white hoops.

Ireland coach Warren Gatland has shelved plans to field a second-rate side against Australia in Dublin on Sunday and is now predicting his World Cup underdogs can topple the Wallabies for the first time in 20 years.

Gatland caused a furore both within and outside the Emerald Isle when he suggested last month the Irish were content to finish runners-up in their pool to Australia, ensuring an easier path through the knockout stages. History should have nudged at Gatland, telling him the preferred route could be taken with his best team anyway. Ireland have not beaten Australia since the 9–3 victory at the Sydney Cricket Ground in 1979.

But a seven-try 53–8 hammering of the USA at Lansdowne Road on Saturday night has Gatland, or is it Garland, looking somewhere over the rainbow.

'We won't be, never would be, going out on to Lansdowne Road to make up the numbers,' he said.

'I said after the second Test against the Aussies in Perth earlier this year (the Wallabies won 32–26 on June 19) that we were looking forward to playing them in Dublin in front of a sellout crowd of 50,000.

'Nothing has changed and we will be putting out a side to beat Australia.'

Gatland, a former All Black hooker, claims the foundation for a passionate Irish performance is cemented in the front row, a trio he contends is the equal of any in the tournament. It is a boast the Australians will not argue with, having had their problems containing Peter Clohessy, Keith Wood and Paul Wallace only four months ago.

The Irish lineout is also sound, while a touch of killer instinct, shown in the three tries the home side scored in the final 12 minutes against the Americans — all finished off by hooker Wood — was the legacy of their down under visit.

'I think initially when we arrived in Australia earlier this year, we were caught short because of the pace and intensity of their guys coming out of Super 12,' said Gatland. 'By the end of the tour we were looking sharp and here tonight we didn't ease up. It was a good start for us. A bit rusty at times but we're pleased.'

Despite the lift in Irish spirits as they hurtled past their previous best effort against the USA — an 11 point win in 1994 — even former Test forwards who wore the green are looking elsewhere to find a northern hemisphere contender for the title.

Second rower Neil Francis, who played in all three previous World Cups, has tipped Ireland's arch rival England to end the southern hemisphere stranglehold.

In his irreverent column for *the Sunday Tribune*, Francis predicted Lawrence Dallaglio will emerge as forward of the tournament, that coach Clive Woodward is one of the few weak links for England because of irrational selections, and that the All Blacks have blundered in picking Christian Cullen at centre.

On the issue of English personnel, he has urged Woodward to dump firebrand hooker Richard Cockerill and promote the younger, more mobile Phil Greening.

'One, Greening's loose play and darts are far superior,' wrote Francis. 'Two, Cockerill is a tosser.'

———

Even the most resolute of All Blacks is starting to fret. As the northern hemisphere challenge for the World Cup title rumbled into view at the weekend with England leading the charge, former New Zealand Test captain Sean Fitzpatrick sensed the impending danger.

Where the Kiwis were less than impressive despite downing Tonga 45–9, the English were the form team of the opening round with a 60–point mincing of Italy. At Twickenham this weekend, England host the All Blacks, the first major showdown of a civil war that has been split along equatorial lines.

In one camp are the Kiwis, Australia and South Africa. In the other England, Wales, Scotland and France with the underlying question of this fourth World Cup: can a team from the north finally take home the William Webb Ellis trophy?

The England–New Zealand pool match will give, if not a decisive answer, a sound indicator before the knockout stages.

'It's obviously a huge game for both teams and England look very focussed, especially in the forwards,' said Fitzpatrick. 'They would have watched the All Blacks against Australia in August and seen we were exposed up front. The All Blacks have a lot of work to do.'

Former Springbok captain Francois Pienaar was also edgy after South Africa's win over Scotland, where the defending champions trailed with 20 minutes to play. Pinpointing England as the major northern hemisphere flag bearers, he looked ahead to their clash with the All Blacks and suggested: 'England will be confident and I would be too.'

Former Wallaby skipper Michael Lynagh, who led Australia's 1995 campaign, was also drawn into the north-south debate.

'Maybe it's about time the title came to the northern hemisphere,' he said. 'But they still have to contend with what you might call the bloody-mindedness of teams from the south. South Africa showed it in the way they eventually put away Scotland.'

The Wallabies, albeit against lesser opposition, were the most impressive of the Tri-Nations sides. But they are adopting a low-key approach.

'We're pleased,' said captain John Eales. 'But England did look good, didn't they? They'll give the All Blacks a good run for their money.'

New Zealand coach John Hart went even further, although it must be said he is a past master of mind games. According to Hart, England should be the new tournament favourites, the standing his own team has held since the start of the year.

October 5

Wallaby five-eighth Stephen Larkham finally thumbed his nose at the injury demons when returned to the Test team today after an 11–month absence, four operations and a season of World Cup fears. For the first time this year, the Australians will field a full-strength team on Sunday with Larkham's long-awaited comeback part of a three-change tweak for the clash with Ireland at Lansdowne Road.

Joe Roff re-claimed a wing position to squeeze Jason Little out of the side and flanker Matt Cockbain was recalled to the backrow, fitness pending, for Owen Finegan. Mark Connors is on standby if Cockbain falters with a muscle strain to his left thigh that forced his late withdrawal, and Finegan's promotion, for the Belfast bashing of Romania.

But the significant development for the World Cup contenders was confirmation that Larkham is back — hot on the heels of skipper John Eales — after his frequent flirtations with setbacks and surgeons. Since playing England at Twickenham last November, the 25–year-old has been plagued by injury. He underwent a hernia operation in the off-season then played only a handful of games before dislocating a knee and mangling ligaments during the early rounds of the Super 12 series in a match for the ACT Brumbies. An operation to repair the damage — and further work on an old injury — left a cloud over his World Cup prospects. But even when that hurdle was cleared, and Larkham returned for Canberra club games and the three-way interstate series in September, the curse continued. A broken thumb, just one week before the Wallabies went into camp to prepare for their World Cup departure, threatened his place in the 30–man squad.

'It's been a long wait,' he said. 'There were stages throughout the year when I didn't think I'd be playing again this year. When I did my leg, my first thought was the World Cup. 'And when I got my hand injury my thoughts again were I'd end up missing the tournament. But I'm here now, it's a bit of relief, and I've just got to get out there and do my best.'

The Australians struggled to settle on a five-eighth in Larkham's absence, first trialling Nathan Spooner, falling back on Tim

Horan and eventually calling in Rod Kafer, who debuted against the All Blacks and retained the job for the World Cup campaign opener four days ago in Northern Ireland. All the while, coach Rod Macqueen and his co-selectors had their eyes on the horizon.

The weight of expectation is immense. Larkham is the key playmaker in the Australian side, his form in the knockout stages vital to how far the Wallabies advance. But the burden sits easily on slender shoulders. 'I'm certainly not going out there with the idea I have to do something special every time I get the ball,' he said, with his thumb just five days out of a splint. 'Rod Kafer played well and the team played well around him. Hopefully I can add something too.'

Not that Larkham expects his re-initiation, against an Irish side on their home patch, to be a walk in the park. 'When you step up to the next level, and I haven't played a Test in a year, fitness comes into it and your reaction times have to be quicker,' he said. 'Coming back from injury and playing club games in Canberra, and the Ricoh interstate series, I was also a bit worried about re-injuring myself. 'That was down to the fact that I thought I'd miss the World Cup if it happened. But I'm here now, I've made it, so there's no point in holding back.'

While Larkham for Kafer — who also missed a spot on the bench — and Cockbain for Finegan were expected, Little's demotion was cruel. On form, he deserved to stay. The problem is three wingers — Little, Roff and Ben Tune — into two positions does not go. On potential and his second half display against Romania, Roff had to return. But it is Tune who will now have the heat turned up with Little awaiting his next opportunity.

In the Irish camp, prop Peter Clohessy is in doubt for the Dublin encounter with a combination of flu and back spasms. If he is ruled out, it will be a major blow to the home side. In partnership with Keith Wood and Paul Wallace, Clohessy gives the Irish one of the most respected front rows in the world.

The Australian team: Matt Burke, Ben Tune, Daniel Herbert, Tim Horan, Joe Roff, Stephen Larkham, George Gregan, Toutai Kefu, David Wilson, Matt Cockbain or Mark Connors, John Eales (c), David Giffin, Andrew Blades, Phil Kearns, Richard Harry. Reserves: Jason Little, Nathan Grey, Chris Whitaker, Mark Connors or Tiaan Strauss, Owen Finegan, Dan Crowley, Jeremy Paul.

Australian skipper John Eales has recalled the great escape of eight
years ago in warning the Wallabies that Sunday's clash with Ireland is
a potential Dublin disaster. It was at Lansdowne Road in 1991,
on the road to World Cup glory, that Australia survived a quarter-
final scare, falling behind to Ireland with three minutes to play
before Michael Lynagh and his try in the corner brought the visitors
late salvation.

According to Eales, history should not be ignored, especially
when on a broader canvas the Great Divide between southern
hemisphere powers and their long languishing northern cousins has
shrunk from chasm to crack. After the opening round of matches at
this fourth World Cup, Eales said the popular theory that Tri-Nations
hotshots Australia, New Zealand and South Africa would again
dominate the game's greatest stage has been left with a hollow tone.
And England, he added, were not the only side closing in on the
southern triumvirate.

The Welsh, Irish and Scots, while still a rung below the best,
are unquestionably on the rise. Whether Ireland can make the step
up this weekend when their raw resources are still well below what
the Wallabies can boast in personnel, and when only a few weeks
ago their coach Warren Gatland was virtually conceding defeat,
remains a mystery.

But to Eales, the signs are clear. 'If we have an off day
against Ireland, we'll be beaten,' he said. 'I know people will
say I'm just talking them up. But look at it this way. This Irish
side is much better than the Irish team we beat in 1991. I'm sure
amongst the general population there is still a belief that there's
this yawning gap between the teams from the southern and
northern hemispheres.

'But you saw the other day when South Africa played
Scotland. While the Springboks got there in the end, they had to lift
to do it. Perhaps in previous years you could play below your best
and still beat the teams over here. That's no longer the case. Have an
off day and you're gone.'

Eales believes southern 'spies', the men recruited to rebuild the
game in Ireland, Wales and Scotland — England have worked from
within — were chiefly responsible for a turnaround in fortunes. He

spoke of New Zealanders Graham Henry and Warren Gatland, now coaching Wales and Ireland, and of Kiwi centre John Leslie in the midfield for Scotland. And of the increased Test match contact between teams either side of the equator since the game turned professional after the 1995 World Cup.

'If you read the history of Queensland rugby, they were the poor relations to New South Wales many years ago. They really struggled to compete,' said Eales.

'But people like (former coach) Bob Templeton took them on trips to New Zealand, to play against quality opposition. They learned what it was all about.

'Now you have someone like Graham Henry going to Wales. He's a guy who's been at the cutting edge of the game for years. He's brought them a consistency and a new dimension. The same with Gatland and Ireland. They have more control about their game now, a real pattern to their play, they're not so scatty. From our point of view that's the concern, the consistency they've been able to achieve. Previously, sides like Ireland would come out and play with a passion that could almost get them through. But to perform week after week you need more than passion, you need the skills and the back-up as well, and that's what they're building. Passion alone is not enough and all the sides over here have more than that now.'

Eales first sensed the northern improvement in 1996 when the Wallabies, despite an unbeaten tour to the UK and Ireland — they did not, however, play England — were stretched in a couple of Test matches. And from a World Cup viewpoint, he said, the home ground advantage at this World Cup could be a significant factor in the European challenge.

'The northern hemisphere sides are a lot more difficult to play over here,' he confirmed. 'What they don't seem to do is travel well, and that can give people the wrong perception about how good they can be. It was the same in 1991. We (thrashed) England in Sydney and at the World Cup they were a different team when we met them in the final.'

If the English upset the All Blacks at Twickenham this weekend, the prospect of another Australia-England final will be a possibility. If the All Blacks win, England will fall into the same half of the draw as the Wallabies for the knockout stages.

'The English are a big, big show of winning this whole thing,' said Eales. 'But there is a lot of pressure building on them through the media and whatever. And for this week, especially, it's only going to fuel the motivation of the All Blacks.'

The Wallabies need no motivating for their showdown the following day. They know, through history, the possible pitfalls of Dublin.

⟶

The first suspensions in a World Cup have been handed down to Welsh flanker Colin Charvis and Argentine prop Roberto Grau. After both were cited for punching incidents in the tournament opener at Cardiff, Charvis has been banned for 14 days and Grau for an extra week. While Charvis will be available for Wales' likely quarter final with Australia on October 23, the World Cup might be over for Grau.

October 6

David Campese predicts a comfortable win over Ireland.

The Australian camp are making all the right noises about how tough their pool match with Ireland will be at Lansdowne Road on Sunday. They have to say it, it's best that they say it, to avoid stoking the fires that always blaze in the bellies of the Irish in Dublin. But the reality is there's still some distance between these two sides in class, skill and fitness.

When Ireland toured in June, I upset the Wallabies with my first Test prediction of a 40–point victory. Instead of being flattered, they were flailing their arms, and playing down a lopsided outcome. The end result was 46–10. Sure, Ireland recovered in the second Test, put up a terrific show and gave the Wallabies a real scare before losing by six. But the reason the gap closed in the space of a week is that Ireland went to school on the first Test and when the Australians failed to change their tactics, the men in green knew exactly what the Wallabies were going to do.

At the risk of copping another caning, and the bruises are still blue from recent attacks, I expect the Wallabies to win comfortably again, in the region of 20 to 30 points, with a flurry of tries at the end.

The reasons? From the Australian side of things, I liked the look of their opening win over Romania in Belfast. Forget the handling errors and the caked on rust that came from not having played in five weeks. There were signs there that gave me hope the Wallabies might return to the backline-driven game that I think they need to employ to win this World Cup in Cardiff on November 6. I just hope they continue in the same vein when they come up against more telling opposition than the willing but outgunned Romanians.

Fullback Matt Burke and winger Joe Roff,

brought on for the second half to collect two tries, most impressed me and looked back to their confident selves.

Burke especially ran the ball with real conviction, and it's a long time since we've seen him do that. The way he cut down the left during the second half to create and score a try after exchanging passes with Chris Whitaker was precisely what I've been waiting for from a player with world-class stamped all over him.

Earlier this season, he seemed reluctant to chance his arm in counter attack, or join the backline with any real vigour. But it was the Burke of old on Sunday.

The Wallabies, across the park, looked relaxed and fresh, and that's another good sign. Perhaps an indicator that they will be peaking as planned around the time of the knockout stages. As for Ireland, they will be full of passion, full of fight, full of running for 60 minutes.

But I am yet to be convinced the northern hemisphere sides have reached the same levels of fitness as the big three from the south. In no way am I saying Ireland will be cast aside easily. They will make it tough for Australia until midway through the second half and, at that stage in the game, there is unlikely to be too many points separating the sides. But when the Wallabies put the foot to floor in the last quarter, I don't think the Irish, for all their improvements under coach Warren Gatland, will stand the pace. This is a far better structured Irish side than others I have seen. But compared man for man with the Australians, there is a significant advantage for the Wallabies from five-eighth Stephen Larkham to Burke at the back.

The game dominating the headlines here however, is the All Blacks-England clash at Twickenham. In short, I can't see England winning. There is no doubting the strength of the English pack but while people are getting carried away with their win over Italy, their backline play had technical shortcomings. Too often they were transferring the ball while standing flat-footed, with no

one out wide hitting the line at pace. Against a good
defence, and the All Blacks have that, the English
threequarters will struggle.

———

To understand how much the Wallaby jersey means to Joe Roff, take
a wander back through time, to when a kid from Canberra on a
family holiday paid a visit to his godfather in Queensland. That the
big bloke he travelled north to see was Greg Cornelsen — the
former Wallaby flanker forever remembered for four tries against the
All Blacks in 1978 — was just part of the thrill.

It was when the presents came out that the boy, who would
later make his debut in the same gold jersey as a teenage wing
sensation, had to struggle to contain his delight. 'I was about 12 or
so,' said Roff. 'He was a good family friend, he'd played rugby with
my dad when they went to university in Armidale.

'We were up at his place in Queensland and I can still see him
bringing out these training jerseys for my elder brother and sister. I
was suitably filthy, as you can imagine, until he went back in and
came out with one of his Test jerseys for me. It was the old Adidas
one, with the three stripes, and the number seven on the back.'

Even now, Roff remembers the welling of pride.

'It's a bit bizarre,' he laughed. 'But I recall asking my mum if I
could give him a hug and she said it might be best if I just shake his
hand. I was stoked. That jumper never left our house. I put it on all
the time and wandered around in it. And yeah, I dreamed of getting
my own.' He did, seven years later, as a member of Australia's 1995
World Cup squad and, for the following three and a bit seasons, was
a consistent figure patrolling the left touchline.

But this year or, more precisely, two months ago, the hiccup
arrived. Roff, after 45 Tests, was dumped from the Wallabies side and
replaced by Jason Little for the Bledisloe Cup decider at Stadium
Australia. One game later, against Romania in Belfast last weekend,
Roff was given his shot at redemption, a second half appearance at
Ravenhill Park in a pre-ordained swap with Ben Tune.

A two-try haul, glimpses of Roff at his best, and the Australian
selectors have recalled him to the starting line-up to play Ireland on
Sunday. 'I'm not going to kid myself and say I wasn't disappointed or

frustrated at losing my place in the team,' said Roff. 'It's made me more determined to get back on the field and make sure I keep my spot. It would be nice to run on wearing 11 again, not 16. And I'm just thankful for the opportunities I got against Romania. The conditions could have made it one of those nightmares for wingers, where you stand out in the cold and rain with nothing to do.

'So when the chances came my way I wanted to make the most of them. My motivation is right up there at the moment, I've got a lot of incentive to do well. I've just got to continue now the same way I played last Sunday if I want to continue to have a part in this World Cup.'

It would certainly make for a more festive New Year's Eve, when Roff travels north again to visit godfather Greg.

Welsh import Jason Jones-Hughes left Australia for the land of the leek aiming to win the Test centre position he craved but failed to secure with the Wallabies. Slowly, but surely, he is getting there, and collecting international caps on the way.

Jones-Hughes has been named in the Welsh starting line-up for Saturday's clash with Japan in Cardiff, but in the unaccustomed role of right wing, where he has played on only fleeting occasions for the NSW Waratahs. In the tournament opener last Friday, Jones-Hughes came on as a second half replacement for centre Scott Gibbs. But coach Graham Henry has retained the midfield pairing of Gibbs and Mark Taylor in making three changes overall after the first-up win over Argentina.

When news filtered back to Australia last week that Wallaby prop Patricio Noriega had damaged a shoulder before the opening game, it was the talk of the Eastwood front-row as they trained for the NSW club grand final.

ACT Brumbies prop Bill Young turned to Waratahs recruit Rod Moore and joked that Wallaby coach Rod Macqueen might soon be on the telephone, offering Moore a trip to Britain. 'You wouldn't believe it,' said Moore. 'Within a day Rod did call, but I wasn't there and he left a message on the answering machine. 'Because it was from a mobile phone it was pretty crackly, and I was convinced it was Bill Young trying to catch me out.'

The call was genuine, Moore flew out for Britain on Monday, initially as a standby player, and learned on his arrival in Dublin he had been promoted to the 30–man squad. Moore will win his first Test cap against the United States next Thursday.

———

Tongan fullback Suia Taumalolo, whose tackling technique revolves around attempted decapitation of the opposition ball carrier, has been rubbed out of the World Cup for 21 days after being cited for his high shots against New Zealand. Taumalolo floored All Black winger Tana Umaga with a swinging arm to the head on Sunday.

But it was his persistent high tackling, rather than a one-off incident, which led a judiciary panel in London to suspend him for the remainder of the pool matches, effectively ending his tournament.

October 7

The Wallabies were put on notice today by an Irishman with an Aussie twang that their stretch of 31 years unbeaten in Dublin will be under threat in a World Cup return to Lansdowne Road on Sunday.

Matt Mostyn, born and raised in Sydney but now residing on Ireland's left wing, revealed the home side have shed the insecurities hoisted on them by history and no longer view the Wallabies through an aura of invincibility.

'That might have been the case earlier in the year when we toured Australia,' he said. 'They took us to the cleaners in the first Test at Ballymore, but the second Test in Perth did wonders for this team.'

A week after being caned 46–10, Ireland held the Wallabies to 32–26 on a June night at Subiaco Oval that Mostyn suggested was more significant than the Australians might suspect. 'It showed that the likes of Australia and New Zealand are not superhuman,' said the one-time NSW flyer who headed offshore last year and wears the green jumper via Irish-born grandparents.

'It made these guys realise the Wallabies and All Blacks are only normal blokes. They're just more accustomed to winning.' For Australia in Ireland, it has long been the case.

The Wallabies have not lost a Test here since 1968, and adopted Dublin as a home away from home when they qualified for the World Cup final eight years ago courtesy of victories at Lansdowne Road over Ireland and the All Blacks.

Mostyn remembers the quarter final that year, and his joy at Australia's advancement, after Ireland grabbed a late lead only to be overhauled in the final three minutes. Now his loyalties demand the Wallabies' downfall.

'We have a great forward pack, and once they get their tails up they can match it with the big guys no problem,' he said. 'Overall, it's a solid team. Obviously sides like Australia capitalise on mistakes and make you pay, and they never let up the pressure.

'What we have to do is go for the full 80 minutes, and if we can do that, at our best, we can beat them. You've also got to remember there's going to be 50,000 Irishmen going bananas in the stands. That will be something to see.'

Mostyn has yet to experience the thrill of playing at a packed Lansdowne Road, having performed before less than capacity crowds in his two Tests there against Argentina in a World Cup warm-up, and last Saturday night against the USA. But the Irish experience he has thrived on is the camaraderie of new-found teammates.

'You've got blokes like Keith Wood, who has to be the best hooker in the world,' said Mostyn. 'He would have every right to be aloof and arrogant, but he's nothing like it. He's friendly, always helping the young blokes, and loves a laugh. When he wants to talk to you it's always the same line — 'step into my office' — and he puts his arm around you and has a chat.

'We call him Fester, after the bald bloke in the Addams Family, but he's getting known now as Dr Evil, out of the Austen Powers movie. We wrote it across his forehead one night and made him go out like that.

'But as a player he's the absolute professional. In sprint tests, he can beat some of the backs over 30m. The guy is just a freak.'

His teammates thought the same of Mostyn, if in a different context, when he was called on to follow team tradition during a bus trip to training recently. 'The Irish do thing a bit differently to what I was used to in Australia,' he said. 'They love their singalongs whenever you're travelling somewhere. They call blokes to the front of the bus and you've got to belt out a tune. It's not a natural thing to do in Australia, not unless you've had a few beers, but it comes so naturally to these guys.

'The first time it happened to me I gave a very poor rendition of 'Hey True Blue'. It's the first time in my life I've ever sung stone cold sober. They thought I made the words up myself and booed me off. 'I went back to my room and practiced for days. The next time it was 'Viva Las Vegas'. That seemed to go down a bit better.

'But some of the guys are brilliant. (Flanker) Trevor Brennan is awesome and (winger) Justin Bishop does a great 'Lady In Red'. He closes his eyes, gives it the whole works. It looks like he's going to cry.'

Living in Galway, Mostyn has no regrets over his move to Ireland. The early homesickness has gone, although it surfaced briefly before the USA game when friends from his former Sydney club

Eastwood left messages on his mobile phone after their first ever premiership triumph on Saturday. 'It was bloody fantastic,' he said. 'I had a quiet celebration of my own that night.'

He can be assured of a larger party if an Irish dream comes true on Sunday.

Wallaby coach Rod Macqueen has spoken out on the Jason Jones-Hughes move to Wales, claiming the NSW centre has cost a stay-at-home Australian the chance to represent his country. 'Personally, we wish Jason the best,' said Macqueen.

'But from an Australian rugby point of view, his presence in a Super 12 side over the past two years has meant someone else, possibly capable of playing for Australia, has been deprived of that opportunity. We only have three teams (NSW, Queensland and ACT) to choose the Australian side from and that's why we have contracts that say our Super 12 players make themselves available for the Wallabies. It's why we invest time and energy into those players.

'As an outside centre, Jason was probably ranked third with a big chance of getting into the Australian squad. Now he's not available, and he has deprived another player of that chance as well.'

Macqueen and others in the Australian Rugby Union will be interested to read the latest comments of Jones-Hughes, who might still be held to his NSW contract for next season, with the deal not expiring until December 31, 2000.

According to the Waratahs midfielder, who is being chased by the Cardiff club for a reported $1 million over three years — his NSW contract is worth around $100,000 a year — he has given up plenty to play for Wales.

'It has cost me a lot of money,' he told *The Independent*. 'I sacrificed a lot to come here, but it has come off. The financial factors are unimportant though when it comes to playing for your country. People knew of my desire to play for Wales. I was approached a couple of years ago but at the time, and at that age, I thought no. But it has always been in my mind to play for Wales.'

Interesting that, considering Jones-Hughes went on tour to Argentina with the Wallabies at the end of 1997.

The likely Australia-Wales quarter final in Cardiff will have added spice if Jones-Hughes stays on the wing where he will play against Japan in a pool match this weekend.

———

All Blacks skipper Taine Randell might well be feeling anxious this morning as the All Blacks consider hauling over another number eight after the World Cup exit of injured utility back Carlos Spencer. Randell has come under fire for his leadership and form during New Zealand's jittery first hour in their opening pool match against Tonga at the weekend. And the prospect of Spencer being replaced by Filo Tiatia or Xavier Rush will give rise to speculation that Randell's position is not wholly secure as the Kiwis prepare for England at Twickenham on Saturday.

To dump a captain mid-World Cup would be a dramatic and almost unthinkable option for coach John Hart to take. Then again, the New Zealanders have been known to take the sword to leaders. Remember Wayne Shelford?

———

Former Wallaby skipper Nick Farr-Jones is to be inducted into the Rugby Hall of Fame during the month-long World Cup festivities, earning him a place alongside his 1984 Grand Slam five-eighth Mark Ella. Farr-Jones is on the latest list of 10 ex-players to be accorded the honour, with others including Gerald Davies (Wales), Andy Irvine (Scotland), Philippe Sella (France) and Brian Lochore (New Zealand).

October 8

POOL MATCHES

SCOTLAND 43 URUGUAY 12

FRANCE 47 NAMIBIA 13

Veteran hooker Phil Kearns, on his final Test campaign for Australia, rates the current Wallabies a better team than the 1991 side he helped lift to the top of the world. Speaking on the eve of a showdown with Ireland in Dublin on Sunday, Kearns was adamant the World Cup winners of eight years ago would struggle if brought forward in time to compete with the professionals of the modern era.

'We're a better side by a mile,' he said. 'The blokes here are bigger, stronger, faster and, across the board, more skillful. I'm not denigrating the 1991 team at all. That was an exceptional side, a great team to be part of, but it was eight years ago. Rugby is now three or four years into professionalism. It would be naïve to think in another 10 years that the team then would not be a lot better than this side is now. A lot of the moves teams employ these days are far more advanced than they were when we won the World Cup.

'More thought goes into it, searching for that extra angle in attack, a flick pass here or something different there to crack an opposition defence. The defences are far more organised. It was definitely more simplistic back then. And the very size and power of players today ... physically they're that much better.'

Kearns has been on the international circuit for 11 seasons, his career straddling both the amateur and play-for-pay days, and this World Cup campaign he has already confirmed will be his last hurrah to the game. He has played in Bledisloe Cup winning sides, captained Australia to a win over the All Blacks, and figured in memorable victories over the Springboks since 1992. But the crowning achievement remains the 1991 World Cup when he was

Joe Roff splits the Romanian defence to score the first of his two tries in Australia's opening World Cup match in Belfast.
Courtesy: Allsport

A familiar sight during 1999 . . . Daniel Herbert brushing aside would-be tacklers to put Australia on the attack, this time against Romania. *Courtesy: Allsport*

Rare chance . . . Nathan Grey takes on the Romanians after coming off the bench to replace Tim Horan in the midfield. Grey spent the tournament as understudy to the 10-year veteran. *Courtesy: Allsport*

Super-sub . . . Owen Finegan was a success story of the World Cup, making an impact every time he was injected into the game as a second half replacement. Against Romania, he was a late call-up to the starting side after Matt Cockbain withdrew. *Courtesy: Allsport*

He's back . . . Jonah Lomu scores the solo try against England that brought memories flooding back of his four-try effort in the 1995 semi final. Lomu finished the tournament as leading try-scorer with eight.
Courtesy: Allsport

Welsh flanker Colin Charvis leaves the Argentine defence in tatters on his way to scoring the first try of the World Cup. *Courtesy: Allsport*

The oldest player at the tournament, 40-year-old Uruguayan skipper Diego Ormaechea, breaks from the back of a scrum against Spain. *Courtesy: Allsport*

Former Wallaby flanker Ilie Tabua, now playing with Fiji, does the two-step as Canadian captain Gareth Ress, the only man to play in all four World Cups, looks content to play touch football. *Courtesy: Allsport*

Japan's Hiroyuki Tanuma wins a lineout against Wales in Cardiff.
Courtesy: Allsport

NSW centre Jason Jones-Hughes, at the centre of a contract
wrangle before being cleared to play for Wales, makes his first
appearance in the starting side on the wing against Japan.
Courtesy: Allsport

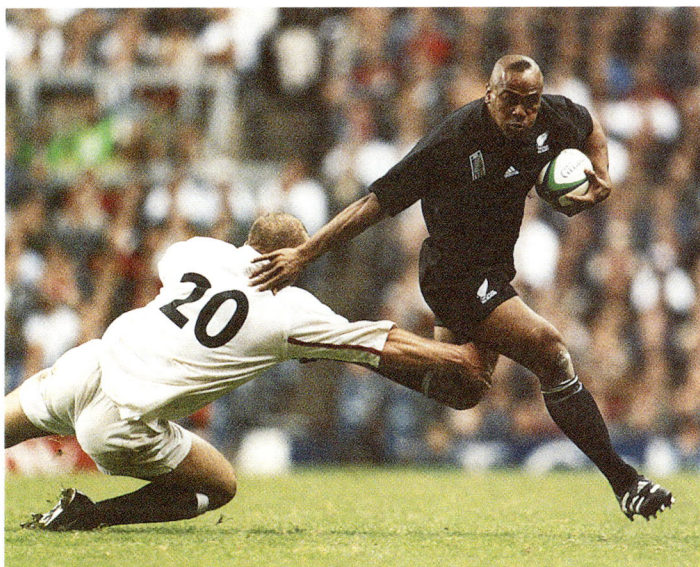

The All Blacks emerged as the form team of the preliminary
rounds, while Jonah Lomu confirmed his standing as the most
feared player in the game. England struggled to contain him, as
Tim Rodber shows with his attempted tackle. *Courtesy: Allsport*

Samoan winger Vai'aga Tuigamala powers past Argentine centre Lisandro Arbizu. *Courtesy: Allsport*

Springbok skipper Joost van der Westhuizen slides past Spanish defenders at Murrayfield. *Courtesy: Allsport*

arguably at the peak of his powers, vying with Sean Fitzpatrick as the best hooker on the planet.

Kearns gave the Wallabies another World XV level player, along with the likes of David Campese, Tim Horan, Jason Little, Michael Lynagh, Nick Farr-Jones, John Eales, Willie Ofahengaue and Simon Poidevin. A team chockful of talent, it was widely acclaimed as the best Australia has produced, with the 1984 Grand Slam winners also in the frame, followed by the side of the mid-1960's when the likes of Ken Catchpole, Phil Hawthorne, John Thornett and Rob Heming helped launch a Wallaby revival.

'If you had to compare all those sides in terms of how they played the game in their own eras, then it becomes very difficult,' said Kearns. 'But even looking at it that way, I still believe this team would be every bit as good as the 1991 side.'

The first test of Kearns' stellar ranking for the 1999 World Cup contenders comes at Landowne Road when the Wallabies face an Irish side buoyed with a new found confidence. Former Test flanker Poidevin, in Dublin for television commentary duties, watched the Wallabies train by the Irish Sea and suggested they were facing a ferocious contest.

'The other mob will reach levels of passion unprecedented in Irish rugby,' he said. 'Anyone who thinks it won't be close has to be on drugs. From what I've seen already, this Irish team would kill the Welsh.'

Kearns and his teammates have already discussed the scenario Poidevin aired on a windswept field adjacent to the famous Portmarnock golf course. 'I pretty much expect it will be like the 1991 quarter final,' said Kearns. 'They'll be pretty niggly, they love a bit of a niggle. And I don't know if they'll do what (Irish backrower) Phil Matthews did from the kickoff in that game, but if they do we'll be ready for them.'

Matthews bolted through at the start of the game and punched Wallaby flanker Ofahengaue squarely on the jaw. 'It was a pretty dumb thing to do,' laughed Kearns. 'Willie belted the living daylights out of him. And if it happens this time, we won't be intimidated. I think our performance against the All Blacks at Stadium Australia showed we won't be intimidated by anyone.'

The worry for both sides, however, is the International Rugby Board's sudden desire to sanitise the game with an unannounced crackdown on foul play. Citing commissioners have already made their mark, hauling several players before judiciary panels after last weekend's opening series of round robin matches.

Three players — Colin Charvis (Wales), Roberto Grau (Argentina) and Suia Taumalolo (Tonga) — have been suspended, with the length of ban ranging from two to three weeks. If the Australians allow themselves to be suckered into a stoush, the aftermath for both sides could seriously jeopardise their tournament prospects.

'We've seen what's happened already,' said Kearns. 'But if someone comes in and plants one on your nose, your first thought is not always 'there's a video guy watching'.'

Several players who were part of the failed 1995 World Cup challenge have already noticed the difference in attitude on this campaign to Britain. The mood, they say, is far more relaxed and there are obvious contributing factors.

Not having the pressure of arriving here as defending champions and tournament favourites, and the glare of publicity that brings, has helped breed an air of nonchalance.

But it does, at times, get to the coach. At training, Rod Macqueen, serious by nature, admitted his blood pressure has risen on several occasions.

'I'm never happy,' he said. 'I'm always saying they've got to be more intense. They're a fairly laid back sort of bunch. Good Australian larrikins. Still, it can be frustrating for me as a coach. The team laughs and jokes and it can get on my nerves. But the good thing about them is they do know when to switch on.'

Macqueen's right hand man, assistant coach Jeff Miller, will re-visit his mixed emotions from the 1991 World Cup when the Wallabies run out against Ireland in front of a sellout crowd. Miller was openside flanker when Australia beat Ireland in that famous quarter final at Lansdowne Road.

But for the semi final with the All Blacks the following week — again in Dublin — he was dropped from the side for Simon

Poidevin. 'It was disappointing at the time because I knew it was all over for me,' said Miller. 'I knew it was my last year and, when I lost my spot, I knew that Irish game would be my last Test. It was obvious that if they went on to beat New Zealand they wouldn't change the team again.'

World Cup goalkickers are grumbling over the footballs being used at the tournament. They claim the balls are too narrow, making the sweet spot smaller, are too pointed at both ends and more closely resemble a rugby league pill than the usual Test match issues.

Hookers are also complaining that the balls, because of their shape, take a different trajectory when being thrown to a lineout. 'When we got one for training last week we thought they'd made a mistake and sent us the runt of the litter,' said one Wallaby. 'Then we got out there for the game against Romania and discovered all the balls are the same.'

Born and raised in New Zealand, growing up in the south island and daring to dream they would one day play for the All Blacks, the Bachop boys were your average rugby-crazed Kiwi kids from Polynesian bloodlines. Unlike most they reached their Nirvana, with Graeme playing 31 Tests as a halfback and his elder brother Stephen a handful in the five-eighth jumper.

But at this World Cup they wear different costumes, are opposed to each other, and with neither singing God Defend New Zealand as their national anthem before each game. In the ultimate have-boots-will-travel tale, Graeme Bachop has hopped from the Land of the Long White Cloud to the Land of the Rising Sun as part of a fair-weather Kiwi horde that have given Japan new-found respect on the game's grandest stage.

Stephen Bachop has preferred to follow his ancestry, and is suiting up for Samoa. He has, significantly, worn blue before, even before he became an All Black, playing for the tiny South Pacific island at the 1991 World Cup.

It is a complexity of the code — many consider it a failing —

that national allegiance has been so easily transferable. But the regulations of the International Rugby Board, the sport's governing body, outline how it has happened.

There are two simple criteria for national team eligibility: that a player has a parent or grandparent born in the country for which he wants to play, or that he has lived there continuously for 36 months. Graeme Bachop qualifies for Japan on the second count, Stephen Bachop for Samoa on the first.

And they are but two of a large 'imports' contingent plying their trade at the highest level, more often than not out of an inability to reach the same heights in the country that initially nurtured their footballing skills.

It is why so many New Zealanders are sprinkled throughout the tournament, clutched to the bosom of other nations, and why a growing number of South Africans and Australians are following the same offshore path to Test match honours. Cruel but true, most were simply not good enough to hack it from where they came. And once hefty monetary offers to head elsewhere are factored in there is, in the professional age, really no choice to make.

There are exceptions, with Graeme Bachop and two current Wallabies high at the top of the list. Former Springbok captain Tiaan Strauss was still at the forefront of the game in South Africa when he accepted a Super League offer at the end of 1995. His two years of rugby league in Australia, plus a season with the NSW Waratahs on return to his union roots, opened the door for Wallaby selection.

Noriega did likewise, heading down under more than three years ago when at the peak of his powers for the Argentine Pumas. The game in South America, even now, is strictly amateur, and when the ACT Brumbies came to him with a six-figure deal to play Super 12, he was not about to shake his head. He now calls Canberra home, and has brought out a dozen or more family members to settle within Australia. Bachop was also impressed by the bottom line when he left New Zealand for Tokyo. But Strauss, Noriega and the Bachops are among the fortunate few — the last of the dual internationals.

From January 1, players who have represented one country will be prevented from playing for another, regardless of residential status or their family tree.

The IRB have brought in the law to prevent an explosion of

country hopping that threatened to undermine the credibility of future World Cups.

Imagine the scenario under the old regulation. Japan, where corporations are prepared to spend millions to improve their company teams, buy up the entire All Blacks side and sit them out of Test football for three years until they qualify to wear the red and white hoops. At the next World Cup, Japan are suddenly title contenders.

The change on New Year's Day will not, however, stop the movement of players such as Sydney born, Sydney raised, Sydney in their system players such as Jason Jones-Hughes and Matt Mostyn. Both had yet to win Wallaby Test honours when they headed overseas, Mostyn to Ireland and Jones-Hughes to Wales.

The Jones-Hughes case was further complicated by the fact he has a contract with the Australian and NSW rugby unions who claim him as theirs even though the IRB ruled in Wales' favour.

Former Wallaby flanker Simon Poidevin, a hand on the heart Australian, sees no problem with the mass movement of players across international waters. 'I think it's contributing to a stronger game globally,' he said. 'If players from Australia, New Zealand or the UK can go to other countries, are qualified to play for them, and can help that nation develop, then it has to be good for rugby.

'Then you also have players like Willie Ofahengaue, who chose to live in Australia after being born in Tonga and spending time in New Zealand. I don't look at Willie as a Tongan. He's a patriotic Australian and I'm proud to have played alongside him.'

Kenji Taguchi, a television producer on tour with Japan — whose Test skipper is Andrew McCormick, a second-tier Kiwi and the son of an All Black legend — echoed the Poidevin sentiments. 'New Zealand have given us soul,' said Taguchi. 'When I speak with McCormick something goes through my body. He makes me very brave. He's the man.'

But the last word belongs to Strauss, who is fulfilling his long-held ambition to play at a World Cup. In 1995, there was speculation he would skipper the Springboks, but Francois Pienaar held on to the job and, in a major shock, Strauss was not even selected in the South African squad.

'I don't see a problem with me now playing for Australia,' he said. 'I've taken up residency, it's my future home. I give the Wallabies 100 percent.'

October 9

POOL MATCHES

FIJI 38 CANADA 22

WALES 64 JAPAN 15

NEW ZEALAND 30 ENGLAND 16

ROMANIA 27 USA 25

Former Australian fullback Roger Gould, part-time coach and fierce protector of the struggling USA Eagles, has warned the Wallabies the Americans will fight like 'cats and dogs' at Limerick in their tournament exit on Thursday. But Gould is also a realist. He knows that domestic pets in a jungle stand little chance of survival.

After Romania beat the USA 27–25 in front of only 2500 in Dublin on Saturday, Gould took a swipe at the International Rugby Board, at Rugby World Cup bosses, and at anyone who dares to denigrate the players wearing red, white and blue.

He pointed to the lack of financial assistance afforded the game in America, and of the limited World Cup preparation for a side forced to take on two possible semi-finalists in their pool in Ireland, based at home, and Australia. The Irish have already accounted for the Americans 53–8.

But with skipper and backrower Dan Lyle — good enough to play club football in England — to miss the game against the Wallabies with a badly injured shoulder, and with morale taking a mauling in the loss to the Romanians, indications are the Pool E finale will be a Limerick landslide.

Leading into the World Cup, England racked up a 106–8 win over the USA at Twickenham. Thomond Park might not rock to a century, with the Australians to rest key players, but a cricket score is expected.

'I've had 12 days all up in the preparation of this team, and for the past year you know how long they've had together to train and play?' said Gould. 'Only 42 days. Compare that to the big boys. Before the World Cup there was no club competition going. They assembled only eight days before flying to Dublin and you had guys running around the block in Atlanta or Philadelphia to keep themselves fit.

'When people say they shouldn't be here, I feel like head butting them. It's ill-informed, ill-equipped, unqualified comment. If they don't want us here, make the qualification harder. But these guys have more passion for the game than blokes from the leading nations. It's the only reason they're here, for the fun of it.'

According to Gould, the camaraderie of the side ties them together. From the handful who have thrown in their jobs to be at the World Cup, to the multi-millionaire who resides on the side of their scrum. Richard Tardits, 34, is a former Winter Olympian for France in the four-man bobsled. He was also a NFL linebacker for the Arizona Cardinals and New England Patriots.

'He played three full seasons in American football and made millions,' said Gould. 'He went to Harvard to get a business masters, has a waste disposal company in New York that's worth a fortune, and now just wants to play rugby. When I die, I want to come back as Richard Tardits.'

American coach Jack Clarke, who says his players still wait in hope that News Corporation will decide to fund a professional league in the USA, described the loss to Romania as a sickening blow. 'We feel gutted,' he said. 'But at the same time, I wouldn't swap one of my players for any other guy at this tournament. That tells you how proud I am of them. When we play Australia we'll be trying to play rugby. There's no sense in us attempting to stifle the game or going out just to keep the score down. That's a cynical approach not in keeping with the American attitude.'

Freddie Kruger has nothing on Jonah Lomu.

When the All Black wing giant raced 60 metres down the left touchline at Twickenham on Saturday, slaughtering defenders along the way to signal to England he was most assuredly back, the nightmares of four years ago returned in a flood. Not only for England, but for any other team in this World Cup with designs

on lopping Lomu and his Kiwi mates in the November 6 final
or before.

In a seven-second burst which turned one of the crunch
games of the tournament, Lomu was again that irresistible force who
dominated the 1995 event in South Africa.

Back then it was a four-try storm in a semi final at Cape Town
that blew the English away, Lomu treating Tony Underwood, Mike
Catt and co. as human doormats on each of his charges to set up a
comfortable All Black victory. At the weekend, almost on the hour,
he brushed aside four defenders in a surge that stopped an England
revival, silenced the singing of Swing Low Sweet Chariot, and set
New Zealand on the road to a 30–16 victory and another virtually
certain World Cup final appearance.

Barring an upset at the hands of Scotland in the quarters and
probably Ireland or France in the semis — and none of those three
European nations are considered the equal of England — the All
Blacks will play the decider. And have the chance to avenge their
1995 loss to South Africa when Lomu was shut down for room and
consistently double-teamed by an onrushing Springbok defence.

England, however, had no answer on Saturday to the menacing
presence of the No.11, who now wears what hair he does not shave
like a tiara upon his head. Or should that be crown? The moment
arrived in the 58th minute, with England and the All Blacks locked
at 16–all. New Zealand pushed the ball to the left and Mehrtens sent
a long pass to Lomu, standing 10m inside his own half. He brushed
off English centre Jeremy Guscott and his marker Austin Healey,
before stretching the famous thighs and setting off over the last 30m
to the English line.

Halfback Matt Dawson and winger Dan Luger chased and
grabbed the runaway, but the left hand went out and the ball went
down before England number eight Lawrence Dallaglio arrived with
an accidental knee to Lomu's face.

'It's not my problem it's his problem,' Lomu said later. 'The ref
said 'cool it' and Dallaglio said he didn't do anything. I just crossed
the line and I got a knee in the face. I was pretty hot about it but I
had these red cards flashing up in front of my eyes.

'You know if you hit them you could be out of the
tournament. You've just got to keep your control.' As for the try,
Lomu said: 'I was just screaming at the top of my lungs for Mehrts to

give the ball. I found the shortest route to the try line and I got there. 'I didn't want to let my country down today. And as I say, the only way I'm coming off that field is on a stretcher.'

Before Lomu struck, New Zealand had been superior with the ball in hand, creating gaps almost at will, while the English hammered away like battering rams, unable to break down the All Black defensive screen.

But the Kiwi sparkle had not provided an edge on the scoreboard. After 18 minutes it was 10–0, a penalty goal to five-eighth Andrew Mehrtens and a converted try to fullback Jeff Wilson leaving England on the back foot.

The English forwards though were not to be snuffed out.

While the boys behind the scrum dithered and showed little enterprise — five-eighth Jonny Wilkinson relying surprisingly on the high kick ploy, a sure sign of frustration — the England pack, led by number eight Lawrence Dallaglio, were doing their bit. From 13–6 down at half time, and 10 points adrift two minutes into the second half, England staged a revival. It took a slice of luck, the ball bouncing off an upright, for England centre Phil de Glanville to score in the 49th minute from a grubber kick by Guscott.

When Wilkinson landed a penalty goal five minutes later, and he kicked only four from eight on the day, the scores were level. Lomu broke open the game and replacement halfback Byron Kelleher stuck the final dagger into England's broken hearts when he crossed 10 minutes from the finish.

England have a horror draw ahead if they are to emulate their final appearance of 1991. The All Blacks have taken the high road. And coach John Hart is more than happy.

'That,' he said later, 'was our best performance of 1999.'

Former Wallaby five-eighth Michael Lynagh will have just three more days to savour his greatest points-scoring landmark. Lynagh's previously peerless 911 points from 72 Tests — a breakdown of 17 tries, 140 conversions, 177 penalty goals and nine dropped goals — remained untouched until Saturday in Cardiff.

Alongside him now on the same world record total is Welsh five-eighth Neil Jenkins, not in the same league as Lynagh as a player but level pegging points-wise, after collecting a haul of 19 in the 64–15 thrashing of Japan.

Jenkins has reached the Lynagh figure in one extra Test match, and will break the record when Wales play Samoa in their final pool match at the Millennium Stadium on Thursday.

—

'I'm a little fed up. I'm over the initial shock of it now, but it's still annoying.' Pensioner Brendan Burke has had calls flooding into his Dublin home from journalists searching for the Wallabies, after World Cup organisers wrongly printed his telephone number in media guides as that of the hotel where the Australians are staying.

The 70–year-old is an indoor bowls fan, not a rugby devotee. But a 'we're sorry' carton of Guinness from World Cup bosses has helped calm his aging nerves.

—

Voices of the downtrodden — the cash-strapped minnows who have come to the World Cup struggling to make ends meet — continue to rise above the din of crowds and on-field action. Fijian coach Brad Johnstone is the latest to scream for assistance from the International Rugby Board after revealing that the islanders, who could knock over France this week, got to the tournament only after their government and a public appeal helped raise the funds to pay for the side's preparation.

'We have spent money the whole year to outfit and develop the team,' he said. 'That left us $800,000 in debt. We had to swallow our pride and go to the government with a begging bowl. There will be a profit of more than $100 million generated from the World Cup. It should be shared out among all the unions, especially the ones who need it.'

—

On the financial front, Romanian players were deeply moved when team management announced a win bonus of $400 a man for their victory over the USA. The Romanian federation are all but broke, have virtually no equipment, and are relying on help from the IRB to pay their players a paltry $25 a day at the tournament.

But somehow, somewhere, around $8000 was cobbled together to reward the Romanians for their victory in Dublin. It is less than a single Australian player will have made for this morning's game against Ireland.

October 10

POOL MATCHES

AUSTRALIA 23 IRELAND 3

SOUTH AFRICA 47 SPAIN 3

ARGENTINA 32 SAMOA

TONGA 28 ITALY 25

Australian hooker Phil Kearns has been forced out of the World Cup, his Test career effectively over, but a further bombshell has rocked the Wallabies with two key players cited after the Dublin disposal of Ireland. While Kearns will be heading home this week to consider retirement after rupturing ligaments in his right foot, the tournament futures of centre Daniel Herbert and number eight Toutai Kefu are in limbo as they prepare to front a judiciary tribunal tomorrow.

Herbert has been called to answer a high tackle charge that left Ireland centre Kevin Maggs dazed and unable to continue during the Wallabies 23–3 victory at Lansdowne Road today, while Kefu is in hot water over the punches he rained on flanker Trevor Brennan early in the second half. Both Australians were cited by one of the independent commissioners appointed by World Cup bosses and ordered to crack down on acts of foul play.

The prospect of losing either Herbert or Kefu will hang heavily over the Wallabies as they head to Limerick for Thursday night's clash with the USA — their last assignment before a likely quarter final with Wales in Cardiff on Saturday week. A suspension of two weeks would rule them ineligible for the quarters and a three-week ban would have them sidelined for the semi finals. Punching offences have already brought players penalties of 14 to 21 days.

For the entire Wallaby squad, and for Kearns in particular, the aftermath of Dublin, a city so cherished when the Australians won crucial knockout matches here en route to World Cup glory eight years ago, has been a series of rolling disasters.

Test skipper John Eales is also on the injured list, with a groin strain likely to sideline him for up to 10 days. 'This is not the way I wanted to go out,' a shattered Kearns, 32, said. But the most capped Wallaby hooker in history with 66 Test appearances refused to confirm his retirement from the game. He said discussions with NSW and Australian officials over the next few days, and with wife Julie in Sydney next week, will decide whether he attempts to take his Test career into an 11th year.

Kearns, who made his debut against the All Blacks in 1989 and racked up a record 46 consecutive Tests to 1995, had hoped to make a fairytale farewell to the game on rugby union's greatest stage. But the mishap eight minutes into the Ireland game, and x-rays that revealed the extent of the damage, have shattered his hopes of leaving the game as a dual World Cup winner. They have also prompted a re-think on his future.

'I've got mixed emotions now about whether I pull the pin or go for another year,' he said. 'The positives are I could keep playing, keep being involved with the team. I've been really happy with my form this year. Hopefully the selectors have been happy as well, because they were continuing to pick me. The negatives are time away from the family and possibly going on too long. I'll need surgery and that means three months to get back to 100 percent. You have different thoughts from one hour to the next. But a couple of the guys have urged me to keep going.'

One problem for Kearns is that NSW have already signed two hookers for next year's Super 12 with the Waratahs resigned to the veteran retiring. 'They have approached me to see if I want to keep going,' he said. 'So the door is still open there I think.'

Australian team physio Greg Craig was treating skipper John Eales when Kearns returned long-faced to the Wallabies hotel after his hospital visit. 'He walked in and just said 'mate it's all over'. But typical of Phil, he's taken it on the chin,' said Craig. 'All he wanted to do after the x-rays came through was get to the after match function, to be there with his mates.'

While Kearns defied even the expectations of his closest allies by returning to the Test team last season after two years out with injury, he also had to graft his way back this season having been

overlooked early for ACT young gun Jeremy Paul. A replacement for
Kearns will not be named until after the USA game, when the
Wallabies will also know the availability of Herbert and Kefu.

→

Former Test coach Alan Jones has joined the court of David
Campese in urging the Wallabies to unleash their backline and parade
the brilliance they are likely to need to win the fourth World Cup.

The mastermind behind Australia's 1984 Grand Slam triumph,
where Mark Ella was the focal point of a free-running side, Jones
aired his concerns about the Wallabies approach in a 23–3 win over
Ireland at Lansdowne Road on Sunday. Speaking on Irish television,
Jones said the Australians were 'making the whole thing too damn
complicated', a tactical affliction he believed was infecting Test sides
around the globe. 'I think we're killing ourselves,' he said.

'We're capable of winning a game like that by 30 or 40 points.
We're capable of beating anyone in the world the way players like
Horan and Tune have the ability to use limited space. But from an
Australian point of view, they couldn't be happy with that
performance, particularly the way some of the other big sides like
New Zealand are playing.

'Australia at no stage put the ball through the hands, bringing
the fullback in and out to the wing. They are making the whole
thing too damn complicated. But it's the modern game, it's not just
Australia. How many Tests have you seen where it's heads down,
bums up, with no movement across the field until late in the game?'

The Jones observations were remarkably in synch with the
season-long thoughts of Campese, whose views on how the Wallabies
should play have been consistently dismissed by team and
management as a simplistic, behind the times notion.

If Jones is now to join the list of those getting under Wallaby
skins, then the Australians can at least be thankful that the breakfast
radio star holidaying here did not rate them as poorly as the Irish.

'They'll be flat out beating Romania if they play like that,' he
said. 'With the ball they were awful. They're all at sea in using it.'

Ireland coach Warren Gatland was not about to argue. 'We felt
we didn't fire a shot there today, we're very disappointed,' he said. 'We
really let ourselves down. But one of the Australian strengths is

defence. They didn't concede a try to Romania, they didn't let one in here and they were very good against New Zealand in August. They will only get better.'

But while Gatland was willing to praise the Wallabies, he was equally happy to land a backhander, almost in keeping with the physical approach witnessed earlier out on the park.

When the Wallabies lost both hookers late in the first half — Phil Kearns to a foot injury and his deputy Jeremy Paul to a head gash — referee Clayton Thomas was encouraged to de-power the scrum, preventing either side from pushing as Dan Crowley, a prop, took over in an unaccustomed role.

'It was a bit of a disgrace that in international rugby you play against a side that has three front rowers and you have to go into uncontested scrums,' Gatland said. 'I could understand it if it was a hooker playing prop, but not a prop playing hooker. And for them to go to uncontested scrums when we were pretty dominant at the time was a bit of a cop out by Australia.'

Macqueen was concerned more with the big picture of the Wallabies campaign, saying there had been a step up from the disposal of Romania a week before in Belfast.

And he was right. While the Australians might still under utilise their primary strength out wide, they did create opportunities, only for the finishing to lack the clinical touch that will be required in the weeks ahead. The raw woodwork was in place. That much is encouraging. What it needs now is polishing.

'We are aware there is a long way to go,' said Macqueen. 'A lot of improvement has to be made. 'We had a lot of trouble getting continuity, we weren't able to string a lot of phases together. There were a lot of penalties at the breakdown, we dropped a lot of ball and we made a lot of breaks that we didn't go on with. The swirling wind out there also made it difficult to throw the ball around.'

The Wallabies led only 6–0 at half time through a penalty apiece from Matt Burke and skipper John Eales, who was called to the job after his fullback missed with two other attempts. There had been patches of promise, a number of chances botched, and nothing substantial to take to the interval.

After the break, Australia stretched the lead to 9–0, with Burke back in the kicking role, before Ireland's only points arrived through the boot of five-eighth David Humphreys. At the 55–minute mark, the Australians finally crossed the home side's line, with man of the match Horan slicing through from a raid into the Irish quarter. Tune provided the finish to another foray in the final 10 minutes.

Australian coach Rod Macqueen has called for the introduction of a Test match sin-bin to weed out the cynical fouls that are stifling attacks at this World Cup.

After the Wallabies accounted for Ireland, Macqueen pointed to the number of occasions on which the Australians were foiled inside the home side's quarter by players happy to give away penalties rather than risk conceding a try.

'A sin-bin would be something really good,' he said. 'It's something that works at Super 12 level and it does stop that sort of infringement situation happening because you know you'll be with only 14 players if you continue to do it. It does make for more free flowing football.

'I think sometimes it can be taken the wrong way that there's not attacking football. What's happening is there's a lot of penalties against the defending side when the other side looks likely to score. We spent the majority of time in their quarter but weren't able to kick the goals when they came.'

Asked if attack or defence would win the World Cup, Macqueen added: 'You've got to have a good defence these days but I hope it's going to be won by an attacking side.'

French legend Philippe Sella, the first man in world rugby to play 100 Tests, admits the famous Tricolours are on the verge of their greatest humiliation as they prepare to play Fiji in Toulouse. A loss for France — even Sella believes what would once have been considered impossible could happen on Saturday — and the 1987 finalists will face a quarter final playoff with England.

'If that happens, it will be over,' said the former champion centre sadly. 'This will be a tense week for the French team. They have to be very serious, very strong in the forwards against Fiji. They need to keep it tight, not play with traditional French flair. At the moment they cannot do it. Playing wide balls is too difficult for this French team. Too many turnovers, too many mistakes. There are worries in our head.'

———

Crowds for most matches, especially those outside of Cardiff, have been poor and the promotion of the tournament even more low-key. It is enough to have South Africa's 1995 World Cup-winning skipper Francois Pienaar wondering about the apathy of the Brits, who seem to take the attitude that the tournament is big enough to generate interest without too much hard work from the orgnising crew.

'I have been surprised by the lack of promotional material, banners, posters and billboards in the great rugby cities of Europe,' said Pienaar. 'The World Cup will be watched by more than three billion people in more than 140 countries. Surely one would think that a tournament of this stature would be promoted to the rafters?'

———

How fortunate for players, coaches and fans that 'Fearless' Fred Howard is enjoying retirement rather than blowing his whistle at the fourth World Cup. Good old Freddie, who did control 20 internationals, has taken a pot shot at the men in the middle here, claiming they are not tough enough, not delivering enough penalties.

'At the moment if they whistle one scrum or one lineout, they feel they are doing their job,' he said. 'The key word is token. I've watched the put-in at the scrum in particular, and I've seen no change to crooked feeds.'

What are they thinking about? Put Fred back in charge. He's just what we need. A few more peeps on the whistle from some pedantic little bloke wanting to play policeman.

———

Tim Horan has developed a liking for World Cup matches at Lansdowne Road. Eight years ago the ground was the scene of his famous semi-final try against the All Blacks, courtesy of an overhead pass from David Campese. Today, he was on the scoresheet again but, more importantly, emerged from the game as Australia's best on the

day followed by Toutai Kefu — he of the flailing fists. Horan
has been in sweet touch in both of Australia's pool matches,
suggesting his decision to stay in the game at the highest level
next season rather than go to England was certainly in the Wallabies
best interests.

His combination with five-eighth Stephen Larkham will only
get better too. Larkham was rusty today, as he should have been,
having not played a Test in almost 12 months. It was not a spectacular
game, apart from the fireworks, but a 20–point win in Dublin will do
nicely at this stage.

Those demanding future World Cups be cut back from 20 teams to
16 because the tiddlers of the tournament are just not up to scratch
should take note of the Tonga-Italy result.

Tonga would not have been here under the old format,
sneaking in as they did through the repechages after Australia, Samoa
and Fiji all advanced to the main draw before them in the Pacific
region. But with the additional teams came Tonga, winners here over
a side considered good enough to have the Five Nations
Championship expanded next year.

This game came down to the last kick of the game, with
Tongan fullback Sateki Tuipulotu landing a 45m dropped goal to
break a 25–all deadlock. Italian five-eighth Diego Dominguez had
drawn his side level only minutes before with a penalty goal from
similar range. For Australian-born fullback Matt Pini, it was another
day of disappointment. Replaced due to injury against England, he
threw an intercept pass for a Tongan try.

Wallaby captain John Eales harboured only one regret as he cast his vote for an Australian republic during the World Cup campaign in Europe. Among the first to vote on the referendum — via a temporary polling booth set-up at a function at the Australian ambassador's residence in Dublin — the Wallabies are planning to be otherwise engaged when the rest of the nation have their say.

The World Cup final, at the Millennium Stadium in Cardiff, will also be staged on November 6 and the disappointment for Eales is that sport and politics will not be in perfect symmetry. 'It would have been good to play England in the final,' he joked. 'We could stuff them on the field and stuff them in the vote. Unfortunately, there's no chance of that now.'

The dye was cast last Saturday. New Zealand beat England in a pool match at Twickenham, handing the Brits a passage through the knockout stages that has them on a collision course with Eales and his teammates a week before the decider.

At least, shrugged Eales, a pre-referendum strike can be made. 'I've gone for the republic,' he said, openly declaring his allegiance. 'I think it's great the history we've had, and the connection with Britain. But for all intents and purposes, Australians make decisions about Australia, there's not a lot of relevance to the monarchy. For that reason alone, as well as others, I voted that way. We don't need to be associated with them and I think it's far more relevant to have an Australian head of state.'

Eales also told of receiving a letter from a leading Australian sportsman, light-heartedly touching on the republican issue. 'He was saying we've never had any special treatment flying into Heathrow,' laughed Eales. 'You've got a line for British passports and a line for the rest. And the other line is always 80 times longer.'

Centre Jason Little was another devout republican. 'Most of the guys are,' he said. 'There's a few monarchists but from my point of view I think it's pretty simple. Being Australians we should have an Australian head of state. It's a sense of independence, of breaking away.'

While most of the Wallabies voted tonight, one member of the

30–man squad did not. Former South African captain Tiaan Strauss, who has been living in Australia for almost four years, is not eligible for citizenship until next year.

Wallaby centre Jason Little will captain his country for the first time when the Wallabies play their final World Cup pool match — and blood two Test rookies — against the United States on Thursday. Little has been chosen to lead a largely second-string side in Limerick as Australian selectors moved to ensure every player in the 30–man squad will make at least one appearance during the tournament campaign. Winger Scott Staniforth and prop Rod Moore, who joined the Wallabies as a replacement last week, will make their Test debuts at the famous Thomond Park, where Irish provincial side Munster once had a legendary win over the All Blacks.

But for the veteran Little, a 10–year Test star, the match will hold unexpected significance after coach Rod Macqueen handed him the captaincy reins. 'It's one of the pinnacles of my career, as it would be for anyone,' said Little. 'Putting it in context, if too many first-choice players had been available, I wouldn't have had the opportunity. But I'm absolutely thrilled to be doing it, really looking forward to it. And a few of the guys have already taken to calling me Slaughter, after (former Test second rower) Rod McCall. He was a one-Test captain — as I'm sure I will be — in the last World Cup when we played Romania.'

Little admitted to limited leadership experience, skippering Queensland against Scotland a few years back and acting as Australian vice-captain on several occasions in 1994 and 1997.

'I can tell you now, the pre-match talk will be short,' he said. 'But in many ways this will be a difficult game for us. It's really a no-win situation. If we score a lot of points it will be expected anyway. Play poorly and there'll be disappointment. What we have to do is focus on the basics and on our own standards. The Americans will be upset with their loss to Romania a few days ago so they'll be up for this one.'

Until his captaincy boost, the World Cup had not been a raging success during the first fortnight for Little. A member of the starting line-up when the Wallabies came away, he lost his place on the wing to Joe Roff after the opening game against Romania. For the clash with the USA, he returns to outside centre to form a new-look pairing with Nathan Grey.

Elsewhere, Chris Whitaker will start at halfback for the first time since last year's World Cup qualifiers with George Gregan one of several frontline players rested for the last of the round robin fixtures. Chris Latham receives his chance at fullback, with Matthew Burke in the side but filling in on one wing.

Only five-eighth Stephen Larkham, needing game time after his injury absence, has been retained from the backline, in the same position, after the win over Ireland on Sunday. The forwards have also undergone a major re-shuffle, with a revamped front-row and second-row, and experimentation at number eight and flanker.

One concern for the Wallabies is an ongoing injury to regular Test backrower Matt Cockbain. He was expected to start the USA match after missing the earlier games with Romania and Ireland. But medical staff have taken the precaution of limiting him to the reserves bench, if he takes his place in the squad at all.

'Matt has had a lingering kneecap problem,' said Wallaby team doctor John Best. 'While there's been steady progress, he didn't really progress much yesterday. He'll be having more aggressive treatment.'

Macqueen is keen for Cockbain's return with the next assignment, after the USA, to be a quarter final showdown with Wales on their home patch at Cardiff on Saturday week. With Cockbain not considered for the starting side, Owen Finegan will play at blindside flanker, with Jim Williams at number eight and Tiaan Strauss on the openside flank.

The selection of Strauss follows his earlier earmarking as the back-up flyer should David Wilson suffer any injury mishaps in the knockout stages.

The Australian team: Chris Latham, Scott Staniforth, Jason Little (c), Nathan Grey, Matt Burke, Stephen Larkham, Chris Whitaker, Jim Williams, Tiaan Strauss, Owen Finegan, Mark Connors, Tom Bowman, Rod Moore, Michael Foley, Dan Crowley. Reserves: Joe Roff, Rod Kafer, George Gregan, David Giffin, Matt Cockbain, David Wilson, Richard Harry, Jeremy Paul (one forward to be omitted).

Wallaby centre Tim Horan, so often the prince of practical jokes, has finally been resigned to the role of victim. As one teammate tells it, under the cloak of anonymity for fear of a Horan reprisal: 'A few of the guys were out the other night and Tim went up to this guy at the bar telling him how much he looked like (Irish dance star) Michael Flatley. 'The guy was going 'do you really think so?' They stood there talking for ages and it wasn't until the next morning that the penny dropped. 'Matt Burke said to Tim 'did you know Michael Flatley was there last night?' You could hear Helmet (Horan) groaning for hours.'

It has been a roller-coaster last few days for Australian centre Daniel Herbert.

The low point was Monday, the morning after the showdown with Ireland at Lansdowne Road, when Herbert was cited for an alleged high tackle of the home side's Kevin Maggs. But three days earlier, on a beach at Portmarnock, a stone's throw from the Wallabies hotel on the outskirts of Dublin, the Queensland midfield strongman was at peace with the world. Herbert proposed to his long-time Irish-born girlfriend. Suffice to say she is now his fiancée.

Wallaby number eight Toutai Kefu was rocked by a 14 day World Cup suspension today and will miss the likely quarter final showdown with Wales in a jolt to Australia's title campaign. Kefu was banned by a three-man tribunal after being cited for punching in Sunday's win over Ireland at Lansdowne Road, leaving him stranded from the Wallabies tournament challenge until the semi finals.

The Tongan-born forward will miss Australia's final pool match against the USA on Thursday, and the first of the knockout games against a fired-up Wales at Millennium Stadium on Saturday week.

For coach Rod Macqueen, the search is now on for a forward to replace the in-form star of the Australian pack from their opening two wins over Romania and Ireland. But finding a stand-in will not be easy. ACT Brumbies backrower Jim Williams will fill the number eight role against the USA, with Tiaan Strauss and Mark Connors also in the frame to take over from Kefu for the battle with Wales.

Australian centre Daniel Herbert was cleared of a high tackle on Irish centre Kevin Maggs.

Wallaby captain John Eales warned today the crackdown on World Cup violence could backfire if title contenders, fearful of losing key players, are left helpless to defend themselves against strongarm rivals. While Eales applauds any moves to stamp out dangerous acts, from stomping to headbutting and eye gouging, he is concerned the clean-up campaign by tournament officials may have been taken too far.

A spate of citings over the past fortnight has included instances of punching in self-defence or retaliation and, according to Eales, there should be allowances made. Former Wallaby winger David Campese has already spoken out against what he describes as an over-reaction from citing commissioners that threatens to turn the game into netball.

Eales holds a slightly different theory. He suggests heavyweight nations will not only be gun-shy but susceptible to intimidation from less skilled opponents as they head towards the knockout stages. 'Everyone wants to play in a clean game, but what exactly is clean?' he asked. 'You're going to expect a bit of rough and tumble. It's a physical contest out there, a body contact sport.

'That they're putting games under scrutiny to look for things is great. If they see someone kicking or head-butting or gouging, they should act. They should get the filthy stuff, the really dangerous stuff, out of the game. But what do you do if you play a side that comes out fighting in a match they need to win to get a spot in the quarter-finals or semi-finals?

'Perhaps they'd be happy to get that far and they'd be willing to come out fighting, just to try and put the other team off. They might see those sort of tactics as their only chance for victory. 'It's a real issue, a real dilemma. What do you do if someone baits you? I don't think two people tussling, one on one, is the end of the world. Hitting someone from behind or hitting a guy not in a position to defend himself is a different matter.

'But you have to draw a line somewhere. 'I'm not advocating open slather. But you do have to be realistic when it's a body contact sport. There are times when it will flare up. 'Now there is the potential there for less talented teams to bait players, even an incentive to bait, because their opposition will know that retaliation could land them in trouble.'

Eales held up the Tri-Nations series as a glowing example for the game. Despite the ferocity of the annual round robin games between Australia, New Zealand and South Africa, there have been rare outbreaks of foul play.

'People don't go overboard, it's very clean rugby all the time,' he said. 'There have been punches thrown on occasions, and I don't condone that. But sometimes things happen in the heat of the moment. I don't think it's hurt the game.'

Eales aired his concerns as Wallaby number eight Toutai Kefu and centre Daniel Herbert fronted judiciary hearings in London.

There was a serious spat in the Wallaby camp last week, kept under wraps until now. But halfback Chris Whitaker — preparing to start in a Test for only the second time when Australia play the USA in

Limerick on Thursday — has lifted the lid on the great lolly fiasco. Welcome to the life of a Wallaby reserve.

The scene was Belfast, on the night of Australia's opening World Cup pool match against the feisty Romanians. It was cold, windy, a miserable night, and with the inactive members of the Wallaby squad in need of their usual sustenance.

Whitaker takes over the tale.

'Someone gets the lollies each week, for the guys on the bench and the management,' he said. 'It's a bit of a tradition in the side. Phil Kearns used to do it but when he got back in the team, I took over, and it's not an easy job. I take the orders, and some guys have different requests. Before the game against Ireland I was down at the mall choosing all the different types, trying to meet the needs of everyone.'

But back up a bit, what about Belfast?

'I forgot against Romania,' he winced. 'The management were filthy, wouldn't talk to me. I was actually surprised I got on the field in the second half. You don't forget the lollies.'

Whitaker was not the only one taken aback when called into action as a replacement for George Gregan with 16 minutes remaining in the 57–9 towelling at Ravenhill Park. For over the past two years, Whitaker has been almost permanently rooted to the bench. Twenty-one times he has dressed for action, to be called into play on only four occasions. Add to that small collection one starting run in September last year against Tonga during World Cup qualifiers.

It is not without reason he is known by the Wallabies as Armageddon.

'The nickname came about because they reckon the world will end before I get on the field,' he said. 'We were laughing about it the other day. I went 13 straight without getting a run until the New Zealand Test this year.'

Levity aside, there are frustrations. There have to be in a competitive environment where ambition is needed to reach the top level.

'The suiting up before each game is not too bad, because you're always thinking you might get on,' said Whitaker. 'It's actually after the game when you come back into the change rooms. It's just a strange feeling. You just don't feel a part of it and it's a bit tough to get over at times. But I've coped with it a lot better this year than I did last season.

'I'm realising I'm better off being where I am, especially here, rather than back in Australia on a month's break before preparing for Super 12 again. This year it's been fine, I've got a bit used to it and they're a good bunch of blokes in this team. At some stages you do feel out of it, but you've got to cop the good with the bad.

'Halfback is not exactly a position you change a lot. Even this year for NSW, I rarely came off unless we were winning or losing by a lot. The halfback touches the ball more than anyone else so it's not the position to change. It's not an impact position like a number eight, and I understand that completely. Besides, I never dreamt of getting this far. I was ecstatic just to play first grade for Randwick a couple of years ago. To get this far is above all the expectations I had.'

But Whitaker still waits for more, and the taste of the good life — wearing the No.9 jumper — arrives again on Thursday against an American side the Australians should dispose of without too much concern.

'It's good to get a run,' he said. 'But it's good for a lot of the guys. Nathan Grey and Jason Little too, we've spent a lot of time on the bench this year. It will be good to get 80 minutes. And it's great that everyone in the squad will get a go at the World Cup. Scott Staniforth and Rod Moore are getting their first caps. It helps make everyone feel even more part of the squad.

'There's not that disjointed team versus the bench type of thing here. Everyone's in it for the same cause.'

That is not to say fringe and second-string players will not be busting their guts to impress the selectors and keep their names in the firing line to displace a mate in the side to play Wales in Saturday week's quarter final.

At the same time, the will to succeed can be a double-edged sword. While it can inspire, it can also breed over eagerness with eventual disappointment the by-product. Whitaker has fallen for it before.

Last season, when the form of Gregan was coming under scrutiny during the Super 12, there was a groundswell of speculation that Whitaker might usurp a halfback who now boasts more than a half century of Tests. Whitaker's form though, tailed off too, before Gregan rediscovered his touch.

'You just try to do too much, try to impress too much,' he said. 'Hopefully that won't happen with any of us against the United States. Certainly for me, with guys like Steve Larkham and Jason Little outside, I won't be hanging on to the ball too much.'

Armageddon is one of several nicknames Whitaker goes by in the side. Hobo is another — 'they reckon I'm a little surfie scumbag' — and there are several he claims that are too rude to mention. But he is used to the ribbing now. Nothing fazes him, except that weekly hunt for lollies.

At least on Thursday, as part of the starting line-up, he can hand on the job to someone else.

October 13

David Campese wonders at the inconsistencies produced by the World Cup crackdown on violence.

Can someone please send these mystery men sitting in front of video replays searching for World Cup foul play incidents a law book and pair of spectacles.

We've heard all the blather about the clampdown on violence, and the citing commissioners have gone gung-ho, pulling in nine guys already for punching, headbutting or the occasional high tackle. Some of the citings have been justified; plenty have not.

But the real joke of this whole judiciary shemozzle is that some genuine acts of foul play that should be stamped out of the game have been left to go unchecked, while the odd fisticuffs are frowned upon.

At the risk of sounding like a parochial Australian, how in the name of William Webb Ellis did they cite Daniel Herbert for his sensational and legal chest-high hit on Irish centre Kevin Maggs but miss the head-hunting effort of Conor O'Shea on Wallaby five-eighth Stephen Larkham?

Slow it down; take a look. Larkham was clearly caught high, and obviously dazed.

What was the commissioner doing then? Did he fast forward through that part of the game. For the life of me, I can't work them out.

The elbow from Irish flanker Trevor Brennan to Jeremy Paul's head was also a shocker. Paul was even looking the other way. How was that not worth a citing?

And if there's one thing in the game that annoys players, rankles with coaches and drives spectators around the bend, it's lack of consistency.

Referees have trouble with the meaning of the

word, and the World Cup citing commissioners, and their mates who sit on the judiciary panels, seem to have trouble finding the dictionary as well.

There have been other offenders who have escaped the eyes of the video police.

I think Lawrence Dallaglio was lucky after his kneeing episode on Jonah Lomu. I know a New Zealand player pushed him from behind, but Dallaglio's knee movements already seemed to be down and in the direction of the big bloke's face. As for Australian number eight Toutai Kefu, who was sensational in the win over Ireland, I have to say he was lucky to get only two weeks for his pummelling of Brennan.

A couple of former Irish internationals, Neil Francis and Brendan Mullin, were on the golf course with me on Tuesday. They rated Kefu's combination as the four finest punches they've ever seen. And both were big fans of Ireland's boxing legend Barry McGuigan. For mine, throwing the punches was not the issue. The fact he continued going on with it, at a time when it looked like Brennan was being held, is what didn't do him any favours.

The Wallabies are talking about an appeal. Two words of advice if I may, even though my suggestions tend to fall on deaf ears these days. Don't bother. Just let it go, walk away. Accept the 14-day ban and get back to the business of preparing for the USA tomorrow and the knockout stages that start next week.

Besides, Wales are not worth the hype surrounding them. Australia will beat them easily in the quarter finals, without or without Toutai Kefu.

What has happened to date also suggests Australia's chances of winning an appeal are slim. The Welsh tried with flanker Colin Charvis, who got two weeks for a couple of love taps on the back of an Argentine's head.

Their challenge of the original finding was thrown out quicker than a Kefu left jab.

On the football side of things, the Wallabies

created plenty of opportunities against Ireland but didn't finish them off on Sunday. It was a plus that they had so many chances to score, but a hint that they need to fine tune in training to get back that clinical edge.

In the first half too, I thought the Wallabies looked ill at ease. They didn't use the ball much. In the second half things got a little more shape, and we saw two good tries taken through some, dare I say it, attacking rugby.

The Australians have the potential to win this tournament. I hope they don't blow it, look back and think, 'if only we'd been more adventurous'.

Maybe they can start tomorrow against the low-flying Eagles.

And the margin in Limerick? I'd have to say 60 or 70 points.

―――

Toutai Kefu, the oversized Jeff Fenech who blasted holes in the features of Irish flanker Trevor Brennan on Sunday, was too scared to pick up the telephone to make the call he was dreading. Cited and suspended over the punching incident, his 14–day ban not only rubbed the Wallaby number eight out of a likely quarter final with Wales in Cardiff, but also torpedoed a planned family celebration.

'My dad and a cousin were coming over, just for a week, that's all they could get, especially to watch that game,' he said. 'I haven't had the guts to ring dad yet.'

Fatai Kefu played for Tonga in their earth shattering upset of the Wallabies at Ballymore 26 years ago. He moved his family, including infant son Toutai, to Australia two years later.

―――

The hit and miss shambles that is the judiciary process here had Kefu concerned when he fronted the tribunal in London.

'I'm obviously disappointed,' he said. 'But I was kind of

expecting around two weeks. At one stage I thought I might get one, but I heard other people saying I could end up with three, which would have meant missing the semi finals (if Australia advance). I'm just filthy on myself and feel as though I've let down the side.'

The concern in the Australian camp was obvious. Wallaby coach Rod Macqueen, at a press conference to discuss the suspension, spoke in animated terms about the ban, adding an appeal might be lodged.

'Obviously it's very disappointing for us because the decision has a significant impact on our World Cup plans,' he said. 'But we also believe there's been a bit of selective citation. There are a number of other incidents and to pick those two (Kefu and Daniel Herbert) astounds us.'

Herbert was cleared on a high tackle charge while Brennan was given two games for the stoush with Kefu.

The inconsistencies though are astonishing. Fijian winger Marika Vunibaka was up on a headbutting charge, far more serious than punching, yet the judiciary panel felt sending off for him was sufficient.

The worry now for the Wallabies is who to play at the back of the scrum against Wales in a quarter final?

Kefu is a damaging ball runner. There is no one from the same mould. Read on for the options.

Tiaan Strauss: Hard, straight runner but lacking the explosiveness of Kefu, and the Queenslander's ability to angle himself into holes. Where Strauss would run through brick walls, Kefu would look for a door.

Mark Connors: High workrate forward who would also improve the lineout. But again he is not a ball in hand gamebreaker.

Jim Williams: The most dynamic of the three contenders, but with little experience at the highest level. Would he be risked in such a big game?

A long-awaited showdown between Jason Jones-Hughes and his former Wallaby teammates in the World Cup quarter finals looks like fizzling out into a non-event.

When Welsh coach Graham Henry named a full-strength backline to play Samoa tonight in their final round robin pool match, the name Jones-Hughes was missing.

It must be taken as a pointer for the knockout stages ahead.

Captain in the clouds . . . skipper John Eales soars in a lineout against Ireland at Lansdowne Road in Dublin. *Courtesy: Allsport*

Player of the tournament . . . Tim Horan was in career-best form at the World Cup. His try here against Ireland was part of a man of the match performance. *Courtesy: Allsport*

Tim Horan's attacking forays were a feature of his peerless World Cup displays. His defence was typically top drawer too, as Irish centre Kevin Maggs discovered. *Courtesy: Allsport*

On song . . . Ben Tune pulls away from the despairing dive of Irish centre Brian O'Driscoll on his way to scoring in Dublin. *Courtesy: Allsport*

And the celebrations begin. *Courtesy: Allsport*

Matthew Burke finished the tournament with 101 points, second
only to Argentine golden boot Gonzalo Quesada. Burke also
passed 500 Test points during the six-match campaign in Britain
and Ireland. *Courtesy: Allsport*

Punching bag . . . Irish flanker Trevor Brennan battered and
bloodied after his toe-to-toe stoush with Toutai Kefu. Both
players were later cited and suspended, Kefu for 14 days and
Brennan for 10. *Courtesy: Allsport*

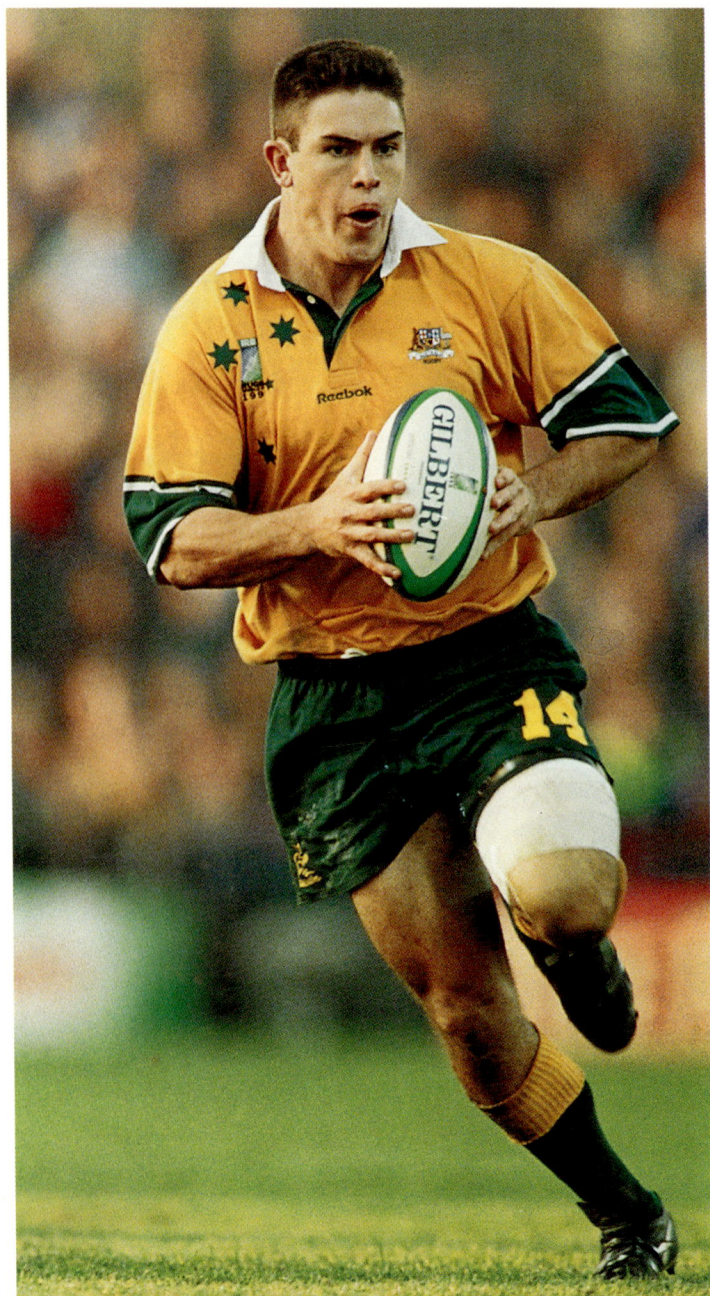

Dream debut . . . Scott Staniforth scored two tries in his first Test against the USA in Limerick. *Courtesy: Allsport*

Jeremy Paul came in for some heavy treatment from the Irish after replacing the injured Phil Kearns during the first half at Lansdowne Road. *Courtesy: Allsport*

Toutai Kefu was Australia's leading forward at the World Cup, with charges like this against Ireland providing the Wallabies with an attacking springboard. *Courtesy: Allsport*

Wild about Harry . . . Richard Harry, in fine form against Ireland, returned to his best during the tournament after being overlooked by Test selectors earlier in the season. *Courtesy: Allsport*

POOL MATCHES

NEW ZEALAND 101 ITALY 3

SAMOA 38 WALES 31

AUSTRALIA 55 USA 19

CANADA 72 NAMIBIA 11

Wallaby coach Rod Macqueen defiantly warned the All Blacks they hold no fears for Australia after the trans-Tasman rivals led the charge of heavyweights into the World Cup quarter finals. While New Zealand left behind the round robin series by steamrolling Italy under a century of points, the Australian campaign continued to stutter during a 55–19 disposal today of the USA in Limerick.

But Macqueen, who faces selection dilemmas at number eight and hooker before the quarter final in Cardiff next week against Wales, Samoa or Argentina, refuses to be intimidated. He maintains the Wallabies are still on track despite another patchy performance, where handling errors and sloppy finishing were in stark contrast to the clinical carve-up hours earlier by the rampant Kiwis.

'They got it all together today,' Macqueen said of the All Blacks demolition job in Huddersfield. 'I've said all the way through they're going to be the team to beat. But from our point of view, we've just got to worry about ourselves. If we meet them in the final, hopefully we'll be able to overcome that hurdle.'

There is a distinct lack of anxiety, almost a quiet air of confidence, in the Australian camp at present, even though they have yet to shift out of low gear and at times today were in reverse with the foot to the floor. It is calmness clearly born of their Stadium Australia win over New Zealand in August.

The Wallabies know if they click they can beat the All Blacks and it breeds a self-belief both England and Italy have lacked the past week in their tilts at the tournament favourites.

'We play against them regularly, and our guys see them all the time in Super 12,' said Macqueen. 'The aura isn't there. Maybe it's something England battled with. But I also think England are unrealistic at times about themselves. They talk up their performances quite a lot and they've got to be accountable for what happens on the field, not what they might be able to do.

'As for Italy, I thought they played very poorly. They didn't tackle. It wasn't a clinical performance from us today like it was from the All Blacks and, at some stage, it would be nice for us to put a performance like that together. But we had a committed side against us here, a team that held the ball well.

I don't think we're far off it. The last three games we've done some of the hard things well. It's that last minute finishing that's letting us down.'

Macqueen's assessment of the Wallabies display against the Americans was generous. Yes, there were concessions to be made. The Australians fielded a side with only a handful of frontline players, they were blooding two Test rookies and had a limited build-up in which to forge combinations. But some of the stuff at Thomond Park did not bear the hallmark of World Cup champions.

The amount of dropped ball was appalling, there were silly penalties conceded, the Americans enjoyed periods of forward ascendancy and, late in the game, one USA raid saw six tackles missed in the space of only 10 seconds. An inability to complete promising raids has been the biggest bugbear for the Wallabies in their unbeaten run of pool matches against Romania, Ireland and USA.

'It has become a bit of a thing for us, it's something we have to get over,' said Macqueen. 'But it's something you can't really train for, not to drop the final pass.'

Australia started the match smoothly enough, with five-eighth Stephen Larkham, in his second game back from injury and appearing more comfortable, making a half break, offloading to centre Nathan Grey and taking the final pass from number eight Jim Williams to score beside the posts.

When halfback Chris Whitaker looped around Larkham, found winger Matt Burke out wide, and fullback Chris Latham joined the attack to send debutant speedster Scott Staniforth across for the first of his two tries, the Wallabies were 17–3 to the good after 16 minutes. But as the errors crept in, the Americans crept closer. Centre Juan Grobler scored out wide on the half hour for 17–10, and only a drive by the Wallaby forwards from a lineout close to the USA line gave them a 22–10 buffer courtesy of hooker Michael Foley touching down.

There was improvement in the second half as the Australian backs found more cohesion. Five tries followed, the best of them to Chris Latham, who hit the ball running straight, and at pace, after two decoy runners were employed in midfield.

The Australians now await their quarter final opponent, with the scoreline and result of the Argentina-Japan clash to decide whether the Pumas, Wales or Samoa advance as the leading side from Pool D. On form, Argentina will beat Japan but will not reach the required total of 69 points to finish on top. Given that scenario, the Wallabies will play Wales next Sunday.

Welsh superboot Neil Jenkins elbowed aside Michael Lynagh as the greatest Test points scorer the game has seen in front of his fanatical Cardiff faithful today.

But the jug-eared redhead — billed in Britain as the goalkicking Ginger Monster — was closer to a crumbling gingerbread man as Samoa sacrificed the World Cup hosts on the altar of their own cathedral. What was to be an afternoon of celebration for Jenkins, and for a Welsh team touted as title contenders before the tournament kicked off, turned into a death march at Millennium Stadium with Samoa called in to play executioners. The islanders are making a habit of leaving the Welsh to lament their rugby woes.

At the 1991 World Cup, Samoa caused a 16–13 round robin boilover, a defeat that cost the men in scarlet a place in the quarter finals. This time it was 38–31 and while Wales have at least one match remaining to restore reputations, they are not yet assured of guaranteed advancement to the last eight of the knockout stages.

Depending on the result and scoreline in Saturday's Argentina-Japan clash, the Welsh will either host Australia in a quarter final in Cardiff, or be forced to take the low road of a quarter final qualifier away to Scotland at Murrayfield.

It was not the scenario the Welsh crowd came to witness on a cloudless Cardiff afternoon.

Jenkins, starting the match equal with former Wallaby five-eighth Lynagh on 911 international points, needed only 13 minutes to hold the record alone. A huge Welsh scrum shove buckled the Samoan front row, led to a penalty try and a simple conversion from in front for the son of a scrapyard dealer.

Signs of success were in the air. After 17 minutes it was 12–3 as winger Gareth Thomas scored the second Welsh try, a dubious effort with television replays showing he crossed the sideline before touching down. But Samoa, hammered in the penalty count by referee Ed Morrison, were not beyond dishing out some poundings themselves.

Their trademark heavy hitting in defence forced handling errors while their aggression in attack, working off the subtle ball play of five-eighth Stephen Bachop, was more effervescent than what the home side had to offer.

A botched Welsh throw to the lineout led to a soft try for second rower Lio Falaniko and when Bachop coolly worked a backline play that led to him stepping inside Jenkins to score, the Samoans trailed only 18–17. Bachop soon after swooped on a loose pass from Welsh number eight Scott Quinnell to put the islanders ahead for the first time and at the break they were leading 24–21.

Jenkins levelled the scores with a penalty goal three minutes after the interval, but he was again the villain on his day of hoped for heroics when a delayed pass went awry and Samoan skipper Pat Lam took the intercept to race 70m for the try. Wales relied on their massive scrum for a second penalty try, forcing another deadlock at 31–all. But with 13 minutes remaining, Bachop delivered a long ball to the right, an overlap was created and fullback Silao Leaega crossed at the corner.

For good measure he landed the conversion, his sixth success from as many attempts, while the usually infallible Jenkins finished with only six from 10.

He was outplayed at five-eighth, outkicked for points. But Jenkins, walking from the field to a deathly hush, could at least comfort himself with a record book entry — a career points tally of 927.

The All Blacks topped the century — the second in World Cup history — as Italy were buried under a Kiwi avalanche in Huddersfield today.

Despite making 11 changes to their top side, the All Blacks romped in 101–3 on a day of shame for the Italians, who next year join the European big boys in an expanded Six Nations Championship.

There were 14 tries for the Kiwis in a power-laden last hitout before the quarter finals with Jonah Lomu becoming the leading try-scorer in World Cups and Jeff Wilson the most prolific try-scorer in New Zealand history

Fullback Wilson grabbed three to take his career tally to 37, two clear of John Kirwan. Lomu crossed twice, carrying him to the top of the World Cup tree with 12, one ahead of former England flyer Rory Underwood.

It was the second biggest victory in four World Cups after New Zealand's 145–17 demolition of Japan four years ago in South Africa. Five tries in 16 minutes before half time flattened the Italians and drew the understatement of the tournament from ex-All Black captain Sean Fitzpatrick.

With NZ leading 51–3 at the break, Fitzpatrick suggested: 'I think coach John Hart will be pleased with that first 40 minutes.'

The latest World Cup ticket fiasco left Australian tourists stranded today when premium grandstand seats they bought for the Wallabies clash with USA failed to even exist. A group of 34 Australians, including Test halfback George Gregan's parents, arrived at Thomond Park in Limerick armed with tickets purchased as part of a $14,000 tour package.

But in searching for their allocated seating, the travelling party was stunned at being told they would have to stand at ground level. 'Their tickets started at number 204, but the seats ran out at 198,' said tour leader Barry Ross.

'In the end the Irish Rugby Union officials found grandstand seats for seven of the group. The others were left to fend for themselves. This is just another example of an ongoing stuff-up. 'Have a look at what's happened at the World Cup so far. The ticketing boss has been sacked, tickets have gone missing, and it's an absolute shambles. 'You turn up here on the day of the match and your tickets aren't even valid.'

Australian Rugby Union general manager John O'Neill said the Thomond Park traumas were only a symptom of broader problems. 'The reality is from the time this match was scheduled there was uncertainty about the ticketing because of the temporary grandstands they were putting in,' O'Neill said. 'Sadly these Australians have been the casualties. These people have paid good money. Built in to their packages, they were probably charged $150 or more for these tickets.'

Ross said Irish Rugby Union officials were not to blame. The ticketing comes through Rugby World Cup. 'But it looks at least like we'll be reimbursed for the trouble,' he said. 'The IRU have written a letter for us to hand on to the relevant authorities.'

POOL MATCHES

ENGLAND 101 TONGA 10

SOUTH AFRICA 39 URUGUAY 3

IRELAND 41 ROMANIA 14

The one-sided romp at Twickenham was finished as a contest
after 35 minutes, once the Tongans had their prop Ngalo
Taufo'ou sent from the field for an act of madness when he
rushed 20m to slam a forearm jolt into the face of England flanker
Richard Hill.

Taufo'ou has been handed a 28–day suspension, irrelevant in
terms of the competition with the Tongans now on their way home.
But the red-card flashed before him by referee Wayne Erickson was
the killer blow for the visitors. They trailed 24–10 at the time and in
the final 45 minutes gave up 77 unanswered points. As England
reached their century with the last play of the game — a conversion
from five-eighth Paul Grayson, who bagged a record 36 points —
the Twickenham crowd erupted. In the television studios they were
gushing as well.

'They have to be the second best side in the competition,'
enthused former England coach Geoff Cooke, placing the Poms
behind only the All Blacks on his World Cup form chart.

But as England learned when topped by New Zealand after
putting 67 points on Italy, there is a difference between looking good
and being good. And they will have to be the latter if they are to
reach the final via a horror draw in the knockout stages.

Despite the ease of the win over Tonga, number eight
Lawrence Dallaglio, with a huge game, underlined how important he
will be to the English chances from here.

The suspensions continue apace at the fourth World Cup as the crackdown on foul play netted another two offenders at the weekend, with the prospect of more to come tonight. Canadian flanker Dan Baugh was banned 28 days for stomping a rival in his side's final pool match against Namibia, while Tongan prop Ngalu Taufo'ou copped the same penalty for his forearm to the face of England flanker Richard Hill at Twickenham. Both players would have exited the World Cup regardless. Neither Tonga nor Canada advanced to the knockout stages.

Other bans during the tournament include:

Colin Charvis (Wales) — 14 days for fighting
Roberto Grau (Argentina) — 21 days for fighting
Toutai Kefu (Australia) — 14 days for fighting
Trevor Brennan (Ireland) — 10 days for fighting
Suia Taumalolo (Tonga) — 21 days for high tackling

POOL MATCHES

FRANCE 28 FIJI 19

SCOTLAND 48 SPAIN 0

ARGENTINA 33 JAPAN 12

As the minnows pack their bags and head for airports across Europe, 10 big fish and one piranha continue swimming the World Cup pool. After 30 round robin matches over the past fortnight, the tournament heads for the knockout stages with New Zealand the nation the rest need to gaffe if the William Webb Ellis trophy is to head anywhere but Kiwi headquarters in Wellington.

The All Blacks have been the outstanding side of the preliminaries — a 30–16 win over England a crucial early strike in their bid to become the first country to win the title twice. But their far from fearsome draw for the quarter finals and semi finals also suggests they are, even now, assured of a place in the Cardiff decider, two weeks before they can ink their names into the centre spread of the program.

New Zealand will not have to meet in sudden death matches en route to Millennium Stadium on November 6 any of the three teams considered to be their only threats at this World Cup.

Australia, South Africa and England have all been directed to the other side of the draw — the Wallabies and Springboks after topping their groups, and England after finishing second to the All Blacks. The Kiwis, by contrast, face a quarter final with the winner of Wednesday's playoff between Scotland and Samoa at Murrayfield and, barring the biggest Test upset of the past 20 years, a semi final showdown against France, Ireland or Argentina. In theory they could field the second string side that ran up a century of points to humiliate Italy and keep their showpiece players in cotton wool until the Millennium Stadium grand finale. The reality will be something quite different.

With a week between matches at the business end, the All Blacks will be on a mission to destroy, and history, combined with their effortless progression to date, indicates the upcoming fortnight will be little more than a dawdle for the tournament favourites.

New Zealand have never been beaten by either Samoa or Scotland, and while France are likely to edge past Ireland or Argentina to reach the final four, their campaign has lumbered along with no suggestion they could stretch the All Blacks.

The French foibles have been so evident that legendary former centre Philippe Sella, on a flight to Toulouse for the Tricolours last pool match with Fiji, suggested he and his friends sip a little champagne. 'We should do it now,' he said. 'Because we might not want to tomorrow night.'

The fears of Sella were not borne out — France beat Fiji 28–19. But had referee Paddy O'Brien not disallowed a seemingly fair Fijian try or given the French a penalty try when it was clearly not warranted, the result could easily have been reversed.

The Fijian performance too, was disappointing. They moved away from the flair that makes them so dangerous to play a more structured field position style. Similar tactics against England in another Wednesday playoff will see them obliterated.

The Scotland–Samoa playoff is a re-match of the 1991 quarter final between the two countries at Murrayfield, won by the Scots 28–6. 'We played them a bit at their own game that day,' recalled former Scotland captain Gavin Hastings. 'And you have to remember the 1991 coach was Jim Telfer, and he's still there. He'll have something up his sleeve.'

Former All Blacks skipper Sean Fitzpatrick also favoured the Scots despite the Samoans last round triumph over Wales in Cardiff. 'That was such a huge game for them, they'll still be on a high,' said Fitzpatrick. 'It will be difficult for them to get down to earth and prepare to play again in a few days time.'

The third playoff will pit Ireland against Argentina.

Irish coach Warren Gatland will be delighted the Pool D placings — Wales from Samoa and Argentina — panned out the way they did. Taking on the Pumas for a spot in the last eight would have been the Gatland preference, albeit offshore in the French city of Lens.

'We will be ready,' said Irish skipper Dion O'Cuinneagain,

who is battling a hamstring strain. 'It's going to be tough but we did the business against Romania in our last match and we'll be up for the next one.'

On the other side of the draw, Australia will take on Wales next Saturday in the only confirmed quarter final. South Africa have advanced to the last eight also and await the winner of the England-Fiji playoff. The Springboks though, are down on their form, down on personnel with five-eighth Henry Honiball hobbled by injury, and with the threat of losing another frontline player when centre Brendan Venter faces a judiciary panel for stomping.

England should see off the Boks, unless the defending champions can suddenly find a level of performance they have not reached all season. But the English campaign, from here, is no paved pathway to the decider. They have to play Fiji, back up four days later to take on South Africa and, providing they win in Paris, face an almost certain semi final clash with Australia at Twickenham.

The Wallabies have yet to display their best, but are confident of accounting for an over-hyped Wales. They should be similarly upbeat about their chances of toppling England or South Africa, who promise to fight out a physical quarter final likely to leave bumps and bruises and have a flattening effect on the winner. So the probable scenario is Australia-New Zealand for the final. Both previous World Cup winners but yet to meet in a tournament decider.

QUARTER FINAL PLAYOFFS

WEDNESDAY
ENGLAND v FIJI at Twickenham
SCOTLAND v SAMOA at Murrayfield
IRELAND v ARGENTINA at Stade Felix Bollaert

QUARTER FINALS

SATURDAY
AUSTRALIA v WALES at Millennium Stadium

SUNDAY
SOUTH AFRICA v ENGLAND/FIJI at Stade de France
FRANCE v IRELAND/ARGENTINA at Lansdowne Road
NEW ZEALAND v SCOTLAND/SAMOA at Murrayfield

Wallaby coach Rod Macqueen has dismissed the weekend wipeout of Wales claiming the World Cup host will still view Australia as quarter final quarry they can kill off in Cardiff to avenge their beatings of the past. Wales were confirmed as the Wallabies first opponent in the tournament's knockout stages when Argentina managed only a 33–12 defeat of Japan at Millennium Stadium.

Despite an upset seven-point loss to Samoa on Friday, the Welsh have, with a scare, topped their pool to advance to a showdown with the Wallabies on Saturday that has been mooted for months and leaves Macqueen wary of potential dangers.

'It will be a difficult match for us to win,' Macqueen said. 'Wales are a side who have shown this year they are a lot better than their performances so far in this World Cup would suggest. One thing about Wales that is a concern is that they have all the ingredients to produce a top performance.

'They are strong in the set pieces, especially the scrum, and in five-eighth Neil Jenkins they have a superb tactical kicker and one of the most accurate goalkickers in the world. They have an effective defensive line, a good coach and the advantage of playing at home in front of a full house.'

Wales strung together 10 successive wins until the Samoans brought them undone 38–31.

But the Wallabies believe 'King' Henry and his on-field subjects have targeted the expected clash with Australia for some time, even before their World Cup campaign kicked off. Taking the formguide approach, the Wallabies have little to fear. The Welsh pack, for all its size, is ponderous and seemingly short of condition.

In the final 20 minutes they frequently look ragged, none more than number eight Scott Quinnell, their attacking anvil in the forwards who had a mistake-riddled game against Samoa and has yet to prove his 80–minute worth. Likewise in the lineout, there are signs of extreme vulnerability.

The Welsh have one specialist jumper in the lanky Chris Wyatt, with the second Quinnell brother, Craig, a 130kg behemoth too heavy to lift as a ball winning option.

But the Macqueen modus operandi before a big Test is to talk up the Australians' opponents. This week he will chart the same course.

But Henry has opted for another psychological tack,

saying the loss to Samoa, in the long run, might benefit his scarlet-clad underdogs.

'Frankly, I hope they don't get over the loss in a hurry,' he said. 'I want them to remember how bad it feels and gain new resolve to make amends. You develop as a team by absorbing the lessons of defeat rather than pretending it never happened. Losing can often give you a much sharper mental edge. You only have to look at the Samoans for proof of that.

'Being beaten by Argentina wounded them, and they came out against us desperate to atone. We possibly didn't have that same mental sharpness. We had won 10 in a row and sometimes you cannot prevent a touch of complacency creeping in. So I don't feel as though this defeat is the end of the world. Sometimes you need that kick up the backside. We're lucky we can pick ourselves up, because it's not as if everything was at stake.'

Wales have not beaten Australia since 1987, in the third place playoff at the inaugural World Cup, when the Wallabies had flanker David Codey sent off early in the game. Since then the contests have been extended humiliation for the Welsh. In 1991, Australia crushed Wales 63–6 in July and three months later at the World Cup dished up a 38–3 hiding in Cardiff.

The following season Australia won 23–6 and, in 1996, completed a two-Test rout with scorelines of 56–25 and 42–3. When the Wallabies toured the British Isles in November the same year, they again saw off the Welsh 28–19.

October 17

Former Springbok captain Tiaan Strauss has been pitched into the World Cup battle zone as the Wallaby forward to wage war with Wales in the Cardiff quarter final on Saturday. As Australian selectors made three crucial changes to their pack for the showdown, the job of attacking arrowhead was entrusted to Strauss in the absence of Toutai Kefu.

The combative South African replaces the suspended number eight in a revamped backrow while Michael Foley takes over at hooker following the World Cup exit and return to Australia of injured rake Phil Kearns. Flanker Matt Cockbain, a regular on the side of the Test scrum this season until a thigh strain sidetracked his World Cup campaign, returns to the line-up for the first time in the tournament.

But the contentious issue for coach Rod Macqueen and his selection sounding boards — until they finalised the line-up — was who to rely on at number eight with Kefu out of action for re-arranging the facial features of Irish flanker Trevor Brennan. Kefu will be available for the semi finals, should the Australians advance as expected this weekend. And, if they do, Strauss is likely to have broken enemy lines to play his part in the host nation's downfall.

The loss of Kefu for two games has been a serious setback for the Wallabies, not for their romp last Thursday over the United States but for this sudden-death tie where Wales will hope to gain a vital ascendancy up front.

Kefu has been the primary powerhouse in the Wallaby pack, the ball carrier saddled with the job of giving the Australians the go-forward they need to provide the space for a backline considered the best in the game. Now, with him gone, the Wallabies need another hard yards man, with Strauss, Jim Williams and Mark Connors in the frame until the first of that trio was given the nod today.

'It's important I get comfortable with what we want to do, to catch them off balance and get in behind their defence,' said Strauss.

But there is another side to his promotion, at least on a personal basis, as Strauss finally fulfills a long-held ambition to play a key role in a World Cup challenge. Four years ago he was the shock omission from the South African squad that went on to win the William Webb Ellis trophy. Tipped at one stage to lead the Springboks into their campaign at home, Strauss was not only passed over for the captaincy — with Francois Pienaar preferred — he was overlooked for the team altogether.

A popular theory for his dismissal is that with two obvious leaders in Pienaar and Strauss — one from the veldt the other from the Cape — the loyalties of players might be divided. Coach at the time Kitch Christie was taking no chances and found no place for Strauss in his squad. While his emotionless features give nothing away, the snub still hurts Strauss deeply. But at Millennium Stadium this weekend he has a chance to exorcise the ghosts of missed opportunity.

'I definitely want to go out there and play well, well enough that they might not be able to drop me,' he said. 'It would be good to stay in there for the next two games. And it's always good to be involved so much more as part of the run-on side; to be part of the decision making and the build-up, rather than getting only 10 or 15 minutes off the bench.

'You don't feel as intense or as good about that. There's added pressure this Saturday, but that's good. It makes it all the more worthwhile. Test matches are all special occasions but this is now do or die in the World Cup. The atmosphere will be fantastic, and that gets more energy out of you as a player. When there's a lot of noise, a full stadium, it doesn't matter who they're cheering for, it pumps me right up.'

The elevation of Foley over Jeremy Paul for the hooking position vacated by Kearns' career-ending injury, has been brought about by the Wallabies desire to pressure the Welsh at their strength in the scrum. Foley is considered Australia's premier scrummager, while Paul, whose forte is mobility and workrate around the field, will be restricted again to the bench, possibly for an entry into the game during the final quarter.

Cockbain, the defensive hitman, was destined to re-claim his position once he had shaken off his quadricep problem. He takes over from Mark Connors. Skipper John Eales, who missed the final pool game against the USA in Limerick with a groin strain, has yet to recover fully but is back in training.

'By the time Saturday comes, I'll be right,' he said. 'It's certainly not something I'm worried about.'

The Australian team: Matt Burke, Ben Tune, Daniel Herbert, Tim Horan, Joe Roff, Stephen Larkham, George Gregan, Tiaan Strauss, David Wilson, Matt Cockbain, John Eales (c), David Giffin, Andrew Blades, Michael Foley, Richard Harry.

Wallaby skipper John Eales rates the current Welsh side the best of his generation and a genuine threat to Australia in Saturday's quarter final at Cardiff. But the tribute from Eales, as heartfelt as it might have been, is not the backslapping compliment it might first appear. Whether he knows it or not, Eales is only washing Wales in faint praise.

Since arriving on the Test scene in 1991 — against the Welsh in Brisbane in a clash remembered not for any on-field dramas but for the after-match stoush between rival cliques in the touring party — Eales has played only easybeat teams in red.

His first Test was a 63–6 walkover, months later it was 38–3 in the World Cup, and the thrashings have been ongoing. In 1992, the Wallabies won 23–6, and in three games in 1996 the lopsided scorelines read 56–25, 42–3 and 28–19.

'But this is the best team they've put out in my memory,' Eales said on arrival in Cardiff. 'We look at them as one of the top sides in the world. There's no doubt about their strength. They proved that with victories over England, France and South Africa this year.'

Welsh observers suggest the side former Auckland coach Graham Henry has developed might well be the finest the principality has had in two decades, going all the way back to the glory days of the late 1970's. That was an era when Wales were feared, when they boasted a backline of legends, including Gareth Edwards, Gerald Davies and JPR Williams. More than 20 years on, hope is rising again, now that Henry has arrived on the scene. The frowning former headmaster enjoyed enormous success with the Auckland Super 12 side, and guided Wales to 10 successive wins until upended by Samoa last week.

Wallaby coach Rod Macqueen knows the difference Henry can make. 'Obviously we were coaching Super 12 teams at the same time,' he said. 'And the last time we met was the Super 12 final of 1997 when Auckland beat the ACT Brumbies. Hopefully I can make amends this time. But they will see this as a real stepping stone for them.'

The quarter final is a stepping stone for the Wallabies as well — hooker Michael Foley in particular. After starting the World Cup campaign as number three rake, behind Phil Kearns and Jeremy Paul, he has jumped to the front of the queue. With Kearns out injured, Foley has been called up to steady the scrum, taking over the number one role for the first time since 1997 against Scotland.

The Welsh are already cranking up the patriotic fervour, with one newspaper proudly leading the media in a jingoistic bashing of all things Australian.

In a double page spread, the Wales on Sunday ran a cock-eyed comparison of the two countries under a headline screaming: Poor Skippy's Bounced Out.

According to 'The Paper that backs Henry's Men', the weather, the music and the soap operas of Wales are all clearly superior — despite an admission the annual rainfall here is at least three times that of Australia. Even down under beer takes a hammering, with the local Brains draught given thumbs up over Fosters.

As for the Australian anthem, the paper went to town.

'The Aussies lose points for the line 'our home is girt by sea'. Girt? Any ideas? Also the line 'in hist'ry's page, let ev'ry stage' is a bit dodgy. You can't just go leaving letters out when they don't fit.

'Off hand, we can't think of anything bad about the Welsh anthem.'

Quote of the week: 'There were occasions when we didn't have enough balls' — the Japanese translator getting into a twist trying to explain the coach's anxiety at not winning enough possession against Argentina.

October 18

Welsh coach Graham Henry has a Hollywood future as the next Woody Allen if he continues to polish the straight-faced comedy act he performed for the world media in Cardiff today. Four days out from a quarter final showdown with Australia at Millennium Stadium, Hangdog Henry was flying the white flag, suggesting his side had no chance of stopping a well-tuned, well-coached Wallaby juggernaut.

It was a classic routine, delivered with feeling. But if you believe the declaration of surrender that spilled from the lips of the once super-successful Auckland coach, then also expect the Easter Bunny to appear in the Welsh front-row, complete with boots and skullcap.

Henry told how the World Cup had arrived too early for Wales, that they were only a small way along the path to becoming a side capable of matching the best on the planet. Were they, however, far enough advanced to topple the Wallabies?

'I wouldn't think so, no,' he said. 'You've got to be rational about it. Australia is probably one of the best two teams in the world. And I think they might have been biding their time a bit. I don't know that they put everything into the Tri-Nations series. I think they wanted to come good right at the end, which they did against the All Blacks.

'I wonder too if they've been keeping their powder dry in Ireland and they're ready now to fizz. Rod Macqueen is a very good coach, I've known him through Super 12. So he'll have the team ready and there's some very experienced, highly capable athletes in the side who are also highly intelligent.

'I haven't taken much notice of their pool matches, but you don't need to go past that All Blacks match. Australia won by 21 points. We're taking on one of the mights of the rugby world.

'All we're going to do is our best. This side is still developing. We're proceeding but we won't get there for a couple of years, and making the quarter finals in itself is an achievement. If our guys give it their best shot, give it their all, you can't ask any more than that.'

Traditionally though, the Welsh public have asked for more,

thirsty as they have been for success during a barren past two decades. And the expectations of late were running artificially high after a run of 10 successive Tests unbeaten.

Last week's upset loss to Samoa caused a re-think on just how good the current Welsh team are, but Henry believes there is still a lack of acceptance about the quality of their opponents this weekend.

'I don't know whether the public realise how great this battle is going to be, how high this hurdle is for us on Saturday. I think they want the unexpected,' he said. 'They think when you pull on the Welsh jersey you're bullet proof, you can walk on water. But that's fine, the fans are marvellous, they're very supportive.'

But Henry admits from the playing perspective, he is still coming to grips with mental attitudes far removed from what he was used to in New Zealand. He also saved another tribute for the Australians, only on a wider scale, beyond their rugby talent.

'As a Kiwi and a guy who has coached New Zealand players, they take defeat a lot more to heart than people do in this part of the world,' he said. 'I'm not talking about just the Welsh, I'm talking about people in Europe. They don't take defeat as inwardly as the All Blacks do for example. That's why UK sport under achieves.

'The best country in the world in sport is Australia. They are hugely determined that they do well, whether it's hockey, rugby, cricket, swimming or whatever it might be. They are a marvellous sporting nation and that's part of the education system and part of their pride in their country. They value that hugely, more than it is valued here. And I do see a difference in general.

'The All Blacks for instance would go in their shell for two or three days over a loss and then come out and go mad on the rugby field. It's just the different way they've been brought up in their own rugby culture.'

THE MID-TOURNAMENT REVIEW

Most Improved: FIJI.

Have finally built a competitive pack under the tutelage of former All Black prop Brad Johnstone. The brilliant backs have always been around — hence the sensational Fijian record at Sevens — but a soft underbelly in the forwards has long been an albatross. Now Johnstone has brought order up front, the islanders have the raw talent to be a world force.

Mightiest Minnows: URUGUAY.

With less than 500 adult players involved in the game back home, there were fears the South Americans, on their World Cup debut, would be cannon fodder for South Africa and Scotland. But where sides as highly regarded as Italy and Tonga had 100 points put on them by opponents, Uruguay never conceded 50. Their best player was 40-year-old number eight, Diego Ormaechea, who admits retirement is now an option.

Biggest Flops: ITALY.

After they failed to win a match, and let in 101 points to England, respect for an Italian side allowed entry from next year into the new, expanded Six Nations Championship, has fallen through the floor. World Cup organisers have drawn up a temporary rankings system from the round robin series and it has the Italians in 19th position. Only Spain was placed lower on the pecking order. Canada were 12th followed by Romania, Tonga, Uruguay, USA, Namibia, Japan, Italy and Spain.

Best Players Division A: JONAH LOMU.

Again threatening to dominate the World Cup and an automatic choice in the combined team from the nations still in the tournament. Lawrence Dallaglio has been moved to blindside flanker to squeeze him in the following side: Jeff Wilson (NZ), Gareth Thomas (Wales), Daniel Herbert (Australia), Tim Horan (Australia), Jonah Lomu (NZ), Stephen Bachop (Samoa), Matt Dawson (England), Toutai Kefu (Australia), Josh Kronfeld (NZ) Lawrence Dallaglio (England), Simon Raiwalui (Fiji),

Abdel Benazzi (France), Phil Vickery (England), Keith Wood (Ireland), Christian Califano (France).

Best Players Division B: PETRE MITU.

The livewire Romanian halfback, would be given the captaincy of the following team: Sateki Tuipulotu (Tonga), Daisuke Ohata (Japan), Andrew McCormick (Japan), Romeo Gontineac (Romania), Gheorghe Solomie (Romania), Gareth Rees (Canada), Petre Mitu (Romania), Dan Lyle (USA), Fafita Mo'unga (USA), Al Charron (Canada), Rob Gordon (Japan), Carlo Checchinato (Italy), Tevita Taumoepeau (Tonga), Fe'ao Vunipola (Tonga), Rod Snow (Canada).

Best Try: JONAH LOMU.

For his 60m effort against England.

Best Tackle: TIAAN STRAUSS.

For his massive hit on an unsuspecting American forward.

Best Kick: SATEKI TUIPULOTU.

For his 45m dropped goal to give Tonga an injury time win over Italy.

Best Game: SAMOA v WALES.

The islanders securing a quarter final playoff against the odds.

South Africa's title defence goes from bad to worse with centre Brendan Venter suspended 21 days for stomping Uruguayan flanker Martin Panizza. Venter will only be back if the Springboks make it through to the final and, with five-eighth Henru Honiball still sidelined, that looks extremely doubtful.

The World Cup will break the one million barrier in crowd figures with the staging of the three quarter final playoffs. Already 931,778 people have attended matches, more than watched the entire tournament in South Africa four years ago. The average per game is 31,059.

The breakdown per country with six matches played in each is:

Wales 277,024	at an average of 46,170
England 273,776	at an average of 45,746
France 155,030	at an average of 25,838
Ireland 129,250	at an average of 21,541
Scotland 96,698	at an average of 16,116

David Campese suggests Wales are in for a bleak afternoon against the Wallabies in Cardiff on Saturday.

There is nothing quite like the Welsh in full voice when Test matches come to Cardiff. They sing their hymns and Land of our Fathers, and they pump their chests out with pride.

But on Saturday at Millennium Stadium, they'll want to be able to hum as well because there are no words to the death march. Wales are no chance against the Wallabies in the World Cup quarter final, and I don't say that as an ignorant or big-headed Australian.

I say it with a firm belief that the Welsh are vulnerable in key areas and the Wallabies are building to a major performance that will stamp their imprint on the tournament. It is the strength and speed of the Australian outside backs that will be the undoing of Wales.

Samoa showed last Thursday how the host nation can be rattled when someone steps outside the square rather than relying on a conservative, structured game plan. The Samoans moved Wales around, made them think, and the Welsh did not have the necessary answers.

Neil Jenkins at five-eighth is a fine player but even his game started to come undone. As for their number eight Scott Quinnell, who everyone raves about, he made plenty of errors when the Samoans started putting in the big defensive hits. Sure, Quinnell was willing, he carried the ball something like 20 times.

But his handling was terrible, coughing it up on a handful of occasions, and you have to ask if that was just a bad day or if it was the pressure the Samoans exerted through the tackle.

The Welsh can expect to be hit hard again this Saturday.

The Australian defence is just about the best in the business, and Wales are not in the same class as the Wallabies either in the midfield or out on the wings, so they will not have too many gaps to cruise through.

There is another problem for this Welsh team. To me, they don't look that fit. They don't have that lean, athletic appearance of the Wallabies. They will be tough in the scrum, that's their number one area of attack, but look for them to be sucking the oxygen with 20 minutes left to play.

As for the Australians, this World Cup campaign is starting to bear an uncanny resemblance to the winning challenge of 1991. Eight years ago we started quietly, as the Wallabies have done here. We struggled to beat Argentina, we struggled to beat Western Samoa, we struggled in the first half before running over Wales, and we almost got beaten by Ireland in the quarter finals.

There was no peak reached until the semi final with the All Blacks.

This team is doing something similar. They have not been fantastic yet, and their finishing has certainly let them down despite comfortable wins over Romania, Ireland and the USA. They haven't hit top gear, but perhaps that day is closer than we think. It will want to be. Now that we're into sudden death, there cannot be all the dropped ball that butchered try after try against the Irish.

I just hope the Australians have taken note of the Samoan success, seen that it was achieved out wide, and attack the Welsh there too.

They need to impose their authority where they hold all the aces and that is clearly in the threequarter line where Horan, Herbert, Roff and Tune have it all over their Welsh counterparts.

One obvious concern is the loss of in-form number eight Toutai Kefu to suspension, while there must still be question marks over five-eighth Stephen Larkham. He's had only the two Tests back from injury, and was knocked senseless by a high shot in the first of those against Ireland.

But if the Wallabies put it together, their winning margin could be anything from 10 to 30 points.

Everyone has been praising England, and I think they'll go on to beat South Africa in the quarter finals, which would put them up against the Wallabies in the semis at Twickenham a week later.

I would still back the Australians there, putting the Wallabies into a final showdown with, guess who, the All Blacks. No one will beat the Kiwis on the way to the final. And only Australia can beat them once they get there.

———

Alec Evans would bet a pound to a penny, as they do over here, that when the national anthems strike up on Saturday before the World Cup quarter final in Cardiff, tears will be flowing from some of the biggest and meanest players in the game. And they will all be wearing the red of Wales.

Sporting a Wallaby tracksuit and the little frown that rarely leaves his brow, Brisbane-based Evans did not need to second-guess the Welsh or the impact the Millennium Stadium showdown will have on their emotions.

He has seen them at first hand, laughed and cried with them through a World Cup campaign, and a disastrous one at that when he accepted, at short notice, an offer to be head coach for the South African adventure in 1995.

Of the 30–man Welsh squad at this tournament, 11 were part of that Evans trek four years ago. Nothing much, he suspects, will have changed.

'They really work themselves up before the game, they're very passionate, very emotional. Tears and anger,' he said. 'They get very emotional even before they get out there to sing the national anthem. And when they do, even if they've been out there 50 times before, it's an empowering sort of feeling they get. It's a stirring thing. If you're the opposition you can feel it.

'It's beating the drum basically, like going to war. They're very passionate about going out and playing for their country and what it means to everybody.

Sometimes it works for them and sometimes they go over the top. It's something they don't seem to be able to control.

'Watch when the crowd starts singing during a game. You can see them visibly lift and, when the singing stops, they seem to back off again. It's a real link with the crowd, very transferable. It's a blood relation thing. They really feel it.'

Imagine then, suggested Evans, their emotional state on Saturday when they stand in front of a home crowd of 72,500, playing for a spot in the World Cup semi-finals in a match being billed in some quarters as the most important in Welsh history.

Is it shaping then as a case of the cool, clinical Australians against the fire and passion of Wales?

'It will be like that,' he agreed. 'And we have to cope with what will be a very, very tough first 20 minutes. They'll go for it and if they get their tails up, get points on the board, they could become hard to stop.'

Samoa beat Wales at the same ground only seven days ago. Logic suggests the Australians should have no problems doing the same. But Evans warned that those who believe the Welsh fire was doused for good last Thursday have a rude shock coming this weekend when the initial outpouring of national pride will hit with tidal wave force.

'People who think it will be easy just don't understand,' he said. 'This is a rugby nation, a genuine rugby nation where the live for the game. You've got New Zealand, you've got South Africa and you've got Wales.

'I think it's a blessing in disguise for them that they did get beaten. They'll lift again now. They had a run of 10 games undefeated where they were building and building and building. Suddenly they get a kick in the pants and it's a bit of a shake-up for them.'

A shake-up on a broader scale, far more wide-ranging than a loss to Samoa, has also been what Welsh rugby needed, and it arrived in the shape of Graham Henry, the former Auckland coach who was given a $3 million five-year deal to resuscitate the Dragon.

Henry arrived a little more than 12 months ago and Evans is aware of the massive task he faced. Of the battle to forge a team spirit, a oneness that Australians take for granted when the Wallabies pull their jumpers on before any international.

'The Welsh are very tribal,' said Evans. 'Athletically they're very good. There are some very big, very fast and very physical athletes here. But they haven't always had the discipline and this tribal thing in Wales was a big problem. You really need an outsider, someone with no club loyalties, to blend it together. Now that Graham Henry is here, he's managed to get them to work collectively.

'It's different to back home. When it comes to the crunch there, NSW, Queensland and ACT players come together for Australia. In a three cornered contest between themselves it's tough and it's blood and guts but when they come into the Wallabies they can leave that behind and put the powers together.

'It hasn't happened here before because you're talking about a couple of hundred years of tribalism. If you could get a team like Cardiff, from the capital city, and take them up into the valleys, you would see the animosity that exists.

'Or a city like Swansea and a city like Llanelli, when they play each other it's like World War III. There's so much hate in it. The toughness of the game is unbelievable but they do throw rugby skills out the window.

'Their club rugby is probably the toughest rugby in the world but it's not the best rugby in the world. What Henry has done is got all that wasted energy and channelled it into skills, into power and thrust.

'I've seen them lose it a little bit now and then at the World Cup but if they get it together at the weekend it's going to be a tough game. At the same time, if we play to our potential we will win.'

For Evans, there are several dangermen in the Welsh side. He pointed to five-eighth Neil Jenkins, the superboot, who will punish any indiscretions inside the Australian half.

He spoke of halfback Robert Howley, 'a world class player', and prop David Young, a Welsh international in the late 1980's who toured with the British Lions, turned to rugby league and eventually headed back to his roots.

'Young is a tough campaigner,' said Evans. 'He knows what it's all about and he can handle himself. Scott Gibbs is another one and Gareth Thomas on the wing is a big unit.

'But I think the major strike force they've got is from fullback. Shane Howarth has lifted his game. He was in the doldrums for a while but Henry has lifted him back, given him confidence.

'So you blend that together and they become a bit of a handful. Even at number eight, Scott Quinnell is not an 80 minute player but the problem is you don't know when he's going to strike. He's very big, very strong. When he decides it's time to go he could be ranging up anywhere. He could be on the wing, at outside centre or halfback. You don't know where he'll bob up.'

What Evans does know is there'll be electricity at Millennium Stadium on Saturday, charging the Welsh for the battle ahead. It will be up to the Australians to turn out the lights on them.

QUARTER FINAL PLAYOFFS

ENGLAND 45 FIJI 24

SCOTLAND 35 SAMOA 20

ARGENTINA 28 IRELAND 24

Wallaby skipper John Eales has swept aside the carefully packaged pre-match patter to declare Saturday's World Cup quarter final a non-negotiable result for Australia.

After a week of psycho-babble — with Wales coach Graham Henry trying to convince anyone who listens that he's ready to concede defeat and the Australians paying daily respects to a 'great rugby nation' — Eales confronted an issue most have tried to avoid.

What if the Wallabies lose? What if their four years of preparation is flushed into the Taffy River that runs alongside Millennium Stadium and they crash from the tournament at the same stage they made their disastrous exit in 1995?

'It would be, um … it would be unthinkable,' Eales said as a gentle rain fell on Cardiff. 'It would be shattering, and everyone in this team would feel exactly the same way. We've done a lot of work as a team since the last World Cup.

'We've come a long way. We've had some hard times and some difficult matches but each year we've improved a bit, we've learned our lessons and we've produced some good performances. But this has always been the goal. The World Cup is what it's all been about. To play here and to win here. And because of that we're not even thinking about defeat.

'We have to win. From our point of view, it's the only result. If we don't win, we won't get to see out our dream.'

Eales knows the chasm that separates the emotions of World Cup winners and those who head home early as also-rans. He's been there. In 1991, he was a rookie second rower in the side Nick Farr-Jones led up the steps of the Twickenham grandstand to receive the William Webb Ellis trophy from the Queen.

Four years later he was part of an Australian outfit booted from the tournament at the quarter finals stage when English five eighth Rob Andrew piloted over a 45m dropped goal in injury time.

Now, as captain, Eales is tunnel-visioned on which path he wants his side to follow, starting with victory over Wales.

'This match will be a huge challenge for us and there will be the pressure that every game from here is a knockout, there are no second chances,' he said. 'But we're simply not thinking about it ending here. We're thinking what we have to do to win the game, and we're confident we can.

'It's not a rash confidence, more a feeling based on what we know this team can do. And I think everyone will feel we've failed if we don't play up to the best of our ability, because we know if we do we'll win.'

Perhaps this self-belief is the difference between the 1999 and 1995 Wallaby sides. There is certainly a different atmosphere surrounding the current team.

Where an early pool loss to South Africa set the tone for an intense but anxiety-filled campaign four years ago, the 1999 side is relaxed, laid back, almost too laconic for their coach Rod Macqueen. And never was it better evidenced than at a press conference in the team hotel today.

Fullback Matthew Burke, not known as a master of mirth, was reflecting on how stress-free the players had been away from the pitch.

'Back home, people must think we're on a golfing holiday,' he said. 'Every time we're shown on television footage it seems as though we're out on the course.'

So how did most of the Wallabies plan to spend their impending day off in the run up to such a crunch game?

'Golfing,' he smiled.

Eales carries the story further, to give an insight into the positive aspects of a preparation that has mixed high-powered sessions on the training paddock with an ability to escape the pressure once the boots are removed.

'In a sense it's quite a different feeling here to what it was in 1995,' he said. 'I don't think we had the same confidence as a team back then. Not that that means anything unless you can transfer it into performance. But before that quarter final against England, I remember there was almost a sense of dreading the 'what if?' scenario. This time it's something we just haven't even spoken about.'

The Wallaby skipper was adamant, however, that the Australians' self-assuredness should not be construed as complacency.

'It's not as if we're up against a side that's no capable,' he said. 'They are a team, on their home turf, and have won 10 of their past 11 Test matches. They have beaten South Africa, they've beaten England and they've beaten France, and under all sorts of conditions.'

The Wallabies are also confident on another front. Flanker David Wilson is progressing well with an ankle ligament injury and is on track to recover in time for the Cardiff clash.

'He's an integral part of our side,' said assistant coach Jeff Miller. 'And if he's not right we won't risk playing him. But at the moment he'd be 60–40 about being there.'

———

England advanced to the World Cup quarter finals with a flattering win over Fiji today, but are already counting the cost as key players were floored by injury just four days out from a showdown with the Springboks.

After a torrid 45–22 victory over the islanders, England coach Clive Woodward was left to survey a dressing room casualty ward as five eighth Jonny Wilkinson (suspected concussion), fullback Matt Perry (shoulder), and wingers Austin Healey (back) and Dan Luger (groin) were forced from the field.

Scoring four tries to three, the home side trudged from Twickenham bruised and exhausted, and now prepare for defending champions South Africa, with the winner likely to play Australia in the tournament semi finals. England led 21–3 at half time but the margin deceptive as the innovative, brilliant Fijians butchered two clear try scoring opportunities in the closing stages of the stanza, both wingers spilling final passes after being left unmarked only metres from the line.

The English were far more clinical. They created two chances in the first 40 minutes and capitalised on both through Luger and flanker Neil Back. Wilkinson stretched the lead to 27–3 with two penalty goals shortly after the break and the quarter final playoff looked likely to be a procession.

But Fijian coach Brad Johnstone, the former All Black prop, has steeled their resolve in the forwards and in defence. And three tries came from the islanders over the last 28 minutes.

While England were expected to advance, the shock result was Argentina's upset victory against Ireland in Lens. At the start of the tournament, the Irish fancied their chances of reaching the semi-finals in what was considered the weaker half of the draw.

Now, they have to live with the embarrassment of failing to make the final eight. The future of coach Warren Gatland, the former All Black hooker, does not look too rosy. Not in Dublin at least.

Jason Little played every match of Australia's World Cup campaign. He was twice in the starting line-up, against Romania and the USA. *Courtesy: Allsport*

Limited opportunities . . . Jim Williams made his only appearance of the tournament against the USA. *Courtesy: Allsport*

Held up . . . Chris Latham runs into a dead end against the USA.
It was the same scenario on Test selections, with the goalkicking
of Matt Burke shutting out Latham's claims for a spot in the side.
Courtesy: Allsport

Mark Connors rises above American rivals to claim lineout ball at Thomond Park. *Courtesy: Allsport*

Tiaan Strauss taken in a tackle by American fullback Kurt Shuman. *Courtesy: Allsport*

Tom Bowman prepares to use the hip and shoulder on American backrower Rob Lumkong while second rower Luke Gross awaits the outcome. *Courtesy: Allsport*

Canadian prop Jon Thiel finds rare resistance from the
Namibian defence in the form of halfback Riaan Jantjies
during a pool match in Toulouse. *Courtesy: Allsport*

Samoan surprise . . . fullback Silao Leaega scores the
match–deciding try for the islanders in their upset victory
over Wales at Millennium Stadium. *Courtesy: Allsport*

Australian referee Wayne Erickson shows Tongan prop
Ngalu Taufo'ou the red card at Twickenham. *Courtesy: Allsport*

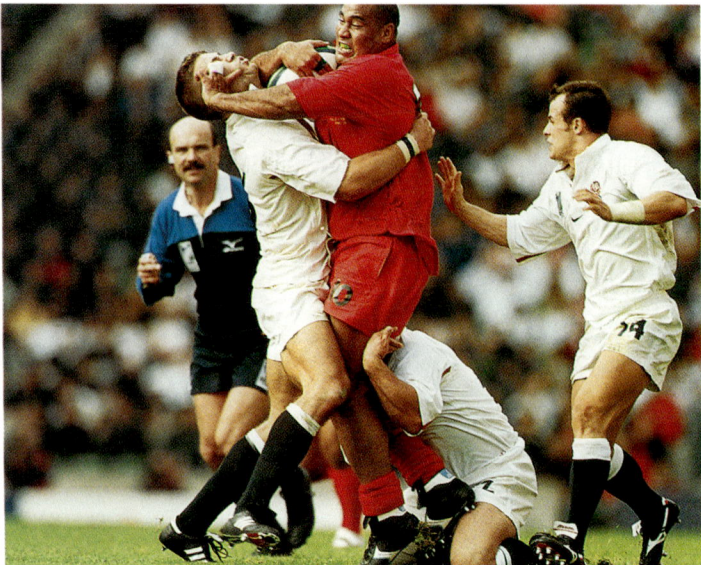

Tongan second rower Falamani Mafi does not take kindly
to the attention of the English defence. *Courtesy: Allsport*

Flying high . . . Irish captain Dion O'Cuinneagain prepares to secure lineout possession against Romania at Lansdowne Road in Dublin. *Courtesy: Allsport*

Hands off . . . Argentine prop Mauricio Reggiardo pushes away from hooker Masaaki Sakata in a pool match against Japan at Cardiff. *Courtesy: Allsport*

A battle for the high ball as France take on Fiji in Toulouse. *Courtesy: Allsport*

Scotland five-eighth Duncan Hodge skips through the tackle of Spanish fullback Ferran Velazco en route to another try for the home side at Murrayfield. *Courtesy: Allsport*

If Australia are clinging to a four-point lead in the dying minutes of
Saturday's World Cup quarter final and Wales launch a last-ditch
salvo, their fullback Shane Howarth will anxiously search for the
smallest man on the Wallaby team.

And hope he is nowhere close by.

The sight of halfback George Gregan, in a desperate dive,
knocking the ball from the grasp of All Black winger Jeff Wilson to
ensure victory in the Bledisloe Cup clash of 1994, is embedded in
the folklore of Australian rugby union. It is also a recurring
nightmare for New Zealand-born Howarth.

On that night at the Sydney Football Stadium, in his previous
life as a Test footballer, Howarth was wearing a black jumper, and
close in support as Wilson prepared to touch down.

'In the photographs of that tackle, I'm the stupid bugger you
can see in the background jumping up and down, thinking we were
about to score,' said the former All Black, now a key element to a
Welsh side coached by another Kiwi, Graham Henry.

'Goldie (Wilson) did incredibly well to get through the
defence, to get where he was. Then all of a sudden this little terror in
the number nine jumper came across and turned a great night into
one to forget. I wish the bastard had picked one of the other 999
times out of 1000 that he wouldn't have made that tackle. It was my
last Test for the All Blacks, and my only loss.'

Five years on, Howarth, 31, has been reborn as a Test player. At
the Millennium Stadium in Cardiff on Saturday, the Aucklander will
play his 16th Test for Wales — 12 more than he appeared in for his
native New Zealand. He is also the form player in a Welsh side still
bristling over their shock defeat to Samoa in Cardiff more than a
week ago.

Howarth has brought an edge to the Welsh, a bit of Kiwi steel,
not so much physically — he weighs only 84kg — but mentally. He
has that hard-nosed, no panic All Black approach. He is a leader on
the field. He is also a rugby realist.

'We know the Aussies are very strong,' he said. 'Theirs is,
without doubt, the best backline in the world, the best backline I've

ever seen them field. A lot of their moves are copied around the world. We've done it here in Wales, and I'm not ashamed to admit that.

'I also think they haven't peaked yet. They've waited for this phase of the World Cup and that doesn't bode well for us. I'm not being defeatist. The World Cup might have come a year early for us. But we also realise we don't have a year. Our guys have got to stand up.

'To be realistic, we'll have to play at 120 percent and they'll have to be at 80 percent for us to win. But Graham has a few ideas. We'll tell you about them after the game.'

The Welsh game plan though, should hold no surprises for the Australians. With a suspect lineout and only one specialist jumper in second rower Chris Wyatt, they will opt for variety, reducing the set piece to three men on occasions.

They will kick for field position, not wanting to open the game up, knowing Australia have the edge out wide. They will rely heavily on their scrum, having pulled together the biggest eight they could muster, including the heavyweight Quinnell brothers, Scott and Craig, who both weigh 130kg.

Scott Quinnell will be the spearhead of their attack from number eight, consistently charging into the Australian forwards to get his side in behind the Wallaby defence.

They will also niggle and harass the Australians — Argentine coach Alex Wyllie claims there was a lot of off-the-ball sneaky stuff in his side's tournament opener against the Welsh. By baiting, they will hope to unsettle the Australians, even draw penalties for five-eighth Neil Jenkins to convert into points.

The Wallabies will be prepared. Do not expect Australia to run ball in their own half for the opening 40 minutes. They will also fall back on a kicking game, to protect themselves from Jenkins' goalkicking.

Australia's backs, for the first half anyway, will be restricted to making their assaults inside Welsh territory. When they do, they will trouble the Welsh for pace in midfield. Watch for them to try and isolate Jenkins in defence, then run the big outside backs, on the angle, in his direction.

Howarth is right. The Welsh do need to play out of their skins and have the Wallabies fall short of the mark. But the

Australians, relaxed and confident, are unlikely to stumble. The Wallaby caravan should be headed for Twickenham, and the first semi-final next week.

———➤

They sat side by side on an aeroplane — the monster and the magician — heading home from a sevens tournament in Uruguay early this year. David Campese, whose twinkling feet and sleight of hand have now been consigned to retirement, and Jonah Lomu, whose powerful presence has again cast his shadow across a World Cup tournament.

Campo suspected it would, nine months ago, when the pair left South America behind and their chat turned, inevitably, to what lay ahead.

'He had a look in his eyes,' said Campese. 'And he told me when he got to the World Cup it would be a chance to complete some unfinished business. While he was the star of the previous tournament in 1995, the All Blacks did not win the final, and the Springboks managed to shut him down in the decider.

'He wanted to go one better. This World Cup is what he wants. This is it. And if the All Blacks do win it, I wouldn't be surprised if he walked away from the game, maybe took up an offer to play American football or even rugby league.'

English league clubs are queuing with open cheque books, and US football teams are said to be interested too, as they were after his spectacular performances as a 20–year–old at the last World Cup.

A lot has happened in the intervening four years. Lomu married, separated, contracted a life-threatening kidney ailment, was stood down from rugby as his weight fluctuated wildly, worked his way back into the game, and eventually returned to the All Blacks. When he did, there were many ready to say his best days were behind him.

Those same observers were given no argument when during this season, All Black coach John Hart left Lomu out of his starting line-up. Christian Cullen had been moved from fullback to wing to make way for Jeff Wilson at the back, and Tana Umaga was handed the other wing jumper. Jonah was reduced to being the impact player coming off the bench. Or was he?

According to Campese, there may have been another motive behind Hart's decision.

'I reckon they left him out to get him a bit more angry, to get him even more fired up for the World Cup,' he said. 'If they did, it seems to have worked.'

Lomu scattered four defenders on the way to scoring a 60m try against England in the pool rounds that screamed: 'I'm back.'

He had already scored two in the All Blacks opening match against Tonga and, by the time he collected another two in a thumping of Italy, he was the leading try-scorer in World Cup history with 12. On Sunday, he will go on the rampage again, with Scotland the side charged with trying to stop New Zealand advancing to the semi finals.

But stopping the All Blacks is only part of the equation. How do you go about stopping Jonah?

Legendary former Welsh halfback Gareth Edwards, rated by a British rugby magazine two years ago as the greatest player who ever lived, has one surefire method.

'Call in the army,' he said. 'But seriously, you've got to keep him as close to the touchline as you possibly can. Then if you don't stop him, the white line might. What else can you say? He's 6 feet 5, he runs the 100 metres in 10.6 and he's strong as an ox.'

Former All Black skipper Sean Fitzpatrick added: 'You have to shut down his space. But if the All Black pack go forward to give him that space, he's unstoppable.'

Wallaby winger Ben Tune will be the man to mark Lomu if, as widely tipped, Australia face the Kiwis in the tournament decider on November 6 in Cardiff.

But while most watch Lomu with a feeling of awe, Tune has no sense of trepidation about lining up opposite 'the big unit'. If anything, he believes poor defence has contributed to the Lomu legend at the fourth World Cup.

'Obviously his confidence is fairly high but his opposition is letting him do what he wants,' said Tune. 'Every guy that's marked him has stood off him. And one thing you don't do with Jonah is stand off him, wait to watch what he's going to do and then try to do something about him. You've got to go in there and grab him before he does anything.'

There is also a sense of the unknown for a lot of players at the

World Cup who have rarely, if ever, tangled with Lomu. The Australians have regular contact at Super 12 and Test level.

But Lomu, Tune agreed, may have overawed the English, especially after his four-try explosion against them in the 1995 World Cup semi finals.

'We do play the Kiwis a helluva lot,' he said. 'We play against the Berrymans, the Vidiris, the Lomus, all those guys out of the same mould … big, fast. So we've become fairly accustomed to them. But guys over here, you don't want to call them soft or anything, but a lot of what they do looks like that.

'Basically, he's very strong on the outside, and a bloke that big, who's also fast and has a good in and away, can be almost impossible to stop if you give him options. So the trick is you don't show the bloke the sideline. You angle in on his outside shoulder and you get to him before he gets any momentum up.'

Tune has lined up against Lomu on half a dozen occasions, for both Queensland and Australia.

'With the exception of my first game against New Zealand in Wellington (in 1996) where he played very well, I don't feel he's had it over me once,' he said. 'I've said all along I'd rather mark a bloke like him than a Jeff Wilson or a Christian Cullen. A Wilson or a Cullen are unpredictable, they can pretty much do anything. They can chip over the top and regather if you corner them. You don't see Jonah doing that.'

At the World Cup so far, he has had no need to. Strength and speed have been enough to blow away rivals and bring five tries. But even if it continues, Tune will sit, and wait, and know he'll be ready to mark the monster.

Jonathan Davies gave Wales fleeting hope three years ago when the Wallabies were last in Cardiff for a Test. Two penalty goals in the second half lifted the home side to a 19–18 lead over Australia with 20 minutes remaining.

The Wallabies eventually saw off the Welsh, and Davies in his last Test, 28–19.

'The Wallabies will be surprised how much Wales have improved since then,' he told Ball and All. 'I'm not confident we can win the quarter final. But we can win. Two years ago you could not have said that. It would have been a foregone conclusion. Australia will need to score at least 20 points to beat us.'

———

Heading deeper into the past, Paul Thorburn was the fullback who captained Wales on their disastrous tour to Australia in 1991.

In his book, *Kicked Into Touch*, Thorburn wrote: 'We were a bunch of whingers and drinkers. For some of our senior players, seasoned internationals, not to give of their best, preferring the wine bottle to the training ground, was inexplicable.'

Eight years on, Thorburn is optimistic about Wales again reaching the heights of international rugby. But it might not be tonight.

'I've actually tipped Australia to be world champions this year,' he said. 'I'm sure the Welsh team will come out full of enthusiasm and vigour. But I seem to recall we did that in Brisbane in 1991. It only lasted 10 minutes. They won 63–6.'

———

Another plucked from the Welsh history pages is five-eighth genius Barry John, a master of the running game. But John this week has called on the current side to forget about being pretty. Go back to 10–man rugby, he's urged.

'Wales simply make too many errors when throwing the ball around,' he said. 'It's the same with England — the northern hemisphere sides simply can't compete with the brilliant backs of New Zealand, Australia and South Africa.'

An unsung Wallaby buried in the dark and private battles waged by front-row forwards will be a silent, mostly unseen key to Australian plans for the downfall of Wales in tomorrow's World Cup quarter final.

There are five head-to-head duels that are set to decide the Millennium Stadium showdown.

ANDREW BLADES v PETER ROGERS

Blades:	Rogers:
Age: 32	Age: 30
Position: Tight head prop	Position: Loose head prop
Tests: 29	Tests: 10
Height: 178cm	Height: 181cm
Weight: 105kg	Weight: 118kg

BLADES: 'They've obviously picked a side geared around their scrum. They've got a huge forward pack, one they want to use as a platform to launch the running game of their number eight Scott Quinnell. The two Quinnell brothers are 130kg each, and Rogers is a monster on my side of the scrum. I've never played him before and only seen stuff of him in the last six months. But he's very aggressive at scrum time, so it's going to be a tough day at the office. They'd have to be the biggest pack around, the biggest we've come up against, and we know they'll attack us up front. They'd also be the best Welsh scrum we've seen in the last 10 years. Some of them haven't been great, in 1996 we had a pushover against them. It will be different this time. But it's just a matter of us knuckling down.'

I see Blades as the Wallabies' scrum doctor, a highly-regarded technician in the most brutal of rugby art forms. As the tight head, he is the rock of the pack. Disrupt him and the Australian forwards will be on the back foot throughout. Rogers is a South African import, a slab of prime beef off the veldt, with a 13kg weight advantage. But scrummaging is not solely about power, and Blades is tough to shift. Expect the Australian scrum to hold its own.

JOHN EALES v CHRIS WYATT

Eales:
Age: 29
Position: Second rower
Tests: 66
Height: 200cm
Weight: 115kg

Wyatt:
Age: 26
Position: Second rower
Tests: 16
Height: 196cm
Weight: 110kg

EALES: 'I don't know a great deal about Wyatt, but I have seen his last couple of games and he looked very impressive in them. They do use him a lot at the lineout, and he's very effective in that part of the game. He's pretty mobile in general play as well. But they've definitely got two different types of second rowers there with Craig Quinnell in for his running.'

Eales could send panic through the Welsh ranks if he starts to dominate Wyatt at the lineout, reason being that the home side has virtually no other targets to throw to, with the other second rower Craig Quinnell, weighing in at 130kg and virtually impossible to lift. Expect the Welsh to use plenty of variation in their lineouts, including the short, three-man alternative. This is a real area of weakness for the Welsh, and has been for many years. When the two sides met in the 1991 World Cup, Eales and Rod McCall slayed Wales 28–2 in the lineout count. Match over. Fortunately for Wales, lifting and supporting has made it easier to win your own ball.

GEORGE GREGAN v ROBERT HOWLEY

Gregan:
Age: 26
Position: Half back
Tests: 51
Height: 173cm
Weight: 80kg

Howley:
Age: 29
Position: Half back
Tests: 38
Height: 176cm
Weight: 82kg

GREGAN: 'Howley is one of the best halfbacks in the world, very dangerous, with a very good running game. We haven't seen too much of that darting from him yet, maybe they've been keeping a few things in reserve. But he also works well with Scott Quinnell at the back of the scrum and we'll have to close both those guys down.

Howley also has a good kicking game and he's got that sort of personality where he'll take control if they need a bit of spark.'

⟶

There's lot of responsibility for Gregan in this game. Equally, the latest member of the Wallabies Test half-century club has an opportunity to show he is not vulnerable on the big occasions. On the tactical side, Gregan has to keep an eye on the home side's two attacking springboards, Howley and number eight Scott Quinnell. Their combination will be vital to Welsh hopes, with both capable of getting in behind the defence. A strength of Gregan's play, however, is his ability to cut down players around the fringes. He should pack a machete today, there'll be plenty of cutting to do.

STEPHEN LARKHAM v NEIL JENKINS

Larkham:
Age: 25
Position: Five eighth
Tests: 27
Height: 188cm
Weight: 87g

Jenkins:
Age: 28
Position: Five eighth
Tests: 74
Height: 178cm
Weight: 90kg

LARKHAM: 'You only have to see how many Tests he's played to know Jenkins is very experienced. He's also the playmaker in this side and a lot of their game revolves around him. So if there's an opportunity to shut him down then we have the chance to shut down the team. He's a very good tactical kicker and if it's wet that will come into play. He also gets very flat in attack and will be prepared to go himself or look for a runner. It also gives you an opportunity to rush up on him, put on the pressure.'

⟶

The Welsh press have taken offence over my potshot at Jenkins on Monday. Billed as the Ginger Monster, I suggested the jug-eared redhead was more like a crumbling gingerbread man when Samoa beat the World Cup hosts in Cardiff last week. He did, after all, throw an intercept pass and badly miss a tackle, both of which led to Samoan tries. But that did not stop the Western Mail referring to sections of my match report as 'criticism bordering on abuse' in a page three article with a front-page pointer. Touchy people these Welsh. They might be even more so come Saturday.

TIM HORAN v SCOTT GIBBS

Horan:	**Gibbs:**
Age: 29	Age: 28
Position: Inside centre	Position: Inside centre
Tests: 76	Tests: 43
Height: 183cm	Height: 178cm
Weight: 93kg	Weight: 99kg

HORAN: 'I don't think the Welsh have used Gibbs as an attacking weapon in the midfield as much as they would have liked. I wouldn't be surprised if they tap a bit of ball off the top of the lineout this weekend and send it wide and flat to him to take it up. Steve Larkham and I will have to be tight in defence. I rate Gibbs very highly and first played against him in 1991, before he went and made a name for himself in rugby league. His strength is his power, he's able to bump people off. But he's not the quickest player on the field, so hopefully we can target that in some way.'

The Welsh have an extremely direct approach to their attack. The Quinnells and Scott Gibbs are battering rams, whose principal aim is to carry the side over the advantage line, allowing for quick recycling of the ball and a feed to Neil Jenkins at five-eighth so he can sum up the kick-run options. But sledgehammers are wasting their time if they think the Australian defensive wall is going to crumble. Wales will have to work out ways of going around or over the Aussies, and the latter might be their option, courtesy of Jenkins' boot.'

It has not been a World Cup to remember for Ireland. Beaten in their quarter final playoff by Argentina, it has also been revealed that assistant coach Steve Aboud had a nightmare preparation. He was locked in his hotel room bathroom for three hours, after the door handle fell off.

According to Irish reporters, the big problem was he missed an entire training session — and no one noticed.

QUARTER FINAL

AUSTRALIA 24 WALES 9

Wallaby centre Tim Horan has led a call for the Millennium Stadium roof to be closed for the World Cup final on Saturday week if wet weather threatens to ruin the showpiece tournament decider in Cardiff. The Australian camp were stunned to learn the stadium pitch was left open to the elements in the rainswept countdown to their quarter final against Wales, won 24–9 by the Wallabies to pitchfork them into the last four.

There was even a suspicion of conspiracy — that with the Welsh basing their tactics around a massive pack of forwards, they would prefer conditions wet and slippery to stifle the Australian backline. We were told the reason for leaving the roof open was that the grass required natural light to grow. Horan raised an eyebrow at the suggestion.

'I thought they would have closed it during the week regardless,' he said. 'We were surprised when we got here today and saw how damp it was after the rain of the past few days. And that was before the first half downpour made it worse. Guys had smaller tags in their boots and had to go and change them for longer ones.

'Why have the roof if you're not going to use it? It's like having a Ferrari in the garage and going out to catch a bus. If you've got it, use it. I know for the quarter final they had to have it open during the match because other teams are playing out in the open. But when it gets to the final, there will only be two teams involved and it will be the same for both.

'The crowd here, and people watching on television, want an entertaining game. But after that downpour 10 to 15 minutes into the match, we had to almost close up shop. When it's pouring like that you can't run the ball and it's very important for us that we do from here on in. It's where our strength is.'

Wallaby coach Rod Macqueen agreed with Horan.

'I think to close it for the final, if there's rain around, would be a wonderful idea,' he said. 'It takes out the elements that make it difficult to play. This is a very slippery surface, and it's when it got even wetter that we got into a bit of trouble.'

But the roof issue aside, by the time the rain arrived in the first half, the Australians should have already had the match in their keeping. They have set a disturbing trend at this tournament, for making then butchering try-scoring opportunities. To put no fine point on it, they are the winning but wasteful Wallabies. And better opposition than they confronted in Cardiff today will punish such disrespect of possession and position.

Macqueen complained of Welsh tactics at the breakdown, of their cynical fouling to disrupt Australia's flow of quick ball, and of the inaction from referee Colin Hawke that allowed the practice to continue without penalty.

'If the opposition are hell-bent on stopping you recycling the ball, and the referee doesn't police it, then you end up with stop start football,' he argued.

'If that's the way the game is going to go, then it's going to be very boring for a lot of people, because you've got to go back to a kicking style of game.'

But the Wallabies need to search their own performance more inwardly. Irrespective of what the Welsh were doing, Australia made enough line breaks to embarrass the home side on the scoreboard. In the first 10 minutes they twice failed to provide finishing polish, once to a dash by five eighth Stephen Larkham when he passed too early to winger Joe Roff, and on another occasion when an overlap was ignored and an inside pass took play back to the defensive traffic.

There were also instances of forward passes and, even more damning in the post-game statistics, a list of 16 handling errors by Australia compared to five by the Welsh. Several of them nipped in the bud promising attacking build-ups.

Wales also got the ball to their wingers on eight occasions, compared to seven by the Wallabies.

On top of all that, two of Australia's three tries should have been disallowed.

The first of the match, in only the fifth minute to halfback George Gregan, should have been called back after Larkham accidentally kicked the ball back into the ruck, and into his own forwards in front of him, during the lead-up. Wales should have been awarded a scrum.

Gregan's second effort, in the final minute, followed a blatant knock-on by Horan as he sought to slip a pass to centre partner Daniel Herbert.

Yet the Australians always had the Welsh measure, if only because the men in red never looked likely to score a try. They were relying on Wallaby indiscretions and the boot of Jenkins, who landed three from three, all in the first half as Australia went to the break just 10–9 ahead.

The decisive score went to the Australians in the 63rd minute when Larkham snaked forward inside the Welsh quarter, cleverly dropped the ball on to his boot and winger Ben Tune ghosted across the stadium surface to slide in for the try that fullback Matthew Burke converted for 17–9.

Pressed on the botched opportunities, Macqueen admitted: 'It's certainly not acceptable. Obviously we're concerned.'

There must be anxiety on some other fronts too. Burke is still below his best at fullback and the groin injury to Eales that had him replaced, will not want to worsen.

The positives were the scrum, an area where Wales had hoped to dominate but failed to gain the upper hand; the number of times flanker David Wilson, earlier in doubt with an ankle injury, snaffled ball from tackled Welsh players; and, most impressively, another flawless defensive effort.

The rain was falling but the tackling watertight. And in 320 minutes of football at this World Cup, the Australians have conceded just one try — to the United States. Romania, Ireland and now Wales have failed to cross the white strip.

The Great Redeemer failed to produce the Miracle at Millennium Stadium a nation had been praying for, but Graham Henry — the Kiwi coach who has rid Wales of their easybeats tag — has not lost faith in the scarlet revival.

Nor has he changed his pre-game opinion that the Wallabies rank, alongside New Zealand, as one of the two finest teams in the world.

'I'm delighted with the progress over the last 12 months,' he said after Wales became the first host nation to bow out of a World Cup before the final. 'It's been beyond my expectations, and I'm very proud of the way these guys tried today. You do hope for miracles but the Australians were too quick, too skilful and too streetwise for us. I don't see any weaknesses in them.

'They were well prepared, they took the power out of our scrum. There are some marvellous teams in this competition. The All Blacks aren't too bad, and obviously you have the Australian side too.

'It'll be interesting to see how it all pans out. But if you're looking for weaknesses in the Australian side, you'll have to tell me where they are.'

Henry denied he was playing mind games midweek when suggesting Wales, at their best, would not beat Australia. And he was standing by his pessimistic previews after the final scoreline, flattering as it was for the Wallabies with two questionable tries, showed a 15–point gap between the two sides.

'The Australians were the better team,' he said, sidestepping the controversial rulings of New Zealand referee Colin Hawke. 'We played quite close to our potential and obviously the guys wanted a miracle so we could go on from here. But I think we've reached the stage where we're at the top of my expectations.

'The crucial question is, how do we get better from here? In Wales for a long time, so they tell me, they go back to the start and say they're simply not good enough. So the heat comes on to the team and those connected with the Test side, which I guess means me.

'I think we need to get all that sorted now. The 30 players involved in this campaign, and the management, have given 150 percent. So other things need to be looked at.'

Australia dominated the midfield tussle in Cardiff, with the trio of Stephen Larkham, Tim Horan and Daniel Herbert far more penetrative than Neil Jenkins, Scott Gibbs and Mark Taylor. The Wallabies were more creative in attack, despite the errors, more solid in defence, more athletic and physically superior.

For Henry, the reasons behind that can be found in the southern hemisphere, in the provincial tournament that made his name as coach of the Auckland Blues.

'If Welsh rugby is going to progress then there have to be

competitions below international level,' he explained. 'We badly need a Super 12 type competition in the northern hemisphere.'

There was also, he said, too much pressure on young players, some of whom at the age of 16 are already playing more than 60 matches a year. According to Henry, youngsters with promise need to play less but at a higher intensity.

'That's what we've got to do as a Welsh rugby nation,' he said. 'If we do those things we'll improve at the top level as time goes on.'

For the moment though, their time has passed.

'The players are devastated,' said skipper and halfback Robert Howley. 'Today was a measure of where we are and we got beaten by a better side. We were in the game at 10–9 but we needed to score first in the second half. At half time we obviously felt this could be the day for Welsh rugby.

'Unfortunately, Australia are an awesome side, they have great defensive qualities. And you couldn't ask more of our players. Sometimes you're best just isn't good enough and today was one of those occasions. You have to accept that and move on.'

October 24

QUARTER FINALS

SOUTH AFRICA 44 ENGLAND 21

FRANCE 47 ARGENTINA 26

NEW ZEALAND 30 SCOTLAND 18

South African five-eighth Jannie de Beer produced the most astonishing individual performance of the 1999 World Cup, with a record five field goals in Paris to push the defending champions past England and into a World Cup semi final with Australia.

De Beer, the freckle-faced redhead with the eyes of a gunslinger — unwanted by the Springboks only two months ago — landed four long-range attempts and another from close range between the 44th and 74th minutes to launch the defending champions to a 44–21 victory.

The irony in the air at the Stade de France was suffocating. Four years ago, it was a dropped goal by England's Rob Andrew in injury time that sent the Wallabies tumbling from the tournament at the same knockout stage. This time it was England on the receiving end, and from a five-bazooka assault by a player who was ready to move to Britain earlier this season after South African selectors made it clear he was not in their World Cup plans. Injuries changed the landscape and de Beer today altered the record books.

Before his second half onslaught, no player from any nation had ever kicked more than three field goals in an international. In also landing five penalty goals, and conversions to the tries by halfback Joost van der Westhuizen and winger Pieter Rossouw, de Beer set a new mark for a South African in a Test with a personal haul of 34 points. His seven place kick successes were also achieved from as many attempts.

The Springboks now head for London and a semi final with Australia at Twickenham on Saturday. And coach Nick Mallett, who was awaiting the return to fitness of his first choice five eighth Henry Honiball, now has no need to worry.

He has found a matchwinner, with magic in his boots.

This was to be the silencing of the southern hemisphere upstarts — the World Cup where England and her British allies were to explode as a myth the chasm between them and the Tri-Nations tall poppies. So much for Rule Brittania.

Entering semi-final week and only France is flying the flag for Europe, and they have yet to meet a heavyweight opponent in the form of Australia, New Zealand or South Africa. England are gone, so too Wales and Scotland, while Ireland made their tails-between-legs exit earlier last week in losing a quarter final playoff to Argentina.

The sad statistic of this fourth World Cup — and it is regrettable if the game wants to be a truly global contest — is that the gap in standards between north and south remains a great divide. At the three previous World Cups, British sides did advance to the final four, and England made it to the final in 1991.

This time around, all four Home Nations were beaten twice during the tournament by sides beneath the equator, and none advanced beyond the quarters.

Wallaby skipper John Eales today admitted his surprise. He believed the gap between hemispheres had closed far more significantly, and before the tournament rated England a leading contender for the crown.

'To look at the results, you would say that gulf is still there,' he said. 'As a player, when you're preparing for a game, even against Scotland and Wales, you know those guys are a chance of beating you if you're not at your best. That's why you get a bit anxious. But I think a lot of it is they don't get the chance to constantly test themselves against the best in the world. From our point of view, even when we've had our lean years in the past four seasons, we're still able to play South Africa and New Zealand twice a year.

'It's good you can measure yourself and set your standards against them. But sides over here, apart from England who are now playing us on a more regular basis, they don't have that same opportunity. If you're not playing at that level regularly, not being subjected to it, then it becomes that much more difficult when you do have to face it.'

Welsh coach Graham Henry, after his side's quarter final loss to Australia, was adamant British rugby needed a Super 12 style tournament to raise the quality. Former England captain Will Carling agrees, saying a high level competition below Test standard is needed to further improve international players.

'Looking at England, we don't have the strike runners who can break the line,' he said. 'But let's not go away and say it's just the players. We've got to look at what these guys play week after week. If we're going to compete with the southern hemisphere we've got to change the competitions.'

Carling also pointed to the defensive strengths of Australia, New Zealand and South Africa, born out of necessity at Super 12 and Tri-Nations level.

'They see it as an offensive weapon,' he said. 'They're going to hit some guy and drive forward aggressively. In the northern hemisphere we always seem on the back foot. We'll tackle the guy but he'll keep moving forward.'

While Britain mourn the loss of their World Cup contenders, there are further problems for the game in the north with allegations that drug taking is rife among players who have appeared at the World Cup. The claims in *The Observer* appear to target players from Europe, not the southern hemisphere, with former internationals saying players have used steroids and stimulants to increase power and performance to enable them to make a living as a fulltime professional.

Former England and British Lions winger John Bentley was quoted as saying a player once hoodwinked a drug testing official by handing in a sample of a teammate's urine.

'That sort of thing makes a nonsense of the whole drug-testing system,' he said. 'It annoys me because drug taking is cheating.'

Former England flanker Peter Winterbottom claimed: 'I played against guys in internationals who had taken steroids and players are still doing it.'

When the Springboks returned to their dressing room, feet not touching the ground, having capped the perfect Paris weekend with a quarter final disposal of England, skipper Joost van der Westhuizen called his players into a huddle. The sort of circular bonding session the Wallabies go through on the field before a crucial match. But in a Bok changing shed, this was ground-breaking stuff.

'It might be a very Australian sort of thing to do, but quite unusual for these guys,' said an observer who was there in the bowels of the Stade de France. 'Joost got them together and told them the win meant nothing unless they went on with it and beat Australia this week.'

The symbolism of the private pow-wow, more than the words delivered by van der Westhuizen, is why the Wallabies are entitled to feel a slight unease about Saturday's World Cup semi final at Twickenham. It showed the South Africans have forged a team unity, are now galvanised by a single ambition, which might not sound so overwhelming to those who follow Wallaby or All Black teams. But in the melting pot of South African rugby, where cultures and creeds collide, team spirit can be left behind the door. And this South African team, despite the denials, was a team divided when they arrived in Britain last month to defend the Webb Ellis trophy.

Former captain Gary Teichmann was dumped during the Tri-Nations series, with coach Nick Mallett suggesting his use-by date had arrived.

The previous season, Teichmann and Mallett ruled the world together as the Boks carried off the Tri-Nations title and set about equalling the global record of 17 successive internationals unbeaten.

When England stopped the Boks taking the record alone last November, the first cracks appeared, as they did for the All Blacks in 1990 when the Wallabies ended their four-year streak without a loss.

The end can arrive quickly for a champion side and when South Africa struggled throughout the southern hemisphere winter, Mallett took a hammer far heavier than the one that carries his name, to re-shape his team. Out went Teichmann, with Bobby

Skinstad, the glamour boy from Cape Town, earmarked to be his successor at the back of the scrum, while van der Westhuizen was handed the captaincy.

The fallout was almost nuclear in strength and, if you listen to those close to the camp, cancers were spreading.

There was a pro-Teichmann faction, others who threw support immediately behind van der Westhuizen, and even a group not convinced that Skinstad was other than a low workrate show pony. There were suggestions that first choice five eighth Henry Honiball faked a hamstring injury in protest at Teichmann's dismissal, leading to his absence from the Test side — an absence ongoing through the World Cup and one that concerned the Springboks until last weekend when Jannie de Beer played unlikely hero.

It has even been alleged Honiball was considering phoning Mallett before the tournament to warn him that unless Teichmann was reinstated he, the five eighth, would step down. By all accounts the call was never made.

To what extent the rumours were based on fact is unclear, but there was, without question, sourness among the Boks, a hangover from the Teichmann controversy. And when a side starts to cannibalise, all the whispers and nods are given. In the Boks case, there were claims that some players left out of the side were bitching about Mallett favouring Cape-based stars over Afrikaners from the veldt.

How deep the disharmony really went only the players will know. But as results continued to go against South Africa this season, Mallett came under increasing pressure, and withdrew from the media spotlight. Last season he was a moth to the flame of publicity.

Now the Boks are into the semi finals — their indifferent early tournament form forgotten — and the relief for Mallett could be seen in his rapid-fire answers to post-match questions. The adrenalin was coursing through his blood, as it was no doubt for van der Westhuizen and co.

One win can mean that much difference. It can turn a side of brooding, out-of-form players into a highly potent unit. And when the Boks are at one with themselves, they are a danger to all. New Zealand can attest to that, via the 1995 World Cup final.

Wallaby coach Rod Macqueen today unveiled the blueprint to snuff out South Africa's dropped goal demon Jannie de Beer in the World Cup semi final at Twickenham on Saturday. Macqueen revealed the only failsafe strategy to prevent a repeat of the Springbok five-eighth's Paris heroics — where a world record five field goals torpedoed England in the quarter finals — was to deny him opportunities.

'It's very difficult trying to defend against someone like that,' Macqueen said after the Wallabies moved camp from Cardiff to London to prepare for a showdown with the defending champions. What we won't be doing this week is going out to practice charging them down. The answer is to play the game in their half.

'And when they do cross the halfway line, you have to make sure you stop their pack going forward which gives him the time and space to get his kick away.'

De Beer was a World Cup after thought for the Springboks, who overlooked him earlier in the year but were forced to fall back on their fourth choice pivot when injuries arrived on tournament eve. Even then he arrived at the World Cup only to keep warm the pivot position until Henry Honiball proved his fitness. Until now.

Having only returned to South Africa this season — to play for the Free State province — after his London Scottish club folded, de Beer has been hailed in Britain as the man who sank England with the 'Foot of God'.

'Some of the things which happened out there were supernatural,' he said. 'God gave us this victory. I am just happy to be part of His game plan. Sometimes things happen in such a way that you just don't have an answer for them. I personally feel God had a hand in this. I believe in my heart that this victory was not just about me as a player. I thank the Lord for the talent He gave me and I thank the forwards for the ball they gave me.'

Macqueen, too, was thankful — that the Wallabies did not have to line-up against England on their home patch this weekend.

'One of the things about playing South Africa is we won't have to worry about the other side having a home crowd and the influence that might have had on the referee,' he said. 'We've seen already during the tournament what effect it can have, so I think we're in a better situation playing South Africa, even though I rate the Springboks a better team than England.'

Macqueen admitted de Beer and his right boot have also given South Africa a new dimension.

'They haven't put a match together for a long time,' he said, drawing reference to Springbok defeats this year against Wales, and in three of their four Tri-Nations Tests. But de Beer had a complete game and his field goals will give them enormous confidence.'

Former Springbok captain Francois Pienaar, having confirmed there had been internal strife in the South African camp following the pre-World Cup sacking of skipper Gary Teichmann, agreed de Beer had done more than kick England out of the tournament.

He had resurrected their confidence.

'The guy was awesome,' said Pienaar, who led the Boks to their 1995 World Cup triumph. 'South Africa have wanted to get Honiball fit, and get him back in the side. But de Beer ruled the roost in the quarter final from the word go.

'The drop kick is one attack you can't defend against, and no-one will again achieve the feat he performed. It was the best kicking display I've ever seen.

'South Africa will win the semi final now. They will have so much confidence from this one. They'll go and play for each other, they'll be on song.'

Pienaar also questioned the strength of the Australian pack, especially their scrum.

'They've had a couple of problems in the forwards,' he added. 'And the Springbok scrum is very powerful. They outmuscled England in the forwards and their mentality was right. I knew the guys would be up for the quarter final after all the criticism they'd received, and all the people who were on their backs.'

Springbok coach Nick Mallett, who was under increasing fire for the Springboks indifferent displays through the pool rounds, was equally enthusiastic about de Beer's haul in their 44–21 disposal of England.

'With defences so well organised, and with him an excellent drop goal kicker, I told him before the game to go and have a bash,' he said. 'When he stuck one or two, I knew it was his day, but I didn't think he'd end up with five.'

Australia has been warned.

David Campese questions whether the All Blacks have what
it takes to win the World Cup after their average showing
against Scotland.

The hallmark of great All Black teams down through the
years has been the ruthless manner in which they destroy
their opposition. They have taken delight in humiliation,
in keeping the foot on the throat long after the fight has
gone out of their rivals. But after watching the World
Cup quarter finals at the weekend, I have to wonder
whether this current New Zealand team has that same
killer instinct.

I know they put 100 points on Italy in the
pool games, which is no mean feat. But Scotland were
there for the taking at Murrayfield on Sunday and the
Kiwis let them wriggle free and escape what should
have been a slaughter. For mine, it gives the French just
the slightest ray of hope for their semi final at
Twickenham. And they certainly need something to
cling to at this stage.

Looking at the match from all sides, only one
thing can stop New Zealand, and that's complacency.
But perhaps that dreaded disease has started to work its
way into All Black bones.

The Kiwis came out all fired up, played at a
million miles an hour to blitz the Scots and put 17
points on the board, and then, for some reason, appeared
to sit back and take it easy.

I only have to go back three years, to a Bledisloe
Cup Test in Wellington against the All Blacks, to know
that has not traditionally been their way.

On that afternoon at Athletic Park they smashed
us, and kept piling on the points until we limped off at
the end having lost 43–6.

The All Blacks had the leadership then of players

like Sean Fitzpatrick and Zinzan Brooke. Players up front who set the tone for the rest of the side.

They led, the others followed, and that pair was never guilty of going easy on anyone.

The real worry for All Black coach John Hart is that a whiff of complacency within the ranks can be dangerous, because it eats away at a player's concentration. If one week he's on cruise control, and the next he has to be on top of his game for the entire 80 minutes, it's not always easy to make the adjustment.

I still can't see France causing the upset on Sunday, but that Scottish performance suggests the Kiwis are not travelling quite as well as many might assume. And the Wallabies and Springboks will take heart from that.

The Kiwis can talk up the Scottish performance all they like. The bottom line is they had the Scots on the rack and loosened the ropes, allowing a team of honest, hard-working players to outscore them 15–5 in the second half. Sean Fitzpatrick is still close to the team and I heard him say it was a good victory, and that the boys were going well.

I wonder if the Kiwis might be kidding themselves a little. They made a lot of mistakes in the second half, and while they knew they were always going to win, there were some weaknesses shown up in their game.

The All Blacks scrum and lineout is not as good as it should be. They will not trouble Australia in either area should the two teams meet in the final.

Conditions at Murrayfield were obviously poor, with rain falling throughout. But losing ball on their own throw to the lineout is a problem they will want to rectify in a hurry.

Jonah Lomu was not at his best either, but gave me the impression he didn't want to be out there. His two handling errors from Scottish kicks were the perfect example of losing concentration. With Jonah though, you're never going to keep him out of the game altogether. He's too good for that. He still managed to score one try, and have a hand in another when he drew in five Scottish defenders during a first half charge at the line.

There's no doubt the All Blacks have numerous weapons in their backline — they don't always rely on Lomu. But I was surprised we didn't see more of Christian Cullen against Scotland. Perhaps he's still getting used to the midfield, another area where the All Blacks might just be a bit vulnerable.

As for France, it's great to see them running the ball like they did against Argentina. When they do use their backs they're a very dangerous side. Some of those tries in the quarter final were classics, typically flamboyant, typically French.

———

All Black coach John Hart has tossed aside trans-Tasman rivalry and tipped Australia to beat the Springboks in Saturday's opening World Cup semi final.

Describing the first of the weekend Twickenham showdowns as 'a close one to call', Hart said the strike force of the Wallaby backline should provide the edge to launch the Bledisloe Cup holders into the final on November 6.

Pointing to the playmaking skills of five-eighth Stephen Larkham, the experience and thrust of centres Tim Horan and Daniel Herbert, and the finishing power of Joe Roff and Ben Tune on the wings, Hart suggested the Boks had a multi-skilled band of marauders to counter.

But a Wallabies win would be conditional, he added, on Australia matching the forward firepower South Africa will rely on, and play to, through their halves combination of Joost van der Wethuizen and kicking wizard Jannie de Beer.

Australia have rushed back number eight Toutai Kefu from a two-week suspension in a bid to bolster their forward ranks for the clash. Kefu, the one true ball runner in the Wallaby pack, replaces Tiaan Strauss, who now misses the chance to play against the country he formerly captained, in the only change to the side that beat Wales 24–9 in the Cardiff quarter final last Saturday.

Out of touch fullback Matthew Burke retains his position despite an ongoing lack of form, and can thank the goalkicking job for holding off the challenge of Chris Latham for a semi final that Hart believes will go down to the wire.

'I'm not surprised both of those teams have got to this point,' he said as the All Blacks prepared on the outskirts of London for Sunday's second semi final with France. 'And it's clearly a battle of the Australian backs against the South African forwards. The Springbok pack might have a slight dominance. It's where their strengths are, around the forwards, and with their halfback and five-eighth. They're not playing a very expansive game.

'Australia, however, do play expansively and that's where South Africa might be vulnerable. The Australian backs look to have too much class. Larkham is an exceptional player. If the Australians get any sort of parity up front, I think they'll win.'

Hart disagrees with the notion that the Wallabies have been unimpressive to date in seeing off Romania, Ireland and USA in the pool rounds, followed by Wales at a rainswept Millennium Stadium.

Despite the scoring opportunities they have bungled and botched, Hart senses a side on the rise.

'They know where they are,' he said. 'They're making progress and you saw the step up in their win over Wales. They have the ability to do that again next weekend. In those early games it's hard to get a fix on how teams are really going because of the disparity in the quality of the opposition.

'It might also be that Australia's depth is not as great in some positions as South Africa, so that can be misleading when they rest a few guys. But when they get their top squad together they show their ability.'

Hart was more reluctant to fashion imaginary outcomes for his own side's battle with a French side that showed glimpses of their traditional flair and confidence in a 47–26 quarter final win over Argentina in Dublin.

'The danger of this French team is they can wake up in the morning, feel good, and produce something special,' he said. 'They looked as if they had lost confidence but they found their way back against Argentina. You have to be very wary of them. If they get it right they're extremely dangerous, and they will be on a high.

'They've probably got as far as they thought they might, maybe further than it looked like being a couple of weeks ago, so they'll throw caution to the wind. That makes them dangerous again.'

———

Each week the Wallabies jump on the scales so team management can monitor any fluctuations in weight. With most forwards, keeping the weight down is important. But for one of the World Cup party, there is a philosophy of 'the heavier the better'.

It explains why he turned up to the weigh-in this week, hiding a bunch of solid silver knives in his shoes, worth at least a couple of kilograms.

———

Quote of the quarter finals came from Taine Randell when, after the win over Scotland, he was asked in a television interview what he thought about playing France in the semi finals. The French had qualified more than an hour before the Kiwis match kicked off.

'Oh, France is it? Great.'
'You didn't know?'
'Uh, no.'

October 27

David Campese predicts a change in fortunes for South Africa's Jannie de Beer in the semi-final against Australia.

Springbok hero Jannie de Beer — a World Cup hero one week, off by half time the next. That's the scenario for the semi final at Twickenham on Saturday, unless I miss my guess. There is no denying his five dropped goals was a fantastic effort against England — a once in a lifetime performance that will ensure his name is linked to this tournament well into the next millennium.

But there is no way de Beer, with all due respect, is in the same class as the player he is likely to keep on the bench for the game against Australia. Henry Honiball came to the World Cup as the Springboks injured first choice five-eighth. South African coach Nick Mallett has been waiting for him to regain fitness and he was still short of the mark for the quarter final, hence the retention of de Boot.

Now, Mallett has little choice but to keep his king of the kicks after his 34 points against the Poms. Maybe Mallett — and my sources tell me did not rate de Beer at all two years ago — will have the courage to make the change and name Honiball in his starting line-up tonight. But I somehow doubt it, and the Wallabies will not be complaining.

Honiball is a superb defender, a strong runner and a very good ball player. Apart from goalkicking, and the ability to bang over long-range field goals, he has the edge on de Beer in every department.

There is, however, scope for Mallett to use both his pivots. He can send de Beer out with instructions to grab as many early points as he can. And with the game sure to be an arm wrestle in the first half-hour, de Beer will fit the bill, kicking for field position then taking every possible opportunity to kick the Boks into a lead.

If he does, his job will be done, and if the South Africans want to sit on their advantage, then Honiball can come on to provide a more robust presence in midfield. The way I see it, the longer de Beer is in the game, the more vulnerable the Boks will become.

The Australians are, no doubt, already planning ways of exposing him. He made a great tackle on Phil de Glanville in the quarter final, a driving hit that knocked the English centre sideways. But defence has not always been his strong suit and the Wallabies, if they share my views, will probably try to bring Daniel Herbert back on the angle to aim his bulk at de Beer. Force him to make a few tackles, sap his strength, or make him a little tentative, and the rest of his game, including his kicking, might not be so flawless as it was in Paris.

I expect to see Honiball out there before half time, maybe as early as the 20–minute mark.

One member of the South African back division who will not be targeted as a weakness is inside centre Pieter Muller. I rate the guy highly, the linchpin of the South Africa backs. He rarely misses a tackle and he was so important to the Springboks last week getting them over the advantage line in attack.

From there the South Africans can bring their backrow into the game, and the trio of Bobby Skinstad, Andre Venter and Johan Erasmus are the real backbone of this side. Venter was everywhere against England. He's big, he's strong and he can cause havoc. He was one of the stars when the Boks beat the Wallabies in their last encounter in Cape Town.

Skinstad is an impact player, and almost in the mould of a modern-day five-eighth the way he runs with the ball, throwing dummies and playing the link man for outside supports.

People keep talking about the South African scrum and the danger it poses to the Wallabies. But I thought the Australian scrum went well against Wales, so

I don't see them getting shoved around. That's why the Bok backrow are the key to their hopes.

The contest between Skinstad, Venter and Erasmus, up against Toutai Kefu, David Wilson and Matt Cockbain will be, for me, the decisive head to head battles in the game. As a backline, I don't think the South Africans will try too much in the way of fancy stuff. They'll be the silent partners to their forwards.

October 28

When Wallaby prop Andrew Blades crawls from his bed on Sunday morning and stares into the bathroom mirror, he expects to find his face sprinkled liberally with a score of tiny red blotches. It will be the unavoidable legacy of tangling with a Springbok monster in Saturday's scrum battle at Twickenham that is likely to shape the opening World Cup semi final.

Os du Randt is considered the world's premier loosehead prop — a lover of steak and red wine whose massive 130kg frame will slam into Blades on around 20 occasions in the most confrontational of on-field contests. Blades will give away 21kg and 12cm to the Man Mountain nicknamed the 'Ox'.

But the Australian scrum guru, with a reputation built on his shrewd tactical approach to the unarmed violence that is international front-row play, is approaching the collision with sadistic glee.

'I know I'm going to be very sore the next day, but this is why I play Test rugby, I love the challenge,' he said. 'I'll be taking it to him as much as possible. Come Sunday morning there'll be red spots on my face. It happens sometimes after a big game because of the amount of pressure in the scrum. It tends to burst a few tiny blood vessels.

'But the pain will be everywhere. It takes it out of you. The next morning you sort of roll out of bed and crawl to the bathroom. Mainly around the neck and the lower back you'll feel it because when you hit in the scrum it's like hitting a brick wall, or being hit by a Mack truck. It's muscle soreness and muscle fatigue and it's a matter of getting in the pool for a few hours to work it out so you can get ready for the next day's training.'

If Blades paints an uncomfortable picture, he has no choice. There is no way to soft soap what is coming Saturday. With a World Cup final berth on the line, the clash up front will be brutal, and retreat cannot be considered, for if Blades and the Australian scrum falter, the Boks will have an ascendancy that could catapult them to the Cardiff decider.

'When you look at the sides we play, the South Africans are

the guys that most physically confront you,' said Blades. 'They are a great forward pack, physically huge. When you look at Ox and look at me there's a big difference there. He's a monster. But it's something I enjoy, taking up that sort of challenge.

'I've played these guys before, I know what to expect this weekend. You've just got to steel yourself for it. You've got to look at it tactically, try a few different things. You've also got to make sure you concentrate every scrum.

'He can probably afford to knock off in a couple and just lean in there. For me that's not an option. And if you don't combine as a scrum against these guys, someone like Ox can tear you apart.'

A father of one, du Randt has a ready smile, God-fearing philosophies and, he says, only respect for the Australian front-row of Blades, Michael Foley and Richard Harry.

Springbok reserve prop Ollie le Roux, cherubic of face but devilish of tongue, was of a different opinion earlier this year. After his provincial teammate Wickus van Heerden was suspended over a biting charge brought by Harry after a Super 12 match last year, le Roux referred to the Australian as a 'soft cock'.

Du Randt today offered only praise.

'I rate the Australian front-row very high, especially now that Andrew Blades and Richard Harry are back,' he said. 'The scrum is won on engagement. If you get the hit on your opponents, get them to shift their feet then they have to make plans to get out of the pressure. But with Australia and New Zealand you don't really get that.

'In the end, it's a mental thing. Our positions are really the only ones in the game where you're man to man and it's a battle out there. You just hit as hard as you can and try to absorb the pressure from the other team. They do it very well.'

While le Roux fired his barb off the field months ago in an Australian magazine, du Randt is more the strong, silent type.

'I haven't grown up doing that,' he said. 'If you come out of the Afrikaaner culture you just do your job, get it over.'

Harry claims that most South Africans have the same approach. 'They just get about their business,' he said. 'There's no talk or hoopla. They're guys who are just good at what they do, and they don't have to talk about it. The northern hemisphere guys love having a bit of a yak, regardless of what the scoreboard says, no

Great start . . . the Wallabies celebrate the fifth-minute try by
George Gregan in the quarter final against Wales in Cardiff.
Courtesy: Allsport

England five-eighth Jonny Wilkinson weaves his way through
the Fijian defence in the quarter final playoff at Twickenham.
Courtesy: Allsport

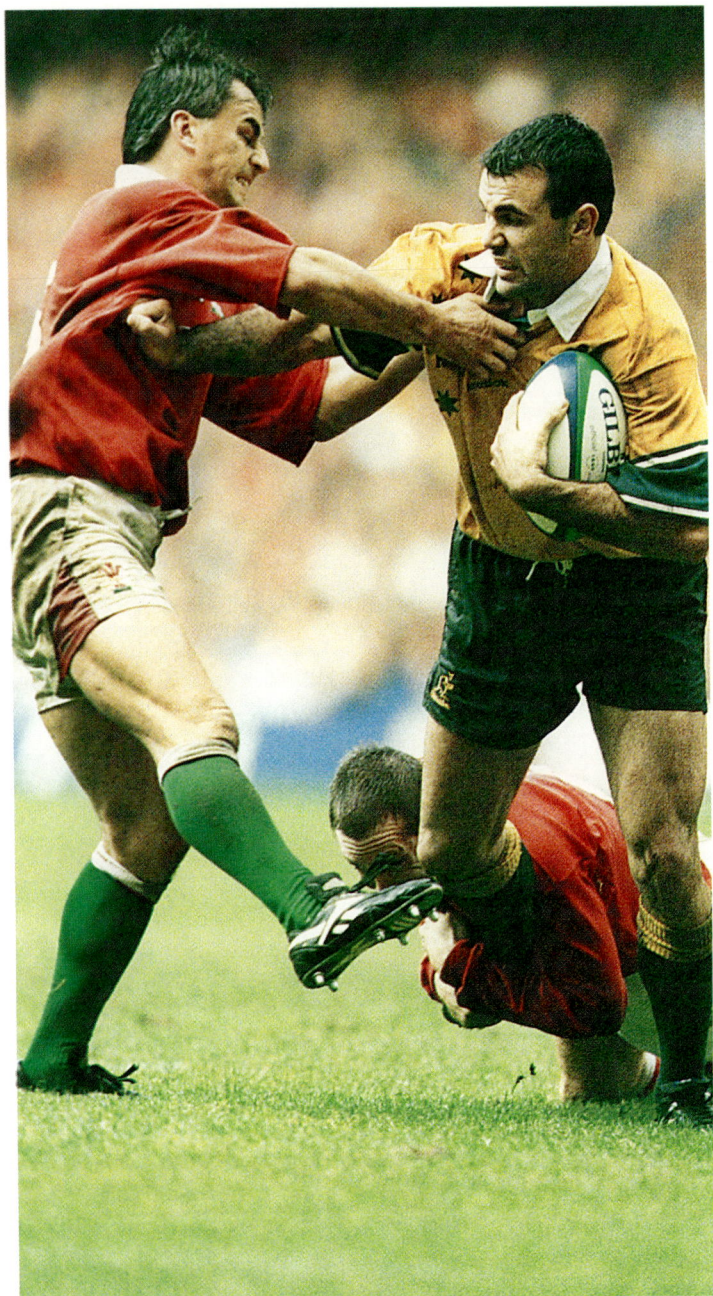

Joe Roff struggles to beat the tackles of Welsh fullback Shane Howarth and utility back Allan Bateman. *Courtesy: Allsport*

Ben Tune slides over to score against Wales after chasing a well-placed grubber kick by Stephen Larkham. *Courtesy: Allsport*

George Gregan, who had a 1995 World Cup to forget, made amends four years later. *Courtesy: Allsport*

Tim Horan prepares to pass, only moments before the force of a tackle forced him to spill the ball forward. Not that it mattered. The ref missed the knock-on and George Gregan crossed for his second try of the quarter final. *Courtesy: Allsport*

Drop goal demon . . . Springbok five-eighth Jannie de Beer kicks one of the five field goals that set a new world record and sent England tumbling out of the World Cup in a quarter final in Paris. *Courtesy: Allsport*

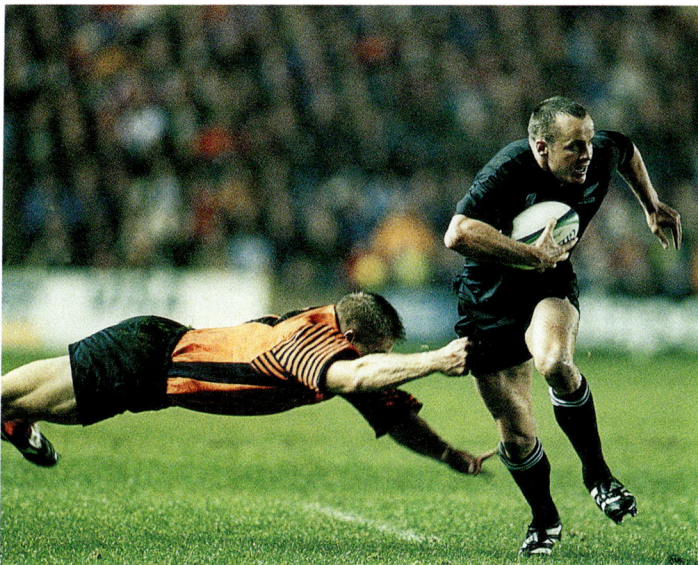

All Black centre Christian Cullen, whose moves from fullback to wing and then wing to centre never really brought out the best in this counter attacking genius, beats the tackle of Scotland fullback Glenn Metcalfe in the Murrayfield quarter final. *Courtesy: Allsport*

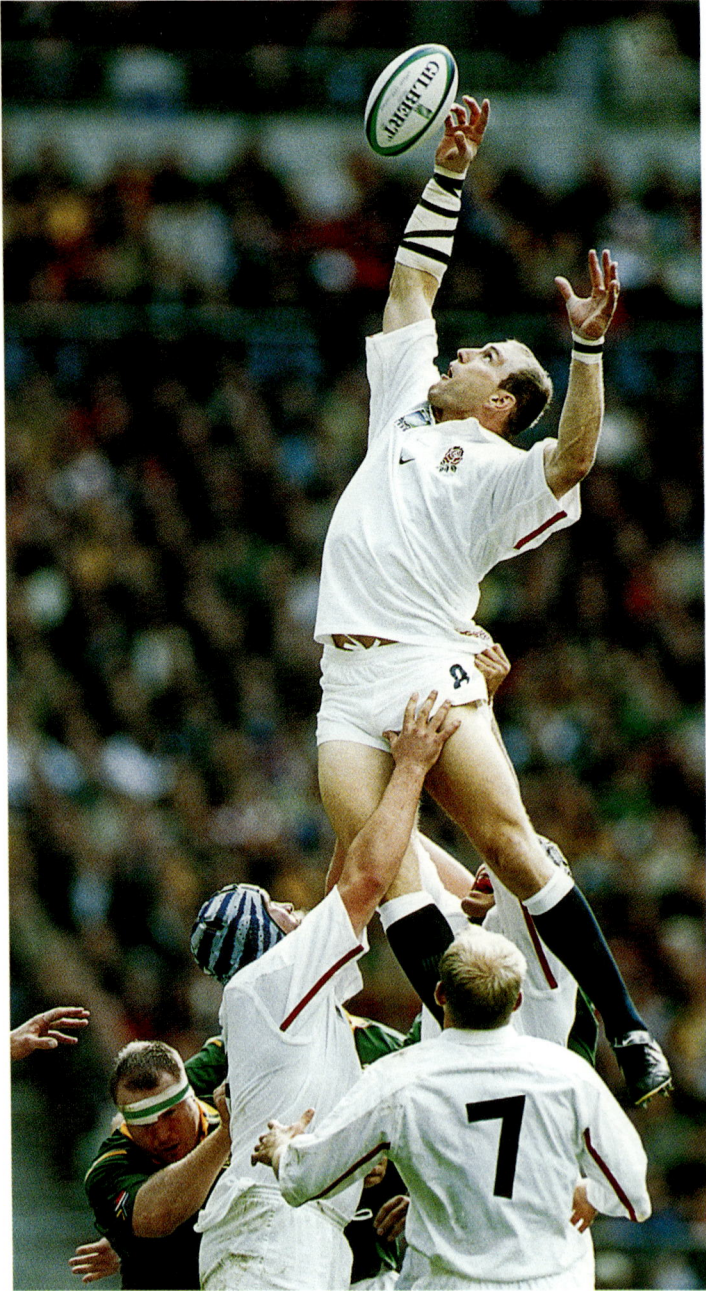

Despite another World Cup disappointment for England, number eight Lawrence Dallaglio was a towering presence throughout. The former captain seen here winning a lineout against South Africa. *Courtesy: Allsport*

French flyer Philippe Bernat-Salles runs in a try against Argentina in a thrilling quarter final at Lansdowne Road. *Courtesy: Allsport*

Miracle kick . . . Stephen Larkham launches his 48-metre drop goal against South Africa in the semi final at Twickenham. *Courtesy: Allsport*

Australian players rush to congratulate Larkham after his stunning extra-time strike. *Courtesy: Allsport*

matter what's happening in the scrum. But someone like Ox never has to utter a word. His actions speak loud enough.'

—⟶

Wallaby forward Toutai Kefu — back after a two week ban for his fistic fury against Ireland — has set himself to land the knockout blow on the bully-boys from South Africa in Saturday's World Cup semi final at Twickenham. While the Tongan-born number eight has vowed not to repeat his rumble in Dublin where flanker Trevor Brennan was left bloodied and bruised, he does intend to punch holes in the Springboks as the Wallabies primary offensive weapon.

South African coach Nick Mallett has already targeted Kefu as a dangerman as the Tri-Nations rivals prepare for a showdown to decide the first team through to the tournament final at Millennium Stadium on Saturday week. As the only recognised ball runner among the Wallaby forwards, his job is vital to the plans of a backline hailed as the best in the world. Without his raids behind enemy lines, their space to operate shrinks, their effectiveness dramatically blunted.

His commando mission will, for the most part, be a solo assignment, and few Australian players will carry more responsibility.

But in returning from his citing and suspension to make a 24th Test appearance at the expense of former Springbok captain Tiaan Strauss, the explosive Kefu is primed for a performance to swing the semi final in Australia's favour.

'It will be the same as usual for me,' he said. 'My main goal is to get us over the advantage line, to get through their defence and start the momentum that will get our backs on the front foot. They're going to be tough. The Springboks have always been the most physical forwards we play. Games against them are more physical than Test matches against either the All Blacks or England.

'They hit hard these guys. They go in for gang tackles, two or three at a time, but it's always been part of their psyche. They want to bash you. It's that bully syndrome.'

October 29

David Campese talks about another Australian winger with a claim to a place in history.

So Joe Roff will re-write the record books tomorrow with the fastest 50 Test caps on record? Now all we have to do is get coach Rod Macqueen to re-write his game plan and get the big bloke more involved.

Roff is an under used asset in this Wallaby team and if the Springboks are to be sent packing at Twickenham tomorrow, then he has to be cast in the role of gamebreaker.

Earlier this season, Joe was the Super 12 player-of-the-series, winning the award for his fullback performances with the free-spirited ACT Brumbies. He revelled in the freedom to run the ball, to counter attack, to be ever present when the Brumbies unleashed their backline and, under coach Eddie Jones, that was at every opportunity. As a confidence player, it was just what Roff needed, and he delivered like never before.

I'm still convinced fullback is his best position, but there is no point debating that now. He is on the left wing to play the Springboks, and it's from there he has to excel. The only problem is, the ball has rarely come to him during the international program this year, and certainly not enough during the World Cup.

Given the occasional chance in the first half against Wales in last week's quarter final, he showed what impact he can have, outstripping their defence to create the first try with an inside pass for George Gregan. But we are still not seeing enough of Joe, and there are two parties to shoulder the blame.

First, the Wallabies continue to concentrate their attack around the midfield, rather than shifting it wide. Secondly, Joe is not asserting himself as he should. He needs to call more play his way, or have the vision to know where the action is heading and make sure, however unexpected it is, that he is there to get a touch on the ball.

Hopefully though, the Wallabies are also moving to mend their ways. How many times have we seen at Super 12 level the double act of Gregan and Roff work the blindside? They have devastated defences time and again because, when done correctly, it creates a situation where Joe is one on one against his opposite number.

Few players in the game stand much chance under those circumstances, and I would place Springbok right wing Deon Kayser in that very category. He weighs 80kg, Roff tips the scales at 100kg. Tell me that's not a mis-match to be exploited.

Gregan is the key to it though. He needs to mix up his game a little more. George has been playing pretty well during the tournament and came up with two tries against the Welsh in Cardiff. But he has more up his sleeve, if allowed, or prepared, to produce it. The dart on the blindside to put Roff away in the quarter final was the perfect example.

Against Joost van der Westhuizen tomorrow, one of the best halfbacks in the game, he should try a few more options, keep the Boks guessing, because they will be looking to shut down both he and five eighth Stephen Larkham with an on-rushing defence. Put them in two minds, and they will be forced to hesitate, and suddenly the space in the backline opens up a touch.

It should be all the Australians need. They have the backline to get to the World Cup final and win it. What they must do is give that back division the room and time to operate. That's where Gregan, as the organiser, will have to play it smart.

Fullback Matt Burke is another who has to throw himself more into the game. If he starts joining the line, then the Boks will have an added problem to ponder. Otherwise, they can limit their targets to the halves and the centre pairing of Tim Horan and Daniel Herbert. Shut them down and Roff and Ben Tune suffer.

While the threequarters are the obvious matchwinners, they will rely heavily on the eight forwards in front of them.

I mentioned yesterday that the Springbok backrow of Bobby Skinstad, Johan Erasmus and Andre Venter were the backbone of the South African side. To take them out of the game, the Wallabies have to use their big men to drag them into tackles. Once that happens the Australians need to shift the point of the attack quickly, not keep hammering away at the same point.

By taking the play away from the ruck or maul that the Bok backrow trio will hopefully be at the bottom of, you render them ineffectual. Sounds easy, I know, but putting plans like that into action requires precision, pace and timing. There were glimpses of it against Wales, but only early. It will need to be a more sustained effort against the defending world champions.

But the Wallabies should be up for the challenge. After all, they realise how close they are now to the ultimate goal. That four-year dream of becoming World Cup holders is, if they get it right, just 160 minutes away.

***

When their worlds collide tomorrow in a semi-final of rugby union's fourth global championship, Stephen Larkham and Jannie de Beer will share nothing in common but the numbers on their backs and the fate of a nation in their hands.

Bernie and The Boot, the rival five-eighths, offer a study of startling contrasts as they prepare for the cauldron of a World Cup showdown between Australia and South Africa at Twickenham.

The prize for the victors, the Wallabies or the Springboks, is a shot at the title next week, and no two players on the neutral soil of the game's headquarters in London will come under closer scrutiny before a billion-plus audience than the players wearing the No.10 jumpers. Both are viewed as matchwinners in their own camps, as weaknesses by the enemy.

But that contradiction only adds to the mix of an oil and water match-up that has past greats at loggerheads over the pair's potential to carry their countries on to the Cardiff decider.

The softly spoken Larkham, nickname Bernie, is a gifted ball runner, a converted fullback, and an opportunist who plays the five-eighth position for Australia without reference to a textbook. De Beer is the South African traditionalist, a kicking freak, who launched a world record five field goals from his right boot last week to blast England out of the tournament.

Former Wallaby captain Michael Lynagh, hailed as one of the finest five-eighths in history, ranks Larkham among the most gifted talents of the professional era — a prototype for the future.

The former Springbok Joel Stransky disagrees. To the five-eighth whose dropped goal in injury time sealed the 1995 World Cup final, de Beer has a significant edge. It is a debate to be detailed later, and one that underlines the great divide between the two central figures of a heavyweight contest.

But the differences between Larkham and de Beer extend well beyond their approach to a game that has brought them wealth and recognition. A visit to the past also reveals the wildly divergent paths they have trod to the lush turf of Twickers and perhaps, by next week, to a World Cup winners medal.

De Beer was the product of a broken and penniless home in a small mining town in South Africa's northern Free State. His mother, who was left unemployed and destitute as she struggled to raise three children, divorced his father, an alcoholic. When de Beer was in his late teens — having relied on local charity for clothes and, just as importantly, his precious football boots — his mother died at the age of 39.

A scholarship to Free State University in Bloemfontein, after his rugby skills had been spotted by talent scouts, would become the turning point in his life.

'But I'm sure everyone has a story to tell about their childhood,' he said. 'All I will say is that my early experiences did not weaken or strengthen me. One accepts the situation and deals with it. We had our own cross to bear and we just got on with it. I've never been bitter or felt that life's been unfair to me. I will never deny the circumstances of my childhood. It happened.

'It's a bit like having a brother in jail. You might not want to talk about it but you can't deny the situation exists. This life is what you make of it, and your attitude shapes your destiny.'

The Larkham upbringing could not have been more dissimilar. Raised in a middle class family on a sheep farm, some 30 minutes outside Canberra, his was a stable family unit. Even now he visits his parents twice a week for dinner, and they are following his fortunes at the World Cup as part of a supporters' tour. They will be in the grandstands tonight, cheering on their free-running son as he tangles with de Beer of the Boks.

It is a clash of opposites that Lynagh and Stransky could find no common ground on when approached to analyse the impact the five-eighths will have on the outcome of the first semi-final. New Zealand plays France in the other, at the same ground on Sunday.

'De Beer is a better tactical kicker, and a great dropped goal exponent, but in terms of attacking ability, Larkham gives Australia an extra dimension,' said Lynagh. 'He has deceptive speed, he almost ghosts through a defence, and that's something you don't learn. It's an instinctive talent. Steve looks very unassuming, and I'm sure that's what causes problems for an opposition.

'They see this guy ambling towards them and they think 'he's not going anywhere'. Next thing they know he's past them and gone. He's beautiful on the ball and when he gets time and space he's extremely dangerous. The Springboks forced him backward in Perth last year, and that put him and the rest of the backline under pressure. But he's more comfortable in the position now, and his vision is very good.

'You saw that last week in the quarter final against Wales, with the kick in behind the defence for Ben Tune's try. I expect Australia to win. They have more tactical awareness, and Larkham is part of that.'

Stransky is yet to be convinced, not of Larkham's footballing ability, but of his value as a five-eighth.

'He's a fullback playing at No.10, and one of his weaknesses is that he runs the ball from too deep,' said Stransky. 'He's a great exponent of the running game, devastating if you give him a bit of space. But he likes to carry the ball up and a good defence can cut him off by getting in his face. If they stop him running then they can also keep the other Australian backs pinned behind the advantage line.

'I think the South African backline look very ordinary in
attack. They've got pace and strength when they take the ball up, but
they won't break down a defence and score tries. But Jannie de
Beer's game is his kicking, and he's fantastic at it, as he showed
against England behind a dominant pack.

'If Australia get enough ball they could rip the South African
backs to pieces. But the team whose forwards come out on top will
win, and for that reason I go with the Boks.'

Where Stransky believes the South Africans can target
Larkham, Lynagh holds similar thoughts on de Beer.

'I think Australia will target him,' he said. 'South Africa might
have made a mistake in playing him against the Wallabies. If they can
take the Springbok backrow out of play, I'm sure they'll run the big
guys at Jannie. I wouldn't be surprised to see Australia attempt to
exploit him.'

Bernie and The Boot. Let the show begin.

South African coach Nick Mallett has retained for the Twickenham
semi final with Australia the same starting line-up that disposed of
England in the quarters — and former Wallaby coach Bob Dwyer
believes the Springbok mentor has blundered.

Dwyer, who guided Australia to World Cup glory in 1991,
claims Mallett should have bitten the bullet and dropped his five field
goal hero Jannie de Beer to return a fully fit Henry Honiball, the
number one choice at five eighth before injury.

'All the players in the South African team think Honiball is a
genius, and if he's fit you play him,' said Dwyer, who is tipping a
Wallaby victory.

Centre Pieter Muller is the lone survivor from the Springbok side
that emerged from isolation to play and be thrashed by the Wallabies
at Cape Town in 1992.

It was a defining moment for an Australian side that had won
the World Cup the previous year, in the absence of South Africa, and
needed to reinforce their number one ranking. The result was 26–3.

Muller remembers the team captained by Nick Farr-Jones as a professional, physical outfit, quantum leaps ahead of the Springboks. But he rates the current Australian side even more highly.

'The team we played seven years ago were world champions and they taught us a lesson,' said Muller. 'We learnt from them. But this Wallaby team is much stronger than the 1992 team, because of the skills they have developed, and things like the decoy running in their attack.

'But we progressed enough to win the World Cup in 1995 and we have progressed again since then. I wouldn't be making a prediction on this game, I wouldn't be putting my money anywhere, there's nothing in it.'

Muller understands the Australian psyche better than any other Springbok, having spent the 1996 winter playing rugby league with Penrith.

Asked to draw a personality portrait, he said: 'The rugby league guys are hard bastards. Very physical guys. I think the rugby union has a better level of players. But Australian teams in general are tough, mentally strong, and I enjoyed my time in league over there. It made me a better player defensively.'

The crowds, too, were a culture shock. More understanding, he said with a smile: 'South Africa is very bad when it comes to wanting winners.'

SEMI FINAL

AUSTRALIA 27 SOUTH AFRICA 21 (after extra-time)

David Campese pays tribute to a backline star set to share the title of legend.

The big occasions are made for great players and Tim Horan proved himself one of the finest with a semi final performance at Twickenham that has crowned his 10–year career. From the time he came into the Wallaby side as a little-known teenager in 1989, he has always saved his best for those Tests when the pressure engulfs you like a blanket.

Two matches spring instantly to mind, and I had the pleasure of playing in both. There was the 1991 World Cup semi-final, against the All Blacks at Lansdowne Road. When Michael Lynagh chipped ahead and I caught the bouncing ball, there was a voice behind me, it was Horan in support, as two All Black defenders converged.

Out of instinct I knew where Timmy would be so that when the Kiwis were drawn to the tackle, I could release him with a pass thrown over my shoulder without even needing to look. The try he scored put us on the road to the final.

A year later in Cape Town, we were defending the world champion tag against a Springbok side whose fanatical fans claimed we were false titleholders unless we could beat their boys. This time our roles were reversed when it came to collecting the crucial score. Tim made a midfield break, kicked ahead, tackled Springok centre Danie Gerber, got to his feet to rip the ball clear and popped up the pass for my 50th Test try.

Under pressure he plays well. He loves the

challenge and the intensity of the important games, when lesser players struggle to cope. What made this display even more courageous was the illness that sapped him of energy in the 36 hours leading into the match. To see him tearing through the Springbok defence on several occasions — and remember this is a side that has given up only two tries all tournament so well do they tackle — you would never have imagined he was in doubt of playing less than five hours before the Test started.

It was a gutsy performance all round by the Wallabies. Stephen Larkham kicking that field goal when his right knee was crying out to be encased in ice … well, that just came out of nowhere. The forwards too, did a great job. David Wilson was everywhere, and the front-row stood up to be counted against the giants of the Springbok pack.

As for Matthew Burke, finally we have seen a glimpse of him back to the sort of form we know he is capable of producing. He was far involved, as he needed to be, and he put over the penalty goals that mattered.

But Horan was the star of the day in what was a bloody hard game.

If there is to be a note of caution though, looking ahead to the final next Saturday, then the Australians have to make sure of getting support to Horan when he makes those inroads through the midfield.

There was still some frustration for me, watching the Wallabies make a lot of breaks again, and not finishing the good work. They didn't ram home the advantage. In a World Cup final, you have to make the most of your chances, you can't create the opportunities and fail to polish it off with points.

I admit there were times when the Australians looked set to score, only to be foiled by professional fouls. It's a blight on the game and has to be stamped out. But there were also times when the Wallabies had only themselves to blame for not getting across the white strip.

There were breaks by Horan, by Roff and by Herbert, which simply died out because the support players did not arrive in time, did not appear on their shoulders to carry the play on. They can't let that happen next week.

Australia should have scored two or three tries and came up with none. In a match of this magnitude, that's too many chances to squander. There was also evidence in the first half that the Wallabies were going to play it wide for a while. But when a few passes went astray, they pulled it back in and worked closer to the forwards.

Everyone knows my views on not only winning, but winning with style. Bottom line, however, is that Australia are through and on target to be the first nation to win the World Cup twice. At half time, I thought they would do it quite comfortably with a 12–6 lead and the wind at their backs for the last 40 minutes. I even told a few people I was with at the break that there was nothing to worry about, the Wallabies would finish the stronger. Early in the second half, I started to wonder.

The South Africans started to dominate the game, and the Wallabies seemed to sit back and wait for them. But they got back into gear pretty quickly, even if it did come down to the wire, and Timmy Horan was one of the main reasons why.

Stephen Larkham was the Wallabies one-legged hero when a damaged right knee helped swing the boot that launched his miracle dropped goal against South Africa today and sent Australia soaring into the World Cup final. That the lanky five-eighth was nursing an injury which could sideline him from the decider when he delivered the defining strike of a semi-final dragged into extra-time could not, surely, have been topped for sensation.

But the skullcapped Larkham, described by teammates as a footballing freak, had a post-match revelation even the wildest Hollywood scriptwriter would have dismissed as fantasy beyond belief. It was, he smiled, the first field goal of his senior career. From

48 metres and on an angle, Larkham landed a three-point thunderbolt that broke a 21–all deadlock in the closing stages of a 100–minute tryless marathon.

Fullback Matthew Burke added a penalty goal, his eighth, to further bury the title defence of a Springbok side never before beaten in two World Cups.

But it was the Larkham wonder-kick on a wonky knee he injured in the first four minutes that effectively settled a gripping encounter, won 27–21 by the Wallabies.

'I can't remember when I last kicked one,' Larkham said in the bowels of the Twickenham grandstands after an amazing finale to a match forced into an extension by a penalty goal from Springbok superboot Jannie de Beer at the end of regulation time.

'I'm sure I landed one in the juniors, but in senior football, I don't think I ever have. I've attempted some for the ACT Brumbies when playing fullback over the last couple of years, but I've never actually kicked one.'

Last week it was de Beer defying reality with five dropped goals to blast England out in the quarter finals, and Larkham admits the Springbok's haul set the Wallabies thinking seriously when scores were level 18–all heading into the additional 20 minutes.

'The whole thing started at fulltime when (assistant coach) Tim Lane, just before we ran out for extra time, said 'if you get an opportunity down in their half, don't wait for Jannie de Beer to take a field goal, take one yourself'.

So we were just in their half, and all intentions were to run it. But when I got the ball, I looked up and there was a wall of South Africans in front of me, so I decided to put it on the boot. To start with, it was a pretty ordinary drop. The ball was in an awkward position and I thought 'I've got no chance here'. When I kicked it, it sounded pretty sweet and I watched it the whole way over, just to make sure it got there.'

Larkham was more stunned than his teammates as the ball sailed safely over the crossbar with six minutes 42 seconds remaining in the last of two 10–minute extra-time periods. The shock was born from his midweek efforts at training. And from the fact his right knee was corked, bleeding internally, and slightly unstable from a strain to his medial ligament.

'We did a lot of practicing this week after Jannie's effort in the quarter final,' he said. 'Well, some of the boys did anyway. I suppose I had five or six kicks, and probably landed only one out of that. What Jannie did last week certainly brought the idea into our minds. We hadn't planned any field goals or anything like that before. It's not really what Australian rugby is all about, kicking and stuff. We like to run it and keep it in hand when we get that close to the line.

'But after Jannie had such a successful week, it plays on your mind a bit and subconsciously, I suppose, it became an option. Still, it was only a spur of the moment decision, and kicking for me wasn't easy today. I had to keep moving my leg, otherwise it was going to seize up, and after every kick it was sore. But there wasn't a lot of pain after that last one.'

A devout Christian, de Beer claimed the Lord was on his side during his quarter final bonanza. But with the South African kicking only one of five attempts in the semi-final, Larkham was asked if God had switched camps.

'I don't know,' he laughed. 'I'm not a churchgoer but maybe I'll have to consider it now.'

He might also consider the power of prayer as he races the clock to recover in time for the final at Millennium Stadium.

Larkham, at best, will take little part in training this week. At worst, he will watch from the grandstands after lifting the Wallabies to their second World Cup final and putting them on track to emulate the triumphant campaign of 1991.

Having battled back from four operations this season, including major knee surgery and a broken thumb only a week before leaving for the World Cup, it is not a prospect he wants to consider.

'I haven't been thinking about it during the week, how lucky I am to be here,' he said. 'But after an assessment on my leg, and we're still not sure whether I'll play next week, I was sitting in the sheds thinking 'I've come this far, I've come through all this adversity and I'm not going to let a little cork get in my road'. I've had a fair bit of luck getting back from injuries, I don't want it to run out now.'

Nor will the Wallabies, who answered the questions put to them by a South African side short on adventure but never lacking in muscle, grit or the flinty attitude that has hallmarked Springbok sides for almost a century. South Africa were always going to challenge the Wallabies at the scrum, with a front-row a coal truck would struggle to shift. But Australia, outweighed kilos per man, refused to budge as

Andrew Blades, Michael Foley and Richard Harry dug in and delivered a stable platform.

This was not a pretty Test. But it was an enthralling, monumental battle, where the defence was frequently ferocious, and the commitment of both sides beyond reproach. Wallaby number eight Toutai Kefu, returning from a two-game suspension and with his hair specially cropped for the occasion, revelled in the crucial sledgehammer role foisted on him as the only recognised ball runner among the Australian forwards.

Skipper John Eales, still finding his feet in the rough and tumble of Test rugby after an extended injury absence, saw out the entire game despite dwindling energy reserves. His second row partner David Giffin won a crucial lineout from a South African throw on the Australian quarter — instant justification for his selection.

In the backline, no one could hold a candle to centre Tim Horan who, this morning, did not have the energy to blow out a match. But while Horan has excelled all tournament, the return to form of Burke was as uplifting as it was necessary. Saved from the sack only by his goalkicking, Burke reacted to what he called the 'hot poker treatment' from coach Rod Macqueen to turn in his most impactful performance of the season. His eight penalty goals from 10 attempts were even more vital, with de Beer landing six from seven plus a dropped goal.

It was Burke who opened the scoring with a penalty goal on 11 minutes, followed by another midway through the first half. Running into a gale force wind, the 6–0 lead was laced in gold. By half time, with Burke and de Beer involved in alternate penalty goal successes, Australia led 12–6.

From there, the result should never have been in question. But the Boks are like one of those inflatable rubber toys that you punch to the ground and they always bounce back.

By the 51–minute mark, with possession flowing their way, South Africa had levelled the scores, with a de Beer penalty and a close range dropped goal. After 73 minutes, Burke had landed another two penalty goals for 18–12. Five minutes later, de Beer reduced the deficit to three but time had seemingly run out.

The ground announcer claimed only two minutes of injury

time would be played. Referee Derek Bevan saw it differently. When
the second half entered its 47th minute, he raised his arm for a South
African penalty, with replacement forward Owen Finegan punished
for a hand in the ruck. De Beer coolly potted an attempt from wide
out to force the game to extra time where, three minutes into the
first period, his billing as matchwinner looked set to continue with
another penalty that put the Springboks in front for the first time in
the match at 21–18. Burke replied two minutes later. And then it was
left to Larkham to give Australia an advantage they would not
surrender again.

Leading World Cup officials threatened Australia with
disqualification as an ivory tower controversy erupted minutes after
their semi-final win over South Africa in the extra-time thriller
at Twickenham.

Australian Rugby Union general manager John O'Neill
revealed the Wallabies were faced with the prospect of being thrown
out of next Saturday's final after tournament chiefs accused them of
making an illegal replacement in the final two minutes.

The switch involved centre Daniel Herbert and winger Ben
Tune, who returned to the field after leaving the game midway
through the second half.

Under International Rugby Board laws, a player taken off
during a Test can only resume as a blood bin replacement. And World
Cup bosses, having seen Herbert treated for cramp moments before
the swap, claimed the Wallabies were in breach of the regulations by
bringing Tune back to the action.

If proven, the result could have been overturned — for
the first time in Test history — and South Africa bound for the
Cardiff decider.

'There was a suggestion within minutes of the game finishing
that Australia would be disqualified,' O'Neill said. 'I told them it was
a blood bin, they said I'd better check in a hurry. I shot down to the
match official dressing rooms and asked the referee Derek Bevan if
he was satisfied it was a blood bin change. He said he was. I checked
with the third touch judge, who controls players coming on and off,
and he was also happy with it.'

Herbert had suffered a cut over his right eye during the game, and confirmed later that blood was still leaking from the wound when he left the field.

But O'Neill admitted he sought further insurance despite the clearance from match officials.

'I got the Wallaby team doctor John Best to write a report on the spot, and ordered photographs to be taken of the injury before they stitched up Herbert,' he said. 'He had three stitches inserted in the cut, how could it not be a blood bin change? Yes he'd been treated for cramp, everyone could see that, but there was also blood there, even if it wasn't so obvious to people sitting high in the grandstands. 'I felt unhappy at having to get photos taken, but we had to do it with the sniff of disqualification in the air.

'When I returned to the officials box, the disqualification talk was still buzzing. The evidence gathered finally killed it off. But what I don't like, and really resent, is the inference that we manufactured a blood bin change. If anyone cares to make that allegation publicly, they'll face the consequences. They will be saying that the match officials and the Wallaby team doctor have told lies, so they had better be prepared for what would follow.'

It is understood South African Rugby Football Union officials were looking to protest about the replacement immediately after the match. O'Neill said the issue was now dead.

'There were people asking SARFU if there would be an appeal,' he said. 'I've been told it's closed.'

⟶

If five drop goals from Jannie de Beer brought a supernatural feel to Paris last week, then Tim Horan took Twickenham to the Twilight Zone today with a World Cup semi-final display that defied the limits of human endurance.

A mystery stomach virus had forced the Wallaby centre to the brink of withdrawing from the clash with the Springboks the night before the Test, and less than five hours before the game he remained a doubtful starter. Utility back Rod Kafer was secretly placed on standby, told to take his playing kit to the ground, and be prepared to join the squad should Horan suffer a last-minute relapse.

During a day and a half of vomiting and diarrhea, Horan ate

only three pieces of toast and a handful of tablets washed down with water and energy drinks. According to Wallaby team doctor John Best, the virulent bug that attacked his system would have forced the average citizen off work for two days.

But Horan cast off the nausea and cramps that wracked his stomach throughout the match — he required further medication at half time — to produce one of the most commanding performances of his 78-Test career. When he finally left the field, 13 minutes from fulltime, with legs of jelly and empty lungs, he had stamped this match with an imperial seal that left no other options for man of the match.

Stephen Larkham fired the 48–metre drop goal bazooka that eventually wiped out the Springboks, but it was the sniper Horan who helped leave South Africa vulnerable to the final assault. Midway through the opening stanza came the first of several incisive bursts that shredded the Springbok defence. And on three occasions he left in his wake one of the leading flankers in international rugby, the defensively sound Andre Venter.

'He showed enormous courage,' said Best. 'There is no doubt he functioned at a very strong mental level. Tim simply blocked out the symptoms and fatigue. He was still slightly dehydrated when he went out there. 'He'll now be drained, be tired, be in need of a sleep.'

But after the two-day drama that had threatened to sour his last World Cup campaign, Horan sidestepped any suggestion his effort was above and beyond the call of duty.

Asked if there had ever been a chance of him not playing the semi final, he said: 'I thought about it last night, but I wanted to give myself a bit more time. I had two pieces of toast for breakfast and one piece of toast last night. I've been able to keep a bit of water down as well, but I'm feeling hungry now.

'I'm still not sure what it was. I had room service on Thursday night, sat down to watch the movie, and I was fine. But at six the next morning I woke up vomiting. I had a walk that afternoon and still didn't feel too much better, so I went back to bed.'

This morning, Best assessed Horan's condition, discussed the situation with the coaching staff and at 10:30am gave a clearance to play.

'Once I knew I was right to play, I tried to forget about it and just go for as long as I could,' said Horan. 'My legs eventually gave way with about 10 minutes to go. They pretty much went to jelly. The adrenalin had kept me going. On the way to the ground, I had started to feel crook again. There was a toilet on the bus so I sat next to that. But having decided I was going to play, I couldn't worry about it anymore.

'When I spent the day in bed yesterday the guys were suggesting I was just taking a rostered day off. You're allowed eight of them in your contract and I think I've only got one to go. But you can't accumulate them anyway.'

Anyone unaware of Horan's condition might have missed the telltale signs of distress during an epic display. The hands to the knees after a long run, the gasping for breath and the frequent visits by trainers to monitor his levels of fatigue.

It was a match, Horan admitted, he would fondly remember when retirement eventually beckons.

'Oh yeah, the enormity of the game, and everything around it,' he said. 'But, you know, I think our biggest hurdle was getting past that quarter final against Wales. Guys were more relaxed this week, weren't quite as nervous. If we'd been beaten last week we were going home and that would have been embarrassing with all the supporters coming over.'

As he prepared for an early night, with his celebrations restricted to a pint of glucose-enriched water, Horan added a word of warning as the Wallabies now look ahead to the final at the Millennium Stadium on Saturday.

'We made some good breaks and once again didn't finish them off,' he said. 'That's a concern but at least we are making those breaks.'

And Horan was responsible for most of them.

The Wallabies hailed Australian cricket captain Steve Waugh as a prophet during an eerie aftermath to their extra-time victory that plunged South African sport into mourning again over a World Cup semi-final disaster. Earlier this year the Waugh-led Australians advanced to the World Cup cricket decider in remarkable scenes to match the Wallabies fairytale finish at Twickenham.

The South Africans needed only one run to win with three

balls left in the match, but a senseless run out forced a tie and shot them out of the tournament having lost to Australia earlier during the preliminary round robin stages.

But the irony of the Down Under sporting double act was further highlighted when Wallaby skipper John Eales revealed the contents of a message Waugh sent to the footballing contenders on the eve of their Springbok showdown.

'It was a fax to the team which was read out on the bus as we drove to the ground today,' said Eales. 'Steve wished us the best of luck for the game. But he also said there was only one thing better than beating the Springboks and that's to tie with them and still go through.'

At the end of regulation time, Australia and South Africa were level 18–all. In extra-time and with a freakish field goal from Stephen Larkham as the catalyst, the Wallabies surged to win 27–21 and secure a place in next week's final.

'It ended up being quite prophetic,' said Eales. 'That Steve Waugh is something of a sage. And you'd have to say, after our win here, that the planets are all in alignment.'

The significance, too, was not lost on Wallaby forward Tiaan Strauss, the former Springbok captain, who was charged with the task of reading Waugh's fax to the rest of the Australian team.

'You know, I remember that cricket semi-final so well, because Jason Little and I were roommates in Perth and we were watching it on the television,' he said.

'I know some of the South African cricketers, I went to varsity with them and I felt for them the way it worked out. But I thought the wording of Steve Waugh's message was great, it was a real little dig in the ribs.'

Springbok coach Nick Mallett, whose fist-pumping reaction to the penalty goal that sent the match into overtime would be replaced within the next half hour by an air of utter dejection, was beyond feeling the barbs.

Quizzed on whether South African sport would be psychologically wounded by the back to back World Cup defeats, he replied: 'I really don't think so. We have a lot of respect for Australia in both cricket and rugby. We know how good they are.'

The cricket influence did not end, however, with the words of encouragement from Waugh. Eales suggested the effort of

Tim Horan in climbing from his sick bed to star for the Wallabies was reminiscent of the double century Dean Jones scored in the Madras tied Test of 1986.

'It was a phenomenal performance by Timmy,' he said. 'The guys didn't see him yesterday because he spent the whole day in bed basically. So to be able to come out from there and perform as he did was incredible. Somebody mentioned it was a bit like Dean Jones when he was crook and scored that 200 virtually coming out of hospital. It was a bit like that for Tim today. He looked a bit ginger this morning. But we had a lot of confidence in him. Tim's a very tough guy and you knew that if there were a chance he'd be out there.

'He doesn't complain, he just gets on with his business and it's great to have people like that in the team, and there a lot of them like that in this side.

'Sometimes you take it for granted a bit that you have players of that calibre. But his effort today was very special. He's very self-motivated, no-one had to say anything to him. Within the team we never doubted the contribution he would give.'

SEMI FINAL

FRANCE 43 NEW ZEALAND 31

There was a French revolution at Twickenham today and the heads of All Black royalty will roll in the wake of the greatest World Cup uprising in the tournament's 12–year history. A 43–31 semi-final boilover has pitched France — Five Nations wooden-spoonists and a team supposedly divided and torn — into an unlikely title decider with Australia at the Millennium Stadium in Cardiff on Saturday. It has also signalled the end of an era for New Zealand coach John Hart and his team.

All Black legend Andy Haden has predicted the sackings of Hart, captain Taine Randell and a handful of other frontline figures after another fruitless World Cup campaign was brought to an end by a French side lampooned as impostors before the match. With flanker Josh Kronfeld likely to be lured to Japan and winger Jonah Lomu to the UK, the supposedly peerless All Blacks are likely to be gutted before the start of next season.

'That result will rock New Zealand rugby to the core, absolutely to the core,' said Haden, the second row giant of two decades ago. 'This team knew it was Sydney or the bush today and, after that, a lot have effectively retired themselves. There'll be a lot of changes out of this, she's all over for a few of them.'

Haden targeted Randell, second rower Robin Brooke, prop Craig Dowd, centre Alama Ieremia and halfback Justin Marshall as long-serving players whose Test careers will soon be consigned to the past. Hart too is facing the chop after the Kiwis wind up their tournament commitments with the third-placed playoff against South Africa on Thursday.

Canterbury Crusaders coach Wayne Smith, who has taken the province to successive Super 12 titles, is already considered the frontrunner to inherit the Test reins next year. From the unforgiving New Zealand public, retribution will be demanded after the pre-tournament favourites butchered a 24–10 second half lead to fall to a side that only managed to beat Fiji in a pool match last month on the back of two controversial refereeing decisions.

The All Blacks, who started the match at 15/1 on, clearly had one eye on the final, and the French poked out the other with a remarkable comeback that sparked wild scenes and emotional outpourings after the fulltime whistle. Prop Franck Tournaire, overcome by the enormity of the occasion, was in tears as he walked a lap of honour, his three-year-old daughter on his shoulders. Players danced, embraced, and waved French flags.

'This was a revolution,' beamed flanker Olivier Magne, who revealed two French World Cup-winning soccer stars, Frank Leboeuf and Didier Deschamps, had visited the team before the match. 'People know we are here now.'

They knew before kickoff when three Frenchmen turned their backs on the haka.

'We knew we had to prepare for war,' explained skipper Raphael Ibanez. 'Some soldiers sing before going to war and we wanted to sing Le Marseillaise.'

A warning too for the Wallabies from centre Richard Dourthe, one of four try-scorers as flamboyant France racked up the highest ever Test score against New Zealand. 'We can beat Australia,' he said. 'We have the players, we have the spirit.'

That the strike potential is there cannot be questioned, not now that the French have emerged from their World Cup slumber. From the 46th to 59th minutes, France harvested 26 unanswered points to sweep from 10–24 to 36–24. Five-eighth Christophe Lamaison was superlative in his control of the match, both with the boot and the ball in hand.

It was his two dropped goals that kick started the comeback, followed by a brace of penalty goals. Two tries in three minutes grabbed then secured the lead. The All Blacks were aimless and without Lomu, whose two tries were solo efforts of brute strength, they could have been humiliated.

Why they did not use Lomu more — he hardly touched the ball in the second half and had to go looking for it in midfield — was staggering. The massive winger had driven fear into French hearts with his first try as he skittled six defenders like ninepins on his way to the line after 23 minutes. His second score, five minutes after the break, was even more sensational for the fact that French fullback Xavier Garbajosa, in no mood to tackle the big bloke front on, stepped aside to let him pass.

Haden supplied one perspective on the All Blacks preference to get themselves muddled in midfield later rather than give Lomu his head.

'They were clueless,' he said. 'Totally naïve, without the ability to change their tactics.'

Hart wore the look of a man on death row as he fronted the media later, but won admiration for his graciousness in defeat.

'We're devastated,' he said. 'As coach I take full accountability for the loss. We were outplayed today. We made too many errors; we have no excuses to offer. But we should not have lost from 24–10.'

Hart also believes the Wallabies will now be crowned the kings of world rugby on Saturday.

'I think it will be very difficult for the French,' he said. 'If they can reproduce what they did today then they will be competitive. But my view is Australia are a very composed side, very organised, they have the advantage of an extra day's preparation. It will be hard for the French to get up again and be able to repeat that performance. At 24–10 we should have won and I don't think Australia would allow that opportunity to go begging.'

Wallaby coach Rod Macqueen conceded the French success caught him on the hop. Planning for the final — after beating South Africa last Saturday — had already started with the All Blacks in mind.

'We, along with many others, believed the All Blacks would win,' he said. 'But it was a superb French performance, particularly in the second half. The French wingers (Philippe Bernat-Salles and Christophe Dominici) have a lot of speed, we'll have to watch them in the final.

'But where we're used to playing against the All Blacks, we don't know the French very well, and we haven't been watching them through this tournament. So we'll have to do a lot of work this week to bring ourselves up to speed.'

David Campese lauds the French performance and finds his heart warmed by the manner in which the underdogs won.

What a match. What a team. The French have always been unpredictable, but that semi-final win at Twickenham, where the All Blacks simply had no answer to the complete ensemble of Gallic flair, was a classic performance when least expected.

Finally, we've seen a great game of rugby, and it came from a team that everyone, including me, was writing off as World Cup pretenders. They proved us wrong. They were brilliant.

From wingers Philippe Dominici and Philippe Bernat-Salles to the heart and soul of their forwards, second rower Abdel Benazzi, France reached a level they have struggled to get anywhere near for the past five years.

And what a pleasure to see them running the ball, taking adventurous options, and seeing it all pay off at the end with a berth in the World Cup final. This is the sort of stuff I've been screaming for since before the tournament got underway, and I was starting to worry that it might never surface. But the French delivered, it was entertainment plus, the best game I have seen in a long time, and certainly the finest of this World Cup by some stretch.

The question now is can the French do it again, can they turn a tournament of turmoil to triumph, can they complete the double and knock off the Wallabies as well as the All Blacks, in successive weeks, to collect the Webb Ellis trophy as the first northern hemisphere winners?

My tip to the Australians is don't take them lightly. Do not make the mistake of thinking the French have already played their final and will find it impossible to revisit the power of the passion they called on last Sunday when they caught, collared and killed off New Zealand despite trailing at one stage 24–10.

The match should have been over once the Kiwis

grabbed a 14–point lead. There was, presumably, no coming back for France. But they refused to lie down, got a sniff when five-eighth Christophe Lamaison banged over a couple of dropped goals, and from there the All Blacks were in trouble.

I can't speak highly enough of the French display. They mixed their game up, they took risks to create space for the two little wingers with the jet boots strapped to their feet and, in some ways, it could be a watershed for the game.

For so long we have been treated to the power games of the southern hemisphere heavyweights — New Zealand, South Africa and Australia. Everyone has been talking about the lack of physical size in the northern hemisphere as the reason for their being behind the eight ball.

Wrong. France have shown with that walloping of the All Blacks that there is more to this game than brawn. The way they played was totally different to what has become the accepted approach of successful teams — that is, crash it up in midfield, or kick for position, use the ball occasionally in the opposition half but generally try to bludgeon the opposition to defeat.

France preferred the guillotine approach with a real cutting edge to their attack. They would take it wide, use the blind, employ attacking chip kicks, counter attack from deep and mix it all in with some terrific defence and a solid forward platform.

Three of the four French tries were wonderfully worked, the other a runaway for Bernat-Salles after a dropped ball by the All Blacks inside the France quarter led to a long kick and chase by flanker Olivier Magne. Benazzi and Magne were magnificent, with the big second rower everywhere around the park. And New Zealand did not know what hit them. Once they were well ahead, the Kiwis seemed to have one eye on the final in Cardiff on Saturday.

But when their intensity dropped a fraction, the French capitalised, and once you give them the chance to lift their confidence, they can be unstoppable. I must admit the French performance did come out of the blue.

Earlier in the tournament they were playing with the same predictability as a lot of other sides. Their drab display against Fiji in the pool matches, when they should have been beaten, was a perfect example. How different this effort was, coming on the back of a quarter final win against Argentina that unveiled just a few glimpses of the attacking brilliance they possess out wide.

Despite the hope taken from that victory, guys like Serge Blanco, Patrice Lagisquet and Jean-Pierre Rives — all former French greats — did not want to tip their countrymen to knock over the All Blacks, and they had every right to hold that opinion.

Since arriving in Britain, rumours have been rife of ill feeling and discontent in the French camp, even of punch-ups at training. For them to play for each other like they did on Sunday, and to celebrate as a team as they did after the match, suggests those cracks in morale have been cemented over. There was, however, too much indiscipline from France in the first half, and the number of professional fouls they committed did not bring them any credit.

As for the All Blacks, the defeat confirms what many people believe, and that is that this All Black side is not really a patch on some of those from the past.

They relied so heavily on Jonah Lomu and, while Jeff Wilson was one exception, no other back really worried the French.

So the scene is set for France against Australia and I only hope, for the sake of what could be a magnificent spectacle, that both sides are prepared to open up the game at Millennium Stadium.

David Campese looks at the mystery factor surrounding France.

When Rod Macqueen told the world media that the
Wallabies might have found it easier to play the All
Blacks in Saturday's final, most would have smiled and
presumed the coach was delving in madcap mind games.
The old tactic of talking up your opposition so as not
to provide them with ammunition that might further
fire their motivation is one of the oldest in the
coaching manual.

But on this occasion, there is plenty of sense to
what Macqueen is saying. As I mentioned yesterday,
France are far from conventional. They do not play to
the more structured and predictable game plans adopted
by the southern hemisphere heavyweights of Australia,
New Zealand and South Africa.

And therein lies the problem for Australia.
To a large extent, they do not know what to expect.
When they run out against the All Blacks, they always
have a fair idea of what the Kiwis are going to do,
where they're going to attack, how they'll react to
certain situations.

But you can toss a lot of that strategic planning
out the window when the French are involved. Even if
the Wallabies study video after video, as they have been
doing for the past 48 hours after ignoring in-depth
analysis of the French earlier in the tournament, they
will struggle to find too many answers.

France have a tendency to vary their game
depending on the team they line-up against or, of
course, as the result of the mood that takes them on the
day of the game. You can't always predict what they're
going to do because they don't know themselves. That
might sound strange coming from me. Plenty of people
used to say my brain never knew what my feet were

doing. But that is the beauty of the whole thing. In rugby, unpredictable means dangerous.

The French might fall in a heap this weekend and be belted all over the park. Or they might keep the roll going that saw the All Blacks cruising comfortably one minute, mesmerised the next and out of World Cup contention a half-hour later.

But there are a few morsels the Wallabies should devour from that Twickenham semi-final on Sunday.

New Zealand, for instance, caused havoc at times on the counter attack out wide. The second try by Jonah Lomu is the most obvious case in point. Lomu fed Wilson who made the initial surge, and his pass back to big Jonah brought the score.

Sure, Lomu's strength played a big part. But the initial speed of the All Black attack is what created the opportunity. In the back three of Matt Burke, Joe Roff and Ben Tune, the Wallabies also have the players with the pace, size and vision to exploit open spaces when France kick deep. For me, that trio appeal as potential match winners.

The forwards, naturally, will need to gain parity, and Tim Horan in the centres will again be a key with his ability to create holes in the midfield. But if it comes to needing a couple of special, off the cuff moments, then Burke, Roff and Tune are your men.

Their size alone can create problems for France, whose wingers Christophe Dominici and Philippe Bernat-Salles, are two of the smallest speedsters around. For the life of me, I can't understand why the All Blacks did not try to isolate them more in defence.

From counter attacks and by using the blindside, you can manipulate one on one situations. Dominici and Bernat-Salles are brilliant with the ball in hand, but the reason Bernat-Salles has not been a regular in the French side over the past few years is that defence has been his shortcoming.

One of the good things about this Wallaby team is the number of attacking options they have. One of the downsides is that they don't always use them. Across the backline there are players who can turn a match, and that is a prized asset going into a World Cup final. But again, they have to be allowed the freedom to take the initiative, try the unexpected, challenge their opponents and back their ability.

The French defence was good against the All Blacks, but the New Zealanders attack, especially in the midfield, was not what you'd call too intelligent.

Rather than getting it wide quickly to Jonah with a couple of cutout passes, where he would have the time and space that makes him such a handful, they wanted to get fancy with switches and loops. Bad call.

But while I am urging the Wallabies to use the width of this pitch, I am not blind to the responsibility that goes with it, regardless of what some people think of my endless calls to attack, attack, and attack. If you take it wide, you have to make sure you retain possession in the tackle. The one thing you cannot do against the French is turn over the ball when the game is taken away from the heavy traffic zones. If you do, they have the counter attack to punish mistakes.

But flanker David Wilson has the pace to get to the breakdown first, and number eight Toutai Kefu, when he roams wide, is equally effective at carrying the play on. After Macqueen and his coaching assistants pore over the videos, I hope they feel the same way.

A winning team is a happy team, unless you happen to be French and preparing for a World Cup final. The amazing story behind the Five Nations failures' advance to the Cardiff decider with Australia is not that they belted the All Blacks to get here. It is how they avoided self-destruction long before Sunday's famous victory.

Halfback Fabien Galthie, even now, is barely on speaking terms with the coaching staff; backline mentor Pierre Villepreux is on the record describing five-eighth Christophe Lamaison as too ponderous for the position; a player rebellion led to team changes earlier in the tournament; and forward hero Abdel Benazzi had a punch-up with prop Franck Tournaire a week before the World Cup kicked off.

Welcome to the fire, the farce and the fascination that is French rugby to the core. The game in France has always been rife with political by-play and tribal tensions that leaves NSW-Queensland rivalry resembling a tea party chat. As a leading Paris scribe admitted yesterday: 'It's war between villages, and people against people, everyone pulling the cart in different directions.'

Four years ago, when Pierre Berbizier stood down from the coaching post — leaping before he was pushed — current coach Jean Claude Skrela took over. And when assistant Villepreux joined him, there was, according to insiders, a move to dismember the Berbizier influence. Villepreux wanted a return to unbridled flamboyance, rather than the previous regime's dedication to forward power and field position. Experienced players were cast aside, and the search for new faces has been ongoing since. In four years, France have used a staggering 80 players at Test level.

There were Five Nations titles in 1997 and 1998, but the wheels fell off this year, with only one win in the championship, and that by a single point over Ireland. As a result, many of the old guard, discarded at various times by Skrela and Villepreux, have found their way back to the fold. Among them are Lamaison, a star of the win over the All Blacks, Benazzi, Galthie and the gifted utility back Emile N'Tamack.

All have had serious career disturbances under the existing coaching set-up, and the residual angst remains, despite what centre Richard Dourthe said at Twickenham.

'Certain persons have said we are not a close group, but if we do not have solidarity, then 10–24 against the All Blacks becomes a 50-point loss,' he said.

'Two months living with each other before the World Cup helped bring us together. We have demonstrated these people are wrong.'

But former French five-eighth Thierry Lacroix said only last week that French players had been confused by the game plans of Skrela and Villepreux, and the camp was not filled with joy.

Thomas Castaignede, their great attacking hope when the World Cup opened, only to be put out by injury, had a confrontation with Villepreux during a training session at the start of the tournament. The backs coach was showing him diagrams of what he wanted. Castaignede shook his head and replied: 'I don't understand, that just won't work.'

Leading players have apparently forced a revision of thinking and the result is an on-field turnaround that saw France recover from a near loss to Fiji — it would have been certain but for two blatant refereeing errors — to produce the sublime 40 minutes of the World Cup in a second half demolition of New Zealand.

The coaching staff was badgered weeks ago into re-casting the side after early hiccups, and the changes have been as significant as they are many. Benazzi, the finest French player at this tournament and the heart and soul of their pack, did play in the opening pool match a month ago — his first Test in 18 months after overcoming injury and selection vagaries.

But in the same game, there was no room for Lamaison, then the third choice pivot; no room for Galthie, who was not even in the original World Cup squad and was only called up when injury struck; and no room for N'Tamack, who was left on the bench behind Stephane Glas and Dourthe in the centres.

There was also no Philippe Bernat-Salles on the wing or Xavier Garbajosa at fullback. Garbajosa, instead, was played as a winger. When France took the field against the All Blacks, only two of the initial first-choice backs — Dourthe and winger Christophe Dominici — were still in the team in their original positions.

Player power had triumphed and even the captain put in place by Skrela and Villepreux, hooker Raphael Ibanez, is now said to lead the side only in name.

Galthie, still smarting over his initial omission, is considered to be the on-field leader, along with the likes of Benazzi and Lamaison. That trio allegedly convinced Ibanez to kick for touch and not for goal during the second half against the All Blacks when France were nestled inside the quarter.

So perhaps the words of Dourthe have a ring of truth. The players might be united. But if so, it is despite rather than because of their relationships with the coaching staff. That is French rugby to a tee.

Australia, as expected, have retained the same side for the decider, with only one change on the bench, where Dan Crowley returns for Rod Moore.

Australia: Matt Burke, Ben Tune, Daniel Herbert, Tim Horan, Joe Roff, Stephen Larkham, George Gregan, Toutai Kefu, David Wilson, Matt Cockbain, John Eales (c), David Giffin, Andrew Blades, Michael Foley, Richard Harry. Replacements: Chris Whitaker, Jason Little, Nathan Grey, Mark Connors, Owen Finegan, Jeremy Paul, Dan Crowley.

David Giffin ignores the attention of Springbok forwards to win a lineout. *Courtesy: Allsport*

The heavyweight and the halfback . . . Springbok prop
Os du Randt, tipping the scales at 130kg, struggles to shake off
the tackle of George Gregan at Twickenham. *Courtesy: Allsport*

On the run . . . Tim Horan climbed from his sick bed to help
the Wallabies advance to the World Cup final with a victory over
South Africa. *Courtesy: Allsport*

Who wants it? Lineout action from the semi final between Australia and the Springboks in London. *Courtesy: Allsport*

Quicksilver . . . French winger Christophe Dominici steps around All Black fullback Jeff Wilson in the lead-up to the Tricolours first try in the second semi final at Twickenham. *Courtesy: Allsport*

The best of a disappointing All Black side, prop Kees Meeuws challenges the Springbok defence in the third place playoff in Cardiff. *Courtesy: Allsport*

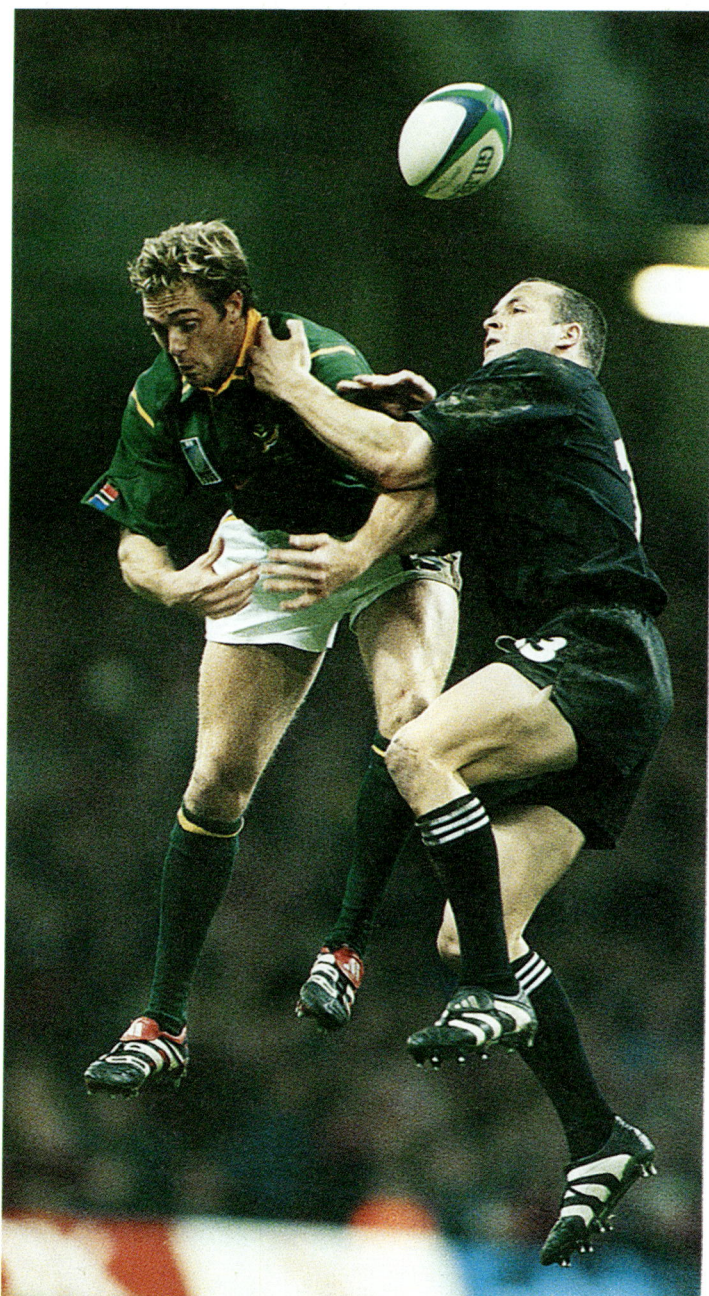

Springbok fullback Percy Montgomery (left) and his All Blacks opposite Christian Cullen come away empty-handed from this mid-air tussle. *Courtesy: Allsport*

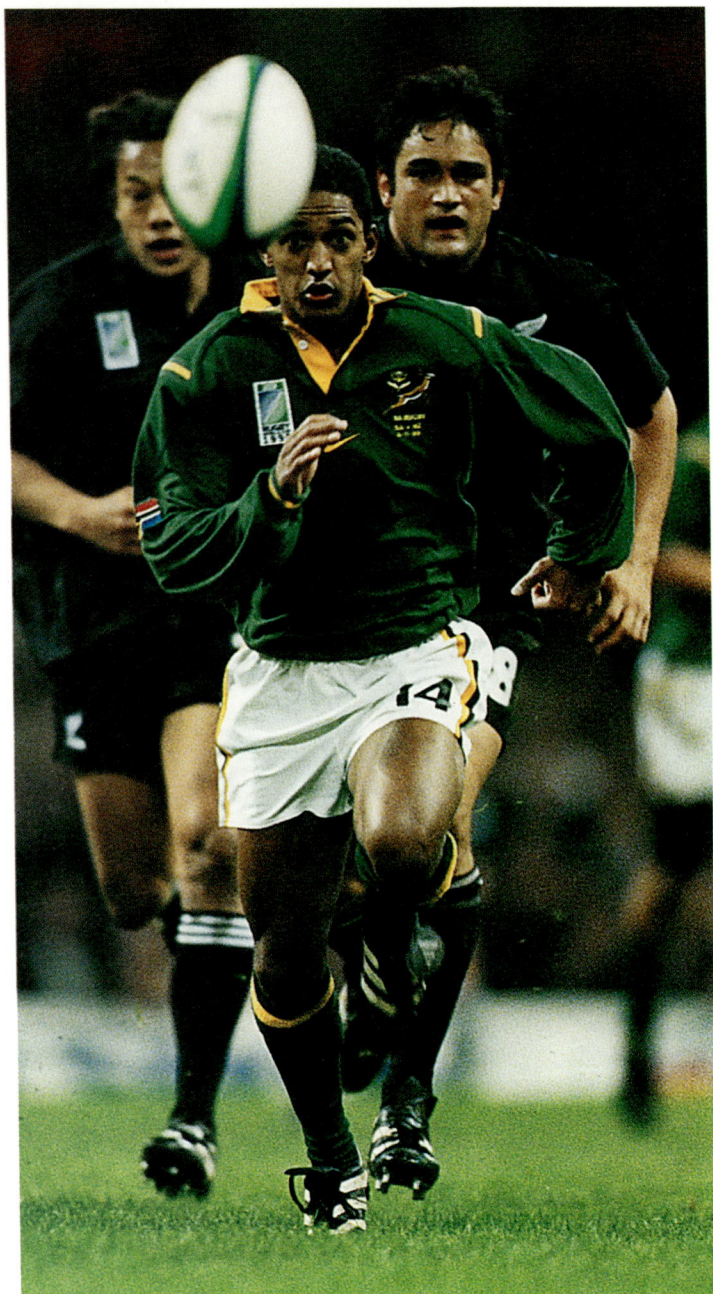

South African winger Breyton Paulse leads the charge for a loose ball as All Blacks Andrew Mehrtens (far Left), Tana Umaga and Taine Randell give chase. *Courtesy: Allsport*

A scene from the closing ceremony at the Millennium Stadium before the final kicked off. *Courtesy: Allsport*

Joe Roff pulled down short of the line by the French back three of Christophe Dominici (left), Xavier Garbajosa (underneath) and Philippe Bernat-Salles. *Courtesy: Allsport*

French centre Emile N'Tamack hurdles the attempted tackle of Dan Crowley in the final. *Courtesy: Allsport*

David Campese profiles a player who has flown the French flag with pride during the World Cup.

It was June, 1990, and having arrived home late from an off-season stint of Italian club rugby, I was dropped from the Australian team to play France in Sydney in the opening Test of the year. I was crushed. Sacked for the first time in my Wallaby career.

But if I felt bad, French second row giant Abdel Benazzi — the Moroccan-born tour de force of the side that will play Australia in the World Cup final on Saturday — was even more heartbroken that same weekend. Benazzi was a baby of the touring team, a player of enormous potential who was selected to make his Test debut as a flanker in the series opener.

He was pumped with emotion, crying as the national anthems were sung, and full of aggression when the game kicked off. Within 13 minutes, he was, like me, watching the Test from the grandstand. In a record he still holds, but never wanted, Benazzi was sent off in his first international. A stomping incident, just one of many foul play acts during a ferocious opening at the Sydney Football Stadium, led to him being marched from the field. He was inconsolable, shamed and humiliated, and the tears streamed down his face.

On Saturday night at the Millennium Stadium, the man whose presence dominates this French team like the Eiffel Tower dominates the landscape of Paris, might well be weeping again. Whether it is with joy or sorrow could well depend on the impact he makes in a clash to decide the next champions of the rugby world.

To reach for an Americanism, Benazzi is the man. He is the guy France looks to for inspiration, and hasn't he given them plenty of it during this World Cup so far. In many ways, he is the John Eales of the French team. A player with all the talents, a complete footballer, a forward who leads by example and urges his players, with actions alone, to follow him into the fray.

Go back to the quarter final against Argentina. It was Benazzi who fielded the ball from a 22 metre dropout, took off upfield, unloaded a brilliant pass in the tackle and set in motion an attacking raid that led to one of those typically spectacular French tries. He is a gamebreaker and the man most likely to break Australia if they let him run riot in Cardiff.

Benazzi is now firmly entrenched in the second row, his backrow days behind him. But I cannot recall a more dominant period during his career than what we have seen here this past four weeks. Whenever I played against him, he was always competitive, always blessed with great ball skills, and never lacking for courage. What he has added during this tournament is a consistency in performance, and the ability to be involved throughout the entire 80 minutes.

At the weekend, in that fabulous semi final win over New Zealand, he was out wide making tackles on the All Black centres, he was in the tight, charging through the Kiwi pack, and he was flawless under the kick re-starts.

There are dangerous players elsewhere in the side. Flanker Olivier Magne was head and shoulders above Josh Kronfeld at Twickenham, and that is a mark of greatness. And I keep coming back to the pocket rockets on the wings, Christophe Dominici and Philippe Bernat-Salles.

They are brilliant on their feet, stepping both ways without dropping pace, and also having the vision to search for support if their path to the line is blocked. But it is Benazzi that holds the key to another unlikely French victory. I must admit, even his best performances of the World Cup to date might not be enough to get them home.

Australia will not, as the All Blacks did, drop the

intensity if they get 24–10 ahead, because there is no need to have an eye on what lies over the next hill.

This is the final, this is the game they have all been waiting four years to be part of, the decider that could write them into Australian sporting history. As it could write Benazzi into French folklore.

The man who was basically unwanted only months before the World Cup campaign, who was only recalled because France fell apart at the Five Nations championship, finishing last, and needing an injection of experience. Benazzi brought that, along with his world class talents.

A sending off against Australia was the lowest of low starts to his Test career. But if he can help France do the impossible two weeks running by skinning the Wallabies on Saturday, he will reach the heights even he might never have thought possible that sunny Sydney afternoon nine years ago.

———

World Cup finalists France stand accused of atrocious foul play acts during Sunday's Twickenham triumph over New Zealand, amid allegations that All Black players were bitten and gouged by rivals. One Frenchman, prop Franck Tournaire, has been cited on an ear-biting charge involving Kiwi skipper Taine Randell. On a list of suggested World Cup penalties, biting carries a recommended ban of anything from one to three years. It is a troubled time for France, who have already lost their other frontline front-rower after Christian Califano was banned earlier in the tournament, until December, for head butting.

All Black coach John Hart, set to resign his post after Thursday's third place playoff against South Africa, has taken a hefty swipe at New Zealand's semi-final conquerors, and the side Australia will line-up against at Millennium Stadium on Saturday.

'There's a suggestion that another player has been bitten, and that's pretty appalling if that's the case,' he said. 'I declined to say anything after the game because it would have detracted from the French victory. But there are a number of reports from my

players of actions taken in the match that have no place in
the game.

'I'm disappointed. I'm a great believer in discipline, always
have been, and the Tri-Nations series (between Australia, New
Zealand and South Africa) has been very disciplined over the years.
French rugby and maybe French club rugby don't seem to show the
same standards.'

Tournaire was cited after a New Zealand television
commentator contacted International Rugby Board executive
member Tim Gresson, also a Kiwi, and asked if Tournaire had been
cited. When told he had not, TVNZ offered World Cup organisers
videotape of the alleged incident.

On the footage, an unidentified player can be heard screaming:
'He's biting me, he's biting me.'

But Randell, a key figure in the controversy, denied any
knowledge of being attacked by Tournaire, who walked a lap of
honour after the match with his three-year-old daughter sitting on
his shoulders.

'I don't remember being bitten, I haven't a clue,' said
Randell, whose stance must have favoured the French prop's case as
he entered the hearing. There were also no marks on Randell's face
or ears.

All Black halfback Byron Kelleher, having received treatment
after the ruck where Tournaire allegedly bit the Kiwi captain,
confirmed there had been other incidents during the game.

'Things were going on, whether it was on purpose, I don't
know,' he said. 'Sometimes it's an accident and sometimes it's not.'

Wallaby five-eighth Stephen Larkham has revealed a long-held secret, speaking for the first time about a childhood illness that almost claimed his life. In the countdown to the World Cup final in Cardiff where Larkham will be the Australian backline linchpin against unpredictable France, he told that, at the age of 12, he contracted a potentially fatal bout of viral meningitis.

After doctors had diagnosed the problem, he was rushed to intensive care, and there was a time when his mother wondered whether the son raised on the family sheep-farm outside Canberra would recover from the ordeal. When he did leave hospital after several weeks, Larkham had dropped a significant portion of his body weight. The needle on the scales limped to just 28kg.

'It was bad strain that meant I could have died,' he said. 'I remember sitting in a hospital bed, having fits and nightmares, hating hospital, hating the hospital food, having bed sores and losing a heap of weight. There was one nightmare where I was just swearing all sorts of rude words. I was in a deep sleep, and I was woken up with mum saying 'what's wrong?'

'All these people down the hallway were wondering what was going on. But from what I remember, I wasn't fazed too much by it all. I don't think I knew it was life threatening or that I should be worried. They might have told me but I was probably too vague to care or realise.'

In year 10 (at age 16), I was still only weighing around 40kg, so it took a while to get a bit of size back. But when I came out of hospital, I went back into school, felt normal again and didn't really think there was anything to worry about.

'Weight was never really an issue. I knew I was a skinny kid but never really cared about it until I started playing senior football. There were times around the age of 16 when I struggled to make the rep sides because of my size, but it wasn't until seniors that I started to worry about putting on some weight.'

Whether the meningitis scare had also suspended his vertical growth for a period, Larkham does not know. But in his late teens there was an amazing one-year spurt that saw him shoot up in height by more than 20cm, from a starting point of just 1.62m. His accelerated growth gave him problems in one knee that prevented him running for about a week.

'But I haven't had anything as serious (as the meningitis) since,' he said. 'I've had a bit of asthma which might be a by-product, but nothing I've ever worried about.'

Maybe, deep in his subconscious, the illness of 13 years ago has steeled a will that has seen Larkham overcome a series of adversities this season — injury dramas that looked likely to claw him away from the Wallabies World Cup campaign. He has undergone four operations — one to each knee after a bad dislocation and ligament damage, one for a hernia, and another last month to pin back into place a broken thumb.

There will be further surgery after the World Cup decider at Millennium Stadium, with the right knee he damaged in the semi-final win over South Africa requiring a further clean out.

'These things happen and you just have to recover from them,' he said. 'That's the attitude I've taken this year. Injuries happen and there's nothing I can do about it, except work hard to get back. Right after the game on Saturday, I put ice on the knee and it was really aching, really sore, and I thought there might be more damage than I first imagined.

'But I figured something as small as a cork and a minor ligament tear was not going to keep me out. I've worked so hard to get to this position. It's been my dream since I started playing rugby to play in a World Cup final. To come this close and just miss out was never really an option. Pretty much nothing was going to stop me from being there.'

His catalogue of mangled muscles, broken bones and stretched or shredded ligaments has left Larkham reflective about the future, however. This World Cup, he says, is likely to be his last. While he has another three years to serve on a contract with the Australian Rugby Union, the willowy pivot does not have any plans, at this stage, to continue on for a further season just to make the 2003 World Cup, to be staged in Australia and New Zealand.

'I just think the number of games you play at that higher level, including Super 12 and international matches, is too much strain for the body,' he said. 'Certainly in the last couple of years I've had more injuries than I've had in my whole career, and I think that's a direct result of the amount of training and playing we're doing.

'Players who have lasted 10 years or longer, like Timmy Horan, I don't think that will be able to be done anymore. It would be nice to play another World Cup, but I am looking at this as my last.'

So for the match winner who last week banged over from 48 metres a miracle dropped goal in extra time to sink defending champions South Africa, there is a once in a career opportunity on Saturday to experience the exhilaration of clambering to the top of rugby's highest peak.

'It's going to mean everything,' he said. 'There'll be a lot of memories flooding back from being a junior in Canberra, sitting in the clubhouse at Wests, watching the previous World Cups, yahooing and carrying on, and how people would say 'if I was out there I'd do this and that'. To have the opportunity to be one of those people who are out there and can make a difference means so much. It sends shivers down your spine.'

French prop Franck Tournaire has been cleared of a biting allegation, with a judiciary panel deciding there was not enough evidence to support the claim.

Tournaire has been named in the French side to play Australia in Saturday's final at the Millennium Stadium in Cardiff.

November 4

PLAYOFF FOR THIRD-FOURTH POSITION

SOUTH AFRICA 22 NEW ZEALAND 18

David Campese makes his prediction for the final, and says France are in for a thrashing.

This will be 1987 revisited for France. Another World Cup final, another 20–point defeat. I can see no other outcome for the title decider in Cardiff because the French, unless I miss my guess, cannot repeat their performance of last Sunday in the Twickenham semi final against the All Blacks.

That was brilliant, and breathtaking, and bloody great to watch, as they tore the Kiwis to shreds in a second half where they played as if touched by the rugby gods.

But this week comes the fall. France played their final six days early. They toppled the All Blacks, celebrated as if there was no tomorrow, and now have to get out there to do it again. It is too high a mountain to climb, as it was back in 1987, when the inaugural World Cup was staged in Australia and New Zealand.

Going back 12 years, the situation was remarkably similar. At the semi final stage, France knocked out the tournament favourites, on this occasion Australia, in a match still regarded as one of the finest on World Cup record. Serge Blanco scored the try that broke a deadlock with only seconds left on the clock, diving over wide out, for the French to take the game 30–24.

The scenes in their dressing room later were chaotic. They sang, they danced and they cried. Their emotions took over as they celebrated a victory they had never really expected. Much like last week.

So what happened in 1987, after they advanced to

the final in such a frenzied state? Quite simply, France had nothing left to give. New Zealand marched over them 29–9, and I have a feeling history is about to repeat itself. Certainly Australia will not fall for the complacency card the All Blacks dealt themselves in the semi final last week, having got to 24–10 ahead early in the second half only to blow the victory entirely.

The Kiwis took the foot off the pedal, their tackling and commitment dropping a little as if they were trying to save themselves for the final. It was just enough to give France a sniff and from there they were men possessed. They ran the ball brilliantly and kicked in behind the All Blacks, both long and short, but always to attack. There were no kicks for kicking's sake. But Australia have the tools to dismantle France and the game plan they used to beat the All Blacks. For a start, the Wallabies defence will be so much better than New Zealand's.

They have given up just one try in the whole tournament and that is an area where they can cause France trouble. If they can shut them down in midfield, the French will become frustrated. That leads to them being irrational, indisciplined, and prone to giving away penalties. If the Wallabies are inside the French half, then Matthew Burke's boot should do the rest.

The kicking game of the French five eighth Christophe Lamaison will have to be stifled as well, and this is where the two Wallaby wingers, Ben Tune and Joe Roff, are likely to have an increased responsibility. They will be charged with covering the backline from the blind wing, sweeping across to clean up any deft little chip kicks or grubbers that Lamaison pops over or through the line.

Australia also have to be wary of the unpredictability factor.

When France attack, there are usually several options open to them, from strategically placing some big men in the backline, to probing the blindside, to giving wingers Dominici and Bernat-Salles the licence to back themselves and take a dip at the defence. After studying videotapes ad nauseum, I'm sure the Wallabies will have some counter measures in place, and they also know unless they get outnumbered that they have the tackling technique to put the French away.

If you do it often enough, France will simply get fed up and kick the ball away, giving Australia the opportunity to attack from the back through Roff, Tune and Matt Burke. Otherwise, I don't see the Wallabies straying too much from the game plan that has brought them this far already. They will kick for field position, keep the ball reasonably close to the forwards, hit it up around the fringes and retain possession for long periods of time.

Number eight Toutai Kefu will be a big part of their game plan, so too will be the in-form Tim Horan. But where they will have to improve is in taking the try-scoring chances they create. If they continue to butcher them the Wallabies will only give hope to France, and we know how dangerous they can become if you let them build some confidence.

I have a feeling this Australian side might just be ready to click. You don't produce too many special performances through a World Cup, it's too intense to stay at a peak for that long. It happened in 1991, and it's happening here. The Australians started off slowly then cranked up the machine. Unless the French can find a way of turning it off, it will run right over the top of them.

Wallaby skipper John Eales has warned France to cut out the filth in the World Cup final or risk the wrath of an Australian side he claims will not be bullied.

As the fallout continues from allegations of biting, eye-gouging and testicle grabbing by the French in their semi final against the All Blacks, Eales said the Wallabies will not be distracted from their ultimate goal by foul play treachery.

He also suggested there were fair and effective methods to make France pay if the showpiece match on the code's greatest day threatens to be marred by underhand violence. French prop Franck Tournaire has been cleared of a biting charge after being cited over an incident involving New Zealand skipper Taine Randell, while Kiwi flanker Josh Kronfeld feared for his sight after twice being gouged by unidentified rivals.

Eales said the Wallabies would not be intimidated if there was a repeat performance from the French firebrands in the title decider at Cardiff, but made it clear any retaliation would be within the laws of the game.

'The worst thing you can do is lose your head and lose the match because of it,' he said, confirming the Australians would not be drawn into fighting nasty with nasty. 'That's what they want. The only reason they would do it is to put us off our game. If it doesn't have that effect, they haven't achieved what they wanted to achieve. We just have to keep our discipline and not let it distract us.

'If it happens, you use it as motivation to get them back in other ways, like around the ground in hard tackles, in the driving play and through our game plan of scoring tries. If we play to the best of our ability it's not going to affect us and you can't let those things worry you. You've got to get on with the game and trust that the referee and linesmen will look after it to the best of their ability. And it's not going to help France as far as we're concerned. We're ready for them if they do try it, but we'll be moving on with the job at hand.'

There were similar outbreaks of French foul play two years ago in Brisbane, where Australia won the second of two Tests 26–19.

Number eight Troy Coker and second rower David Giffin claimed they were eye gouged, flanker David Wilson was punched in the head, kneed in the ribs and felled by a high tackle, while Eales was stomped at a ruck. After the match, Coker was asked why he used French forward Fabien Pelous — a second rower in the current French team — as a punching bag before half time.

'What are you supposed to do when a guy has his fingers buried up to the second knuckle in your eye socket,' he fumed. Eales referred to the 1997 clash when he said: 'If you look back to that game at Ballymore, we got through, we kept our composure, we didn't let it worry us and just kept going.'

Australian coach Rod Macqueen echoed the Eales view when pressed on the prospect of France turning to strong-arm tactics.

'Teams in the past have tried to intimidate us and it hasn't worked,' he said. 'So we've got to have faith that the players will be able to handle themselves again. In a situation like that, they aren't going to lie down, but we will be relying absolutely on the match officials.

'From our point of view, the instructions will be to impose ourselves on France, rather than worry about what they're going to do. If we don't stamp our authority and our pattern of play on them, we'll be starting to wait for them, and watching them, which is what happened to the All Blacks. Then they become a strength and a threat.'

But the words of Kronfeld will be a concern to both Macqueen and match officials, who will fear the black eye the game will receive if the tournament climax erupts in on-field controversy.

'It was quite scary being a victim not once but twice,' Kronfeld said of the alleged French eye gouging at Twickenham. 'It's not something we are used to in New Zealand rugby. It was the shock of it, especially the second one when it took a lot of time to see past the blur. My dad has only got one eye (after being blinded in a childhood accident), so to me it was quite shocking. Eyes are very important.'

After Richard Harry took a daring mid-career gamble and switched from flanker to the front-row ranks, it took only a handful of games to make him wonder whether he was chasing an impossible dream.

Harry was 25, and a useful backrower for the Sydney club Eastwood, when he realised his footballing future would never include a Wallaby jumper. Not if he stayed in the back three of the scrum. That was six years ago. On Saturday, Harry runs out for the Wallabies in the World Cup final in Cardiff — the ultimate justification for a change many lampooned when he first moved to prop.

'I did it because I wanted to play for Australia,' he said on the eve of his head-to-head battle with the controverisal Frenchman, Franck Tournaire.

'I knew I just wasn't going to make it as a backrower. I didn't know if I'd make it in my new position either, but the driving factor was Wallaby selection, and that's where I saw my chance.'

Harry started at the bottom of the well, dropping back to fifth grade to learn his trade during the closing months of the 1993 season. The following year he changed clubs, joined Sydney University, and broke into their number one team. But the doubts were never far from the surface.

'There were times,' he said, 'when I was thinking to myself 'what the hell am I doing here?' One of the first opportunities I got at prop was playing with the Australian Barbarians against Scots College in Sydney. I was packing against a schoolboy and even he sent me into the air, took my feet off the ground.

'Then there was the first grade game for Uni when I packed against (former Maoris prop) Huia Gordon. I'll never forget it because it proved to be quite a watershed match. In the first scrum he hit me so hard I had pins and needles up to my forehead. They took eight tight heads off us that afternoon, it was a very long day in the office. And sitting in the dressing room later I thought 'this is too hard, it just can't be done'.

'That day I could almost have given it away. Gone back to being a backrower. But up at the bar later, Huia said I'd come close a couple of times to having him on toast.'

It was all the encouragement Harry required. By the end of the 1994 season, he had been selected for the Emerging Wallabies. He was named in an extended training squad for the World Cup the following year and, while he missed the cut, he knew his time was approaching.

When Wales toured Australia in the June of 1996, Harry was chosen for his Test debut, less than three years after his drastic positional U-turn. A further 29 caps have followed but, as Harry is quick to point out, the fairytale has fallen on hard times occasionally. Like this season, when he failed to win selection for the early Tests, and slipped so far down the pecking order it seemed the World Cup was likely to pass by without him.

'While I never lost sight of the goal, there were times when it seemed a long way away and I might well have been watching this week's game with my feet up at home on the lounge,' he said. 'I actually thought about the whole move to prop and why I'd done it when I sat there watching the boys play those Tests when I wasn't in the team. I was thinking 'how's it going to end up?' But the opportunities came and when they do you have to take them.'

Harry was recalled during the Tri-Nations series when the Australian scrum was on the skids. In helping to add stability, he booked his World Cup berth.

Now he stands, with the rest of the Wallabies, one step away from history. That gamble he took six years ago is about to reap the ultimate reward.

Defiant All Black coach John Hart refused to accept the inevitable and maintained a stony silence on his future as the New Zealand World Cup nightmare worsened with a playoff loss to South Africa today.

The dominant force in the game for the best part of a century, the All Blacks were driven to despair in Cardiff when a 22–18 loss robbed them of automatic entry to the next World Cup.

New Zealand will be thrown into qualifying rounds against fellow Oceania nations before 2003 in the last twist of the knife to a side that came here as unbackable favourites and leave on Sunday as tournament zeroes.

In losing to the Springboks in a match where a ghastly 33 handling errors provided proof why the meaningless third-place contest should be scrapped from the World Cup format, the All Blacks slipped to their eighth defeat in 18 Tests.

But Hart bristled at suggestions that poor selections this year helped put the side on the slide. Asked about the move of Taine Randell from flanker to number eight, of Christian Cullen from fullback to centre and of Jeff Wilson from wing to fullback, Hart maintained all three were successful.

'You're creating statistics to suit your argument, but the truth is we made those changes this season, and we've won 10 from 13 in 1999,' he said. 'That will be the second best international record this season (behind Australia who go into the World Cup final winning 10 of their past 12 Tests).

'We've got the talent, and I'm sure we had the right players here. But they are still a young side and what we have to do now is sustain their confidence. We're disappointed right now, but it's a small dent compared to the semi final defeat by France. That was a game we could and should have won.'

With this to be remembered as the last Test of Hart's reign, he would have been hoping for better. The Kiwi backline mirrored the strange malaise that has gripped this team with a bumbling performance that bordered on appalling.

Passes were thrown over the touchline, spilled by support players or simply tossed to the wind as the All Black threequarters, all brilliant individuals, combined like a bunch of short-sighted strangers. Their cohesion was virtually non-existent, and it took 26 minutes for wing Jonah Lomu to get his hands on the ball for the first time.

'They didn't play well, that was really disappointing,' said Hart.

(The All Black coach announced his resignation the following morning, claiming: 'After four marvellous years in the job, my time is up.')

November 5

Australian players on the doorstep of greatness admit the chance to be remembered forever, via a weekend the country will never forget, is a driving force behind their desire to win tomorrow's World Cup final against France.

As the nation prepares to go to the ballot box on the republican referendum, the Wallabies are hoping, on the other side of the world, to create a page of history for themselves with a win at the Millennium Stadium in Cardiff. More than 70,000 will pack the ground with millions more watching across the globe when the four-yearly World Cup festival finally reaches its five-week climax. And if Australia defeat the Gallic giantkillers who upset the All Blacks in London last Sunday, they will become the first nation to win the World Cup twice in its 12-year existence.

The Wallabies took the title in 1991, New Zealand in 1987 and South Africa in 1995. But it is the recognition the Australian side of eight years ago still attracts through its triumph that has given an added spur to the team hoping to repeat the deed this weekend. On the eve of the showdown, players spoke openly of their dreams, their fears and their hopes to become a touchstone for future generations.

'The only way I can put it all in perspective, what it would mean to succeed, is to tell of the way that I think about those 1991 Wallabies,' said winger Joe Roff. 'What they did made a lot of people, including me, look up to them. And I'd love to be able to say in 10 years time that I was part of the 1999 Wallabies that won the World Cup in Cardiff.

'It's been a pretty nervous week. I've noticed it when I try to sleep. I put the head on the pillow and can't stop thinking about the game. That's a bit bizarre for me. I never have trouble when it comes to sleeping.'

Number eight Toutai Kefu was, like Roff, a teenager who tracked on television the success of the Wallabies under Nick Farr-Jones, and marvelled at the magnitude of their achievement.

'In Australian rugby, we keep referring back to them and what they did,' he said. 'They were a great team and I think this team could be just as great if not better. At all those dinners we went to before this World Cup, the talk at each one was about the 1991 team, and deservedly so. The guys who came out of that side were legends. Hopefully in years to come, at dinners down the track, they'll be talking about us as well.

'It would be unbelievable to be in a winning side and we'll be going out there to play as hard as we can, to leave nothing in the tank at the end.'

Kefu and Roff will be two of Australia's attacking spearheads against the flamboyant French. Another is five-eighth Stephen Larkham. After a season plagued by injury, with four operations already and another on a damaged right knee to follow the World Cup final, the Canberra-based pivot is relieved just to have got this far. For the Wallabies to be crowned the kings of world rugby would be, in his words, spine-tingling.

'I think everyone who plays the game wants to be remembered as being a great player and being part of a great team,' he said. 'And this team certainly has its special properties. We work well on and off the field so, from that respect, it would be a shame if we didn't come away with a victory. From the people I've spoken to like Timmy Horan, and others who played in 1991, they say the feeling in this team is even stronger than it was with them.

'Hopefully if we win it we will become one of those touchstone teams.'

Flanker David Wilson, who will continue for another year regardless of tomorrow's result, also acknowledged the spirit and harmony that has helped shape the Wallabies and their season.

'It's a wonderful group of people we've got playing at the moment,' he said. 'We've worked so hard to get here, to be so close, I only hope we can put another good performance together. It's obviously the biggest game in everyone's career. Along with all the other boys, I'm very, very anxious, and with this to be my last World Cup, it would just be magnificent to win it, then look back one day when my careers over knowing I was able to achieve it.'

For prop Richard Harry, there are personal issues involved in the mix as well.

'It's hard to put into words,' he said. 'It will be the culmination of a lot of hard work, but also of a lot of sacrifices, like being away from your family, and of training when you didn't want to train. It will be the culmination of a lot of great things too, like some of the games we've played over the years and the way this team has developed.'

Perhaps one of the more relaxed Wallabies is the 10-year veteran Tim Horan. A centre in the 1991 side, he is one of two survivors in the starting line-up, the other being skipper John Eales. But even the cool midfield general is a little on edge approaching an Australian Day to be celebrated on opposite sides of the world.

'It would be fantastic to come off the field and know that in a decade of playing the game at this level you've won two World Cups out of three,' said Horan. 'It is in the back of my mind. How could it not be in a week like this?'

The words of French captain Raphael Ibanez captured in an instant the mystery and uncertainty that surrounds the staging of the fourth World Cup final at the Millennium Stadium in Cardiff tomorrow.

A passionate bull-necked hooker, Ibanez was asked if the French flame that scorched the All Blacks last Sunday could burn as brightly against the Wallabies.

'We are French,' he said. 'We are always unpredictable, and I don't know exactly what will happen in the final. I don't know what we will do.'

If their leader can shed little light on the subject, then the Wallabies are fumbling in the dark. But composure and confidence over the past five weeks have been the pillars of this Australian campaign, and being forced to expect the unexpected will hardly cause a flurry of panic.

The pressure, instead, is on France. It took a monumental comeback for them to beat an All Black side that had clearly turned its collective mind to the following week when leading 24–10 at Twickenham. In the final, there will be no complacency factor for France to feed off and flourish.

It is not to deny the danger of the galloping Gallic horde. Theirs is a game plan that can be formed and revised on the run. They can kick for position, as five eighth Christophe Lamaison demonstrated so flawlessly against the All Blacks; they can break down defences through the clever use of chip kicks and grubbers behind the line; they can mix it in the forwards with second row

Abdel Benazzi as their spearhead and Olivier Magne as the free-spirited runner; and they can, in moments of magic, create tries out of nothing through quicksilver wingers like Christophe Dominici.

A willing defence, especially in the midfield where French backrowers were strategically placed to stop the Kiwi advance, was one element of surprise that shook the All Blacks. Australia will have watched and learned. They will also have noticed the frequent forays to the blindside, led by veteran halfback Fabien Galthie, with the idea is to create one on one situations for wingers whose footwork and speed comfortably offset their lack of size.

Heavyweight Wallaby Joe Roff told The Australian he would prefer, given a choice, to line up against All Black hulks Jonah Lomu and Tana Umaga. The balletic French pair of Dominici and Philippe Bernat Salles are, he admitted, less predictable.

With Lomu and Umaga what you see is what you get, a physical confrontation. Chasing jackrabbits requires more thought. From the Australian perspective, the key is to frustrate France and force them into error. History is laced with examples of French self-destruction where if the game is not going their way, the demon of indiscipline emerges. Wallaby fullback Matt Burke, and his goalkicking right boot, will be ready to punish if it does.

For that reason, do not expect an adventurous Wallaby approach, at least in the early stages. They will not play the game in their own half, relying on the tactical kicking of five eighth Stephen Larkham to launch them into French territory.

And they will, for long periods, keep the play tightly regimented around their forwards unless obvious opportunities call them wide. By not risking turnovers, the Australians will shut down the chance for France to pilfer loose ball and kick start the counter attacks that so often fuel their confidence. New Zealand realised that all too late, and to their peril, at Twickenham last Sunday.

Toutai Kefu will again be the workhorse up front, powering his frame over the advantage line. He has established himself during the World Cup as the finest number eight in the game. Horan has been the other strike force the Australians have used to build platforms from which to recycle possession and maintain their continuity. But the French are expected to target the centre, having already referred to him as the most important player in the Australian side.

If the Wallabies want to throw a curve ball of their own, they might, perhaps, use Horan as a decoy on occasions and bring Daniel Herbert into the play more, back on the angle from outside centre.

Despite their efforts last week, the French midfield is not defensively watertight. Emile N'Tamack, a former fullback and winger, is susceptible to the odd tackling blemish, and Richard Dourthe is known for the rushes of blood that bring him out of the line in search for his opposite number.

It is why the French had their backrowers, and Benazzi too, prowling wide when the All Blacks were with the ball last week. But the Australians, having done their homework, will attempt to tie up the French forwards by pounding down the middle. If they can drag the big men into rucks and mauls, the numbers out wide will be thinner. It is then the Wallabies will turn to a back division where wingers Joe Roff and Ben Tune, and fullback Matt Burke, can capitalise on the open spaces.

Roff and Tune, with their added bulk, could be quite a handful for Dominici and Bernat Salles.

And if the blueprint does not unravel, the Wallabies could well cruise to a comfortable victory. David Campese predicts a 20-point win, and Campo is not known for his conservatism. But if the French fire is doused early, if their laissez faire approach is put to the sword by a disciplined, mistake free Australian performance, the final margin might even be greater.

If tomorrow's climactic showdown between Australia and France can match for excitement and theatre the last World Cup meeting between these two sides, then rugby union's final major match of this century will be hailed as one of its finest. The 1987 semi-final at Concord Oval in Sydney's inner-west has only been topped as a World Cup thriller by the Ellis Park decider eight years later when Joel Stransky, with a right foot dropped goal, delivered the pot of gold for a Rainbow Nation.

France upsetting New Zealand last week is another to challenge for the all-time tag. But rewind the tape to the inaugural tournament, and to a ground that held only 17,000 — empty seats were aplenty — as the match moved into its closing stages, the scores locked at 24-all.

Australia, with the bulk of their 1984 Grand Slam and 1986 Bledisloe Cup winning sides intact, had been favoured to pass by the French and into the final a week later at Auckland. They were not overwhelming favourites as the All Blacks were at Twickenham last Sunday, but the French, as they so frequently are when their most sublime displays emerge, had been cast in the role of underdog.

Now, with two minutes to go, they launched an attack inside the Australian half. French number eight Laurent Rodriguez appeared to knock on, but the handling lapse went unnoticed by Scottish referee Brian Anderson, and the play swept to the left.

Eleven players handled before the incomparable Serge Blanco, drifting up from fullback, made a graceful, effortless run for the corner. Where he was all poise, the defence was in panic. Australian hooker Tom Lawton, somehow calling on massive, weary thighs to carry him across in cover, made a desperate dive. David Campese too, was in on the chase.

But Blanco was just out of reach. He skidded across the line, then raised himself to his knees, arms aloft, face alight. France were in the World Cup final and, in Brisbane, the All Blacks cheered.

As New Zealand captain Wayne Shelford recalls, the Kiwis wanted the chance to avenge their shock defeat to France a year before in Nantes. The following day, New Zealand beat Wales in the second semi-final to ensure that opportunity.

Back at Concord Oval, as the All Blacks advanced, the ground was still wet with tears and champagne from a celebration the night before. After their monumental victory over the Wallabies, the French had walked back into the middle of the field, darkness converging and sang Le Marseillaise.

It had been that sort of match. Not played to a 70,000 crowd like the Twickenham boilover of six days ago, but the emotion was there nonetheless. Thrust and counter thrust from two attack-driven sides had produced a game of sustained brilliance. Australia led 9–6 at half time and 24–21 with seven minutes to play.

Andrew Slack was the Australian captain 12 years ago, and he remembers the turning point of the semi final — the act that allowed the Blanco finale — came in the dying seconds of the opening half. Australia led 9–0 when number eight Troy Coker won a lineout on his own line. French second rower Alain Lorieux moved in swiftly, ripped the ball from Coker's grasp, and crashed over for the score.

It was, said Slack, the softest of tries 'considering the circumstances'. France finished with four tries to two on a day when Campese also made history by breaking the world try-scoring record. His 25th in 32 Tests surpassed the previous mark of Scotland's I.S. Smith, who collected his haul over a nine-year period from 1924.

There have been other momentous Australia-France Tests, including both clashes of the 1989 series in France.

In the opening game, Australia were dismissed as having no hope. Ten of their players had won, between them, only 25 caps. Four were on debut, including Jason Little and Peter FitzSimons, and one, Darren Junee, would come off the bench to also play his first Test.

Tim Horan, partnering Little in the centres, is the only survivor from that game involved in tomorrow's Cardiff final, and he, as a teenager, was playing just his second international.

The match was in Strasbourg and with Horan scoring two of four tries, Campese also getting in on the act, Australia won 32–15. It was against the odds, a result from nowhere, as the Wallaby rookies took on a French side boasting Blanco, Sella, Berbizier, Rodriguez, Champ, Cecillon and co.

Coach Bob Dwyer said: 'If anyone had suggested before this match that we'd score four tries to nil, you'd have told them they were having themselves on. We won't get carried away, but if we were any happier we'd burst.'

A week later their balloon did.

France had made nine changes, including the axing of Blanco, in a stunning shake-up. This time the Wallabies went in as favourites and France were victorious 25–19.

In all, since the first Test between them in 1928, when the Waratahs carried the Australian flag, the Wallabies have played France 28 times — for 13 wins, 13 losses and two draws. To further underline the closeness of the contests, Australia have scored a total of 498 Test points against France, and conceded 481. It works out, on average, to be a scoreline per game of 17.79 to 17.18.

If it looks like being that tight tomorrow, can someone hand me a Valium.

French team officials have accused the All Blacks, and Australian players before them, of inventing foul play allegations against their World Cup final heroes. Reacting angrily to claims of gouging, biting and testicle-grabbing in last week's semi-final with New Zealand, assistant coach Pierre Villepreux has aimed a broadside at Kiwi coach John Hart on the eve of the tournament decider.

He also denied acts of violence took place in Brisbane two years ago, when Wallaby stars levelled similar complaints about underhanded French tactics. At the centre of the Ballymore controversy was second rower Fabien Pelous, who will line up against the Wallabies tomorrow in his 45th Test.

According to Villepreux, France are squeaky clean, despite All Black flanker Josh Kronfeld confirming this week he was twice gouged in the eyes at Twickenham, including one attack that left him with blurred vision.

'I am very surprised,' said the former French fullback. 'I spoke with the All Black manager and coach after the game, and there were no complaints about foul play. If players we respect, and a coach we respect, cannot say to us directly there is a problem, then I think that's really bad.

'When I have something to say to somebody I go to him and say 'I am not happy with you'. They have coaches like me and Jean Claude Skrela, they can come and see us before they speak to the media. I am proud of my players. I know they have never done that type of thing because they will not be in the French team if they do. Show us who do that, show us.

'I have too much respect for what is a rugby player to allow those things. So these people can say what they want. Until they come to me and say 'Pierre, you are wrong with that opinion', I am finished with this problem.'

Manager Joe Maso said French players were primed for the match of their lives, but would still go into the decider as underdogs. According to Maso, Australia proved with their disposal of South Africa that they deserve not only respect, but the tag of title favourites.

He also pointed to the Wallabies success in Paris last year, adding: 'We will go in with the necessary humility, and with the pride of champions. But it will be difficult to play two matches like last week, to get the state of mind back.'

Head coach Skrela said the French were planning to destabilise the Wallabies, how he would not reveal, citing the Australians ability to control and retain possession as a stumbling block for his side.

'They have good continuity and their link between backs and forwards is well organised,' he said. 'They present a lot of possibilities to disturb our defence, that is what we have to overcome.'

When referee Andre Watson whistles fulltime in tomorrow's World Cup final he will signal the end to two Wallaby careers. Props Andrew Blades and Dan Crowley have confirmed the Cardiff clash will be their last Tests and, for Blades, his last game of football.

Crowley, the longest serving Australian player having debuted against the British Lions in 1989, will continue at Super 12 level with Queensland having signed a new two-season deal.

'But I've told the selectors I won't be available for Australia next year,' said the front-row reserve. 'I think it's time and they'll be looking, after this game, towards building for the next World Cup.'

For Blades, it will be a more dramatic exit. No club, provincial or Test rugby next season, only the hope that he can look back with pride on a World Cup final victory.

'While the boys don't believe I'll be able to go cold turkey, this is the end for me, and I've just got to make the most of it,' he said. 'It will be up there with my first Test in terms of throwing myself about. On that day I ran around like a chook with its head cut off and probably got in the way the first 20 minutes. But while the other guys are going on, most will never play a World Cup again, certainly not the older guys. So it is for a lot of us our last chance.

'I spoke to Tim Horan earlier in the week and he said one of his greatest disappointments was losing a club grand final. He had the whole off season to think about it. Well, I've got a very long off season coming up so I don't want to have any regrets.'

Wallaby flanker David Wilson has yet to sign a contract for next season but has every intention of continuing his career as the most capped flanker in world rugby. 'I am looking to play next year,' he said. 'No matter what the outcome is, I'm pretty sure I'll go around. I'm still enjoying it and I enjoy the life of a rugby player.

'I've been reasonably happy with my performances this year and while I've still got something to contribute and can still be competitive against the best, I'll go around for one more year.'

Wilson tomorrow plays his 72nd Test.

Strongly in contention for the coveted player of the tournament award, Wallaby centre Tim Horan expects to be the number one target of France tomorrow. The French camp have spoken in glowing terms about Horan, and the need to shut him down. But the veteran midfielder, a survivor from the 1991 World Cup triumph, is welcoming all the attention.

'I think I will be put under a lot of pressure,' he said. 'But if that happens, then it will allow the players around me to find a bit more space. If the French are looking to target myself and Steve Larkham, that's great, that's exactly what we want them to do. We've never really gone into a game putting pressure on one certain player.

'We were going to try it last week with (Springbok five eighth) Jannie de Beer, but then (halfback) Joost van der Westhuizen started causing problems. You can't afford to do it, just concentrate on one guy.'

November 6

THE FINAL

AUSTRALIA 35 FRANCE 12

> 'There is a point of no return where you have laboured
> so long, sacrificed so much, that you can't go back.
> You must reach your goal and trample on anyone who
> tries to stop you.'

Shortly before the Wallabies boarded the bus that took them to Millennium Stadium and their date with destiny in the World Cup final against France, those words of former Olympic middle distance champion, Herb Elliott, were engraved on their minds.

In a function room at their team hotel, utility back Jason Little read the quote aloud to an audience of silent, reflective Australians, preparing to play for the biggest prize in the game and the honour of winning the last major global sporting championship of the century.

It is a pre-game tradition the Wallabies follow. A phrase for the day to suit the occasion. But never has there been one more fitting.

For two years the World Cup was their focus, and the title was now within reach. As they made the short ride through Cardiff streets, past thousands of spectators making their way to the Welsh cathedral, faces painted in green and gold or the red, white and blue of France, the message was hammered home further.

The youngest player in the Wallaby squad, winger Scott Staniforth, was called on to address the team. 'This is it,' he said. 'Make sure there are no regrets.'

As Little recalled later, it was a build-up of unmatched tension, of gut-wrenching expectation, of a career turning opportunity ahead, of the chance to make history and wear the crown of kings for the next four years.

'It was unbelievable,' he said. 'Earlier, at the team meeting, Andrew Blades got up to make a speech because this was his last

Test. He choked up, and half the guys in the room had tears in their eyes as he told what it meant to him.'

On this tide of adrenalin the Wallabies swept into a stadium of 72,500 and, a couple of hours later, had ground the French cockerel to pate in becoming the first nation in the rugby world to win the William Webb Ellis trophy twice — the scoreline 35–12.

It was a victory of hardship. France, driven to desperate measures in the second half in a bid to stop the Australian advance, resorted to the most brutal and base of tactics, with eye-gouging top of their option list. Several Australian players bore scratches around their eyes later, with skipper John Eales nursing a swollen and bloodshot example of what ferocious fingers can achieve. But Eales spoke later of self-belief and composure, and the Australians had a healthy measure of both despite the French intimidation.

The Wallabies did eventually trample their opponents, with two tries in the final 20 minutes from winger Ben Tune and super-sub Owen Finegan, making the Elliott words even more prophetic.

The glory of the day, however, was not that they finished with two tries to hold aloft the trophy. The significance was in them not conceding a try to the side that ran four past the All Blacks in the semi finals at Twickenham.

Defence has been the cornerstone of the Wallaby campaign. They have given up just one try in six matches en route to collecting the cup from the Queen. American centre Juan Grobler grabbed the score in a pool match on October 14. But Wales, South Africa and France failed to cross the white line in successive weeks.

There was nothing shabby either about the potency of the French attack at times, especially when they ran from depth, and with numbers in support.

The list of crucial tackles though, highlighted the brick wall curtain the Wallabies have brought down on opponents this season.

Jason Little on Emile N'Tamack, Horan on both Abdel Benazzi and speedster Philippe Bernat Salle, Toutai Kefu on N'Tamack in the midfield — they were typical of the way the Australians have guarded their tryline jealousy over 500 minutes of tournament play.

The final itself was not the prettiest contest, with mistakes aplenty particularly in the first half. But when the Wallaby machine moved into a higher gear after half time — they led 12–6 at the break — the French were unable to mount the resistance that overwhelmed the All Blacks.

Still, the final scoreline was deceptively inflated.

Australia led only 18–12 — six penalty goals to four — entering the final quarter of the final.

Then a series of drives through the middle of the French forwards had them quickly on the retreat.

Halfback George Gregan made a sniping run to place himself behind enemy lines. Centre Tim Horan arrived to carry on the play and turned in the tackle of two defenders to unload to replacement Owen Finegan.

In one motion, Finegan threw his hip into two other tacklers, and sent the ball to Tune to dive in at the corner. The conversion by fullback Matthew Burke raised the bar to almost unreachable heights for France.

At 25–12 the Wallabies appeared safe, and by the time Finegan crossed in the closing stages, after he timed his run off an inside flick from Gregan to race 30m to touch down, the World Cup showdown was over as a contest.

In the scrum the Australians had again been rock solid; the lineout functioned smoothly, except for one loss on their own throw; and the backrow trio of Wilson, Kefu and Cockbain were instrumental in closing off avenues for the French to exploit.

Behind the scrum, Gregan had his best game of the tournament, five eighth Stephan Larkham, by comparison, was off colour with the boot, while Horan and Herbert in the midfield again patrolled their area with the diligence of parking cops.

Winger Ben Tune was impressive in what he did, showing power to go with his pace by barrelling through two defenders for the first try.

And two replacements off the bench, Owen Finegan and Little, impressed. Finegan has been a revelation here as a second half impact player. In the final he squeezed more into his 28 minutes than most other players with three times the game time.

The 1991 World Cup winning captain, Nick Farr-Jones, paid tribute to the current side today, saying: 'The biggest thing out of this is what it does for the game in Australia for the next four years, leading up to the next World Cup on our patch in 2003.

'As Rod Macqueen has already said, they worked their arses off for this. They really do deserve it.'

The 1991 and 1999 World Cup teams now share a special bond, having successfully grabbed for glory either side of the disappointment of the 1995 tournament.

But two out of three ain't bad, just ask the All Blacks, who have not won the title since 1987.

Wallaby skipper John Eales threatened to lead his team off the field during the World Cup final in Cardiff as a protest against French brutality that left him fearing for his players safety.

Several Australians required extensive treatment in the wake of eye-gouging incidents, with Eales suffering a torn cornea after a vicious second half attack.

At the height of the foul play fiasco, Eales approached South African referee Andre Watson and could be heard over television microphones warning he would take his players off the pitch unless the French were brought under control.

After the game, with his right eye swollen and bloodshot, Eales confirmed there had been a number of incidents, while the Australian team medical staff counted halfback George Gregan, hooker Michael Foley and prop Richard Harry among the gouging victims.

Flanker David Wilson was kicked in the face.

Eales said he had spoken to Watson: 'I told him the whole thing was getting ridiculous and he had to do something about it.'

But the Australian captain stopped short of confirming what he had already been captured saying to the referee via television sound tapes.

It is not the first time Eales has threatened a mid-match walkoff.

During a Tri-Nations clash with South Africa in Johannesburg last year, Eales again considered the safety factor when Springbok supporters started pelting the field with bottles.

He spoke to Scottish referee Jim Fleming and warned that the Wallabies would leave the field if the situation continued.

'I told him 'if this keeps going I'm going to take the players off", Eales said at the time. 'Fortunately it didn't continue. But it was dangerous. Those bottles were made of glass.'

At the Millennium Stadium, Eales was far more concerned with natural products, like the fingers at the end of the hands of French forwards.

France has been both the beauty and the beast of the 1999 World Cup.

But if the International Rugby Board has any backbone at all, then the flamboyant filth-traders should be heavily censured for the dirt they dished up in the code's showpiece match today before a worldwide audience of more than a billion.

Sport has no place for eye-gougers, headbutters, testicle-tweakers and biters. Yet the French, two weeks running, have embarked on underhanded mayhem and are yet to be even slapped on the wrist for the black eye they have given the game.

What makes it all the more reviling, is that the French camp — so deserving of accolades for their semi final brilliance to topple unbackable favourites New Zealand — have blithely denied all allegations, let alone show remorse.

Their assistant coach Pierre Villepreux was horrified last week that All Blacks coach John Hart, and flanker Josh Kronfeld, would say such things about the players he was 'very proud of'.

But the Australians, privately, were also fuming over the sustained cheap shots they were subject to from early in the second half, after the Wallabies ascendancy left the French desperate.

At a time when the IRB is proudly beating its chest about taking the game to the world, with more than 90 countries now affiliated to the governing body, the French are giving parents across the globe good reason to keep their sons on the sidelines.

It is time for the IRB to show strength, to prove it is more than a toothless tiger happily caged in an ivory tower.

Noises were made at the start of the tournament about how a clamp down on violence was a top priority. Players throwing punches were rubbed out for two or three weeks at a time. But the most foul of acts have gone unpunished.

Agreed, video evidence is needed to cite and suspend offenders, and French prop Franck Tournaire was called to answer a charge of biting after the Twickenham semi final with the All Blacks. He was cleared due to insufficient proof.

But the current farce involving France needs to be acted on, whether or not the cameras are capturing their dirty deeds. A general warning at least is required. Yet the silence from the IRB has been deafening.

If evidence of physical damage is required, the boffins need only visit the Australian camp.

Winger Joe Roff needed stitches to a head wound after another off the ball incident.

And while the Australians were reluctant to speak out about the strongarm tactics by their final opponents, the IRB should not allow an issue vital to the game's well being to be swept under the carpet.

Perhaps they could start by interviewing Watson and taking their investigation from there. Kronfeld one week, Eales the next. Neither player has ever had his integrity questioned. Why would they want to fabricate anti-French allegations?

French captain Raphael Ibanez after the Cardiff final quickly sidestepped talk of foul play.

'The referee went to see me a lot, be he did the same for Australia,' he said.

French coach Jean Claude Skrela, in a delicious irony, suggested the physical approach of the Wallabies was the difference between the two sides on the day.

'What we missed today was that strength,' he said. 'They challenged us physically and we made mistakes.

'What we have to do is have more matches of this intensity if we're going to face up to this kind of physical intensity in the future. We have to re-organise things in the northern hemisphere.

'Australia are world champions because they were physically better. Last week we challenged the All Blacks there and won. But it was the Wallabies physical pressure that has made them world champions today.'

Ibanez agreed, saying: 'They're used to playing at this level. We were like kids playing in the World Cup final. But Australia deserved their victory. I have no criticism of my players, we did the best we could.'

On a cloudless afternoon in Cardiff, as darkness approached and emotions ran riot, John Eales reached out to embrace his family and thought of the sister who could not be there to witness the magic at Millennium Stadium.

As the Wallabies embarked on a victory lap minutes after the French had been foiled 35–12 in the World Cup final, Eales went searching for the clan who had made the trek to Britain to follow his fortunes and those of the Australian team that he led.

'I saw my dad and my wife Lara down near the fence,' the gentleman skipper said later. 'My mother my three sisters and my brother were in the crowd as well. And my sister who passed away, she'll be here somewhere too.'

Carmel Eales was just 20–years–old when cancer claimed her a decade ago. But time has not dimmed the fond memories of a brother whose world was in orbit tonight.

'Yeah, you do think about things like that on a day like this,' he said. 'I'm just grateful for the opportunity we've had. And it's great to know I have someone up there looking after me as well.

'It's just such a special day. When we won the World Cup in 1991, none of my family was able to be there. Having them here today is something I will always treasure.'

Front rower Andrew Blades, in his final Test, did not wait for the victory lap to share his joy.

Shortly after the fulltime whistle, as Australian players leapt into each other's arms, Blades hobbled across the ground, to where two brothers and his wife's father were waiting for him in the front rows of a packed stadium.

A mobile telephone was produced and within seconds, Blades was speaking to his wife Nickey in Sydney.

'I just wanted to share the moment with her,' said the retiring tight head prop. 'She couldn't get over here because of the bub. Amy is four months old now, and I just can't wait to get home to them.'

Replacement forward Owen Finegan, who took an inside pass from George Gregan to race 30 metres for the try that ballooned Australia's winning margin to 23 points, was another to seek out family and friends.

From Irish stock, Finegan has more than 100 cousins in the Emerald Isle, and many of them made the journey to Cardiff for a match he will never forget.

Daniel Herbert starts an Australian attack with French second rower Abdel Benazzi in pursuit. *Courtesy: Allsport*

George Gregan had a hand in both Australian tries in the final but finds his path blocked this time by French captain Raphael Ibanez. *Courtesy: Allsport*

Match sealer . . . Ben Tune crashes over with 15 minutes remaining to give Australia a commanding lead in the decider. *Courtesy: Allsport*

Andrew Blades, in his last, shows the French there is more to his game than technique in the scrum as he prepares to cross enemy lines. *Courtesy: Allsport*

John Eales powers ahead as Andrew Blades (far left) looms in support. *Courtesy: Allsport*

Matt Cockbain manages to fire off a pass despite the tackle of French halfback Fabien Galthie. *Courtesy: Allsport*

It's over . . . the Wallabies celebrate after the fulltime whistle signalled their ascendancy to the title of world champions. *Courtesy: Allsport*

John Eales embraces David Giffin (left) and David Wilson (No.7) as Ben Tune prepares to join the party. *Courtesy: Allsport*

Joy for the front row . . . Richard Harry, Michael Foley and
Andrew Blades hoist the William Webb Ellis trophy.
Courtesy: Allsport

An Australian supporter leaves no doubt where his loyalties lie.
Courtesy: Allsport

The brains trust . . . coach Rod Macqueen (centre) with his
assistants Tim Lane (left) and Jeff Miller. *Courtesy: Allsport*

"Bill" gets a welcome back kiss from Richard Harry.
Courtesy: Allsport

World Champions . . . the victorious Wallabies savour the moment at the Millennium Stadium. *Courtesy: Allsport*

'When I got the ball, I never had in my mind that I would go on and score,' he laughed. 'But when I went through the gap I got a bit greedy. I looked for support then got greedy again and just kept going. They say it was 30m, I think it was more like 60m.'

After the trophy presentation, and before they started their stadium walkabout, the Australians formed a huddle on the field, standing in a wide circle, players, coaches and support staff linking arms in a show of solidarity.

With an almost ceremonial touch, coach Rod Macqueen walked to the middle of the group and tenderly sat the William Webb Ellis trophy on the churned up turf of an underdone pitch.

What followed was a rendition of the national anthem that could be heard high in the grandstands on the far side of the ground.

'That was a celebration for us,' said Eales. 'And a celebration for the people at home as well. It was a happy little circle that one.'

The singing though, was not over. As the Wallabies took in their victory lap, a song written for them by entertainer John Williamson — A Number On My Back — boomed through the loudspeakers.

The Men at Work classic *Downunder* followed.

And in the dressing room later, Rolf Harris, who sang the national anthem with Williamson before the match kicked off, joined the Wallaby frivolities and again opened the famous vocal chords.

It was that sort of day, for the Wallabies and for Eales, who must have been happy that, in the end, the stadium roof was kept open for the final. It would have given eyes from above a chance to follow the action.

Wallaby coach Rod Macqueen was searching for a lift to a nearby nightclub to celebrate with his World Cup champions shortly before midnight on Saturday in Cardiff.

Almost seven hours had passed since referee Andre Watson swirled an arm in the air to signal fulltime and the start of Australian celebrations.

It had been long enough for Macqueen to reflect on the enormity of what had been achieved, both by the players under his coaching regime and by the head man himself.

But when asked to describe his innermost emotions, Macqueen looked only outward.

'What makes me happy is what these guys have achieved for themselves,' he said. 'That's what gives me satisfaction. They really deserve this. They've worked so hard.'

Earlier at the post-match press conference, where the world media wanted to know what lay behind the Australian triumph, he said: 'A lot of work and a lot of preparation. But we also needed passion, to match the passion of the French.

'What I've just seen is probably the most emotional dressing room we've had. But we've been looking for this for two years and we didn't want to give it away.

'I was very happy with the discipline shown, we didn't have any let-offs or dry spots. And you didn't have to look too far past their faces out there to know what proud Australians they are.'

A pride in the Test jumper, and pride in the nation, has been a catchcry from Macqueen since he stepped into the coaching job two years and two months ago.

He introduced a pre-match routine where a former Wallaby presents the jumpers prior to each Test match. Before the final, television commentator Chris Handy, a blood and guts forward from the late 1970's and early 1980s, was chosen for the role.

Macqueen has also gathered around him a coaching and support staff who, he believes, have given the Wallabies an edge on the rest of the world.

One of the recruits, brought in by Macqueen late in 1997, was former rugby league international John Muggleton, whose brief was to stiffen the Australian defence.

Proof of his contribution is tied to one, quite astounding statistic.

In 500 minutes of football on the way to winning the William Webb Ellis trophy, the Wallabies conceded just one try, and that back on October 14 in a pool match against the USA, when American outside centre Juan Grobler crossed in the corner at Thomond Park in Limerick.

'But I don't take any responsibility for that one,' said Muggleton. 'Because I wasn't at the game. I was off spying on (quarter final opponent) Wales.'

On the coaching staff at the North Sydney rugby league club

before being drafted into the Wallaby system, Muggleton admits Macqueen helped salvage his football coaching career.

'North Sydney put the knife into me,' he claimed. 'And I was pretty much on the scrapheap before Rod came along and picked me up.'

Another significant addition to the staff when Macqueen was first appointed was former Test flanker Jeff Miller, one of two assistant coaches.

Miller was a part of the 1991 World Cup squad, and has been a vital buffer at times between players and coach.

'Australian rugby was not in the healthiest of states in 1997,' he said. 'I don't think we'd handled professionalism all that well, and changes needed to be made.

'Players still wanted all the good things about the amateur game but not accept what came with professionalism — all the sacrifices that need to be made when you're being paid to play.'

According to Macqueen, the turnaround was mirrored in the victory over France today.

'There have been a lot of sacrifices to get us where we are today,' he said. 'And not just sacrifices by the players and support staff, but by their families as well.

'It's nice to see them now reaping the rewards. The support we've received from home has also been great. We've had faxes from everybody, from the Prime Minister to the local greengrocer, from leading sportsmen to the commander in chief of the forces in East Timor, Major General Peter Cosgrove.

'There was no way we were going into that game without feeling that we had a lot of expectations to fill. And they went out there and they played for the pride of Australia.'

Forget the referendum post-mortems, the debate to dominate bar-room chat for those with a sporting bent this week will surround the World Cup Wallabies.

More precisely, are they the greatest of all time?

It has always been, will always remain, the domain of the unwinnable argument, trying to compare champions from different eras, sometimes generations apart, in a bid to eke out the defining answer of just who is best of the best.

But call up the contenders anyway, and a two-man panel of experts, and let the dissection begin.

The candidates have been narrowed to three — the ground-breaking Grand Slam side of 1984, the World Cup champions of 1991, and the 1999 team crowned kings of their code on Saturday night.

The judges are Andrew Slack, the Grand Slam captain, and former Test flanker Simon Poidevin, who played in both the 1984 and 1991 teams.

Slack got straight to the point.

'Our 1984 side would give the other two a run for their money, but we are a bit older these days,' he smiled. 'Look, it really is an apples and oranges comparison because the game has changed so much in the past 15 years.

'But I'm happy to recognise that in 1984 we were the greatest ever, in 1991 the World Cup champions could make the same claim and now the 1999 side can justifiably say they're the best we've ever had.

'Time marches on, and very few sporting figures of the past can stand the test of time. Sir Donald Bradman is one, so too his 1948 touring team to England.

'When Australia win the World Cup in 2003, they're going to be the greatest team ever, better than this side. But I would have to say, in 1999, they have more genuine athletes than we had. They have also had the opportunity of being fulltime players.

'If you allowed the 1984 team to be similarly prepared, and we played under 1984 rules, they might just edge us. If you played the way the game is played these days, they'd beat us.'

But Slack paid tribute to the backline he led to a clean sweep of Test victories against England, Ireland, Wales and Scotland, ruling only himself and Michael Lynagh, who was then a rookie inside centre, out of contention for a place in a composite back division.

'We had guys like David Campese, Brendan Moon, Roger Gould, Mark Ella and Nick Farr-Jones,' he said. 'They stand up against any one from any era. And in the forwards, I think someone like (flanker) David Codey would have been a sensation in the modern game.'

Poidevin, who never shirked the job at hand when confronting All Black packs that were determined to chip a few holes in those chiselled features, went looking for a seat on the fence.

'There is no doubt this team is among the greatest we have seen,' he said. 'I'm not saying it's the all time great, that is just too tough a call when you think of the changes in the game over the past 15 years, and the different requirements of the different positions.

'But I do know this side has come through one of the hardest routes possible on the way to winning the title. They had Wales on their home patch in the quarter finals, a fired up defending champion in South Africa in the semis, and a flamboyant French side that smacked the backsides of the All Blacks.'

There would be one indisputable edge for the 1999 side over the others. Their defence, moulded and maintained by former rugby league international John Muggleton, has been close to impregnable.

And, in the modern game, a solid defence is the bedrock of victory. It is why the dropped goal was re-born as an attacking option at this tournament. The tackling has been too good to beat. Tries, except in lopsided contests, have been pretty much at a premium.

'That's why these comparisons are so onerous,' said Poidevin. 'Take the current side. Their halfback-five eighth combination of George Gregan and Stephen Larkham would not, in too many people's eyes, be on the same level as Nick Farr-Jones with Mark Ella or Michael Lynagh.

'But that's if you look at the romantic way of playing the game. In the new era, defence is so important, and I don't think in Farr-Jones, Lynagh and Ella you can come up with a pairing that provides the same defensive capabilities of Gregan and Larkham.

'We all know how well George can tackle, and Larkham is a killer. For 1999, those two fit the bill beautifully.'

Poidevin also dismisses the idea that the current team is not attack-conscious, or as running-minded as the 1984 and 1991 outfits. Eight years ago it was a Wallaby winger, Campese, who stole the show, emphasising the regularity with which the ball was moved wide.

The outstanding players for the 1999 champions have been number eight Toutai Kefu and inside centre Tim Horan.

'But I think they have enhanced the tradition of Australian teams that run the ball,' Poidevin argued. 'Campo might criticise them for not doing it enough, but the defences are tighter and better structured these days. They do have an attitude of wanting to take the game wide.

'At the same time, I think that 1984 backline was something quite extraordinary, and I think Steve Larkham has a way to go before you would put him alongside Mark Ella. While Larkham has done some exceptional things, Mark was just freakish.'

And so the debate continues to rage.

Would the current front-row of Richard Harry, Michael Foley and Andrew Blades — a trio who had question marks placed over them during the knockout stages — be as effective as the 1984 unit of Enrique Rodriguez, Tom Lawton and Andy McIntyre, or the 1991 combination of Tony Daly, Phil Kearns and Ewen McKenzie?

Eales stands alone in the second row for both the 1991 and 1999 teams while the backrow is another endless source of agitation.

Tuynman, Codey and Poidevin, up against Coker, Poidevin and Ofahengaue, up against Kefu, Wilson and Cockbain.

It might just be best to adjourn the discussion. Bourbon and coke please barman.

1984: Roger Gould, Brendan Moon, Andrew Slack (c), Michael Lynagh, David Campese, Mark Ella, Nick Farr-Jones, Steve Tuynman, Simon Poidevin, David Codey, Steve Cutler, Steve Williams, Andy McIntyre, Tom Lawton, Enrique Rodriguez.

1991: Marty Roebuck, Rob Egerton, Jason Little, Tim Horan, David Campese, Michael Lynagh, Nick Farr-Jones, Troy Coker, Simon Poidevin, Willie Ofahengaue, John Eales, Rod McCall, Ewen McKenzie, Phil Kearns, Tony Daly.

1999: Matt Burke, Ben Tune, Daniel Herbert, Tim Horan, Joe Roff, Stephen Larkham, George Gregan, Toutai Kefu, David Wilson, Matt Cockbain, John Eales, David Giffin, Andrew Blades, Michael Foley, Richard Harry.

*David Campese has the final word — would he have it any other way —
on Australia's World Cup triumph.*

The most points by a side in a World Cup final, and a
record winning margin to boot. Australian players are
entitled to feel they could do no more in disposing
of France.

I don't think any of us will fool ourselves into
believing it was a high-class affair. There were a few too
many mistakes for that.

But World Cup deciders have a habit of being a
little bit rough around the edges. It comes with the
territory. These are the biggest matches of your life, and
the nerves can be almost overwhelming.

One player who did not suffer today, at least
with his goalkicking, was fullback Matthew Burke,
who managed to pass the 500–point career mark with
his haul of 25 points — another new milestone for
the tournament.

The first half of the game never really developed
and neither side held a clear ascendancy.

But after the break the Wallabies came out and
they took their opportunities. The French? I get the
feeling the semi final win over the All Blacks took a lot
out of them mentally.

They played their final a week too early.

Besides, they got plenty of good bounces of the
ball against New Zealand, and that never happens two
weeks running.

Today was when they needed them too, because
they could find no way through the Wallaby defence.

The Australians have been superb in that area all
year. John Eales said defence won them the final. I
would go even further and say defence was the real
foundation stone of their whole tournament.

They've worked very hard on tackling techniques,
and power in defence, and obviously that wins matches
in the modern era. Even an old running rugby romantic
like me has to accept that situation.

Back in 1991, we had to defend for 20 minutes as England threw everything at us at Twickenham. And I think it was somewhat similar here for a brief period in the match.

But breaking all the accepted practices of the game, the Australians don't mind if they get caught without possession. They seemed quite happy to let the French have the ball, knowing they had their measure.

Under those circumstances, the French quite quickly get frustrated, and the ill discipline creeps in. We saw enough of that at Millennium Stadium to suggest they still have a long way to go to bring a professional maturity to their game.

But enough of the negatives. The Wallabies in defence were outstanding. They never gave the French much in the way of field position, and from inside your own territory it can be difficult to put pressure on the opposition.

As for the Australian attack, we didn't see as much as we would have hoped, but replacement Owen Finegan stood out when he finally joined the fray at the 52–minute mark.

Every time he has got a run in the World Cup he's brought a sense of urgency and enthusiasm to the pack.

The Australian scrum deserves praise as well. I have a feeling Alex Evans, our old assistant coach from the 1984 Grand Slam side, has had a fair input into this side.

To me, Alex is a hero behind the scenes. He's achieved so much in this game and he's still going.

As far as the Australian tactics were concerned, it was hardly a variation on the theme they have followed right through the World Cup.

I still maintain the Wallabies have been the best team in the tournament. They made it hard for themselves early because they were struggling to find form. But what that tells me is that we haven't seen the best of this team yet.

Stephen Larkham is still finding his feet to a

certain extent at five eighth. He's played extremely well but if you have a five eighth that can run the ball a bit better, then the Australian backline will end up with far more opportunity.

Joe Roff hardly touched the ball in the final and I find that disturbing. He had it all over his French counterpart for size. Why didn't he get more ball?

But improving those areas is something we can now look forward to as we push ahead to the 2003 tournament in Australia and New Zealand.

In making those suggestions, I'm not in any trying to demean the magnificent achievement of the Wallabies. It was a magnificent victory over France, scoring 35 points and never looking in doubt in the second half.

Perhaps it is also the right time to pay credit to Australia's best two players, centre Tim Horan and number eight Toutai Kefu.

I thought Kefu was exceptional despite missing two games through suspension, and he must have run Horan close for the player of the tournament award.

He reminds me a lot of Willie Ofahengaue, with that same explosive acceleration usually not found in a forward of his size. Kefu is still young too, he could lead this Australian pack for some years to come.

The job now for the Wallabies, even though their playing schedule is finished for the season, is to maintain level heads and not let the pressure of being world champions get to them.

In many ways, these guys set the standard, now they've got to continue it. But that's a small price to pay when you have the opportunity to win a World Cup.

Congratulations to Rod Macqueen and his players. A great job from the lot of them. They are very deserving winners.

AFTER THE FINAL IN THE DRESSING ROOM

MATTHEW BURKE: 'That's the greatest moment in my rugby life. It is just great to be part of this team ... 44 guys came away and we all succeeded. It was a tremendous reward for everyone, and our very loyal supporters. The last two years have been a real building phase, and the management has overseen that extremely well. You could not have found a group of guys who could have got on better over seven weeks. We're going to have a good one tonight. There's humility in winning, but we are living it up right now.'

BEN TUNE: 'For my try, I just picked the perfect French player to run at — their fullback. I got the ball, didn't have a lot of room to work with, so I just put my head down, and gave it a crack. I got close enough just to chug my arm out with the ball and it got there. Overall we played a smart game.'

DANIEL HERBERT: 'We played to our game plan and we knew if we hung in there, and stayed in their territory, we'd get the points. Eventually it came. We knew it was going to be a struggle. I didn't think we'd get away with as many points as we did. To our credit, we stuck to our guns. Even though I was on the sideline at the end, it was just so fantastic, knowing that we were not going to be beaten, no matter what. I had to come off with a medial tear, but who cares.'

TIM HORAN: 'It's a fantastic feeling. I don't think it has sunk in yet. It is great for all of the people back in Australia. The Cup has already got a lot of XXXX in it. It's just a sensational feeling. It was a great tournament. We went along quite smoothly. We had a very good team spirit, which is something the side prides itself on. It was a very jovial tour, and we knew when to switch on and off. It is fantastic to finish the week off particularly after the netballers had gone so well, the rugby league side has won, and the cricketers are on their way to a win.'

JOE ROFF: 'I haven't really thought about it much at all. All that matters is that we won the game. I haven't stopped to think about the first half or second half. I just really haven't come to terms with it yet, but over a couple of days I'm sure it will sink in. All I have been thinking about is getting a couple of stitches in my head, the hoopla, and all the drinks I am going to have with family and friends tonight. I can't wait to get home and thank all the supporters.'

STEPHEN LARKHAM: 'A great moment, especially having my folks over here, and for all the supporters at home. I'm sorry I'm losing my voice at the moment. We knew we had a lot of support at home. It was a very tight game for 60 minutes and then we ran away with it. The feeling among us is just unbelievable at the moment. I didn't hit all my kicks right tonight, but in the end it didn't really matter.'

GEORGE GREGAN: 'It will take me a long time to comprehend winning the Cup. I just feel a lot of emotion because a lot of hard work has gone into this. And it's spilling over in the change room. We persevered in the second half, because we knew the French would come and play very well like the week before. It took 60 minutes to crack them. The great thing is that we did it in style.'

TOUTAI KEFU: 'A dream come true. Unbelievable. Ecstatic. Once we get amongst the Australian supporters back home, it will start sinking in. I just thank God I got the chance to play two more games after being suspended. The other guys carried the team through to give me this chance.'

DAVID WILSON: 'It's unbelievable, the highlight of my career. And it's more a relief than anything else after the emotions of this week. It's just great to achieve the ultimate goal after being together for two years, some of us for four years. All the hard work, hours in the gym, weeks away from family — this has certainly made it all worthwhile. When Ben Tune scored and Matt Burke kicked the goal to give us the buffer of 14 points, I thought we were pretty comfortable. But when Owen Finegan went over, the hoopla really started.'

MATT COCKBAIN: 'I remember watching the 1991 World Cup especially staying up late with my father for the Irish game, and being so pumped about what they did. Eight years down the track, it is just a great feeling to do what that team had done. I had so many years on the edge of selection. To be involved in the last two seasons has been fantastic. I embraced my wife, Sally, at the end of the game, and that was pretty emotional. The tears were flowing.'

JOHN EALES: 'The team performed so well, and to be able to lift the Cup in the end, is the highest accolade you can achieve. We knew we didn't have to play our best football in the first match of the tournament, or the fifth, just the sixth. We did that.'

DAVID GIFFIN: 'It is going to be a very, very big night, celebrating a World Cup and a birthday at the same time. We knew it was going to be tough and reasonably tight. We had it over them for the entire game, but we didn't really carry on with it. The tries thankfully came towards the end, which was great.'

ANDREW BLADES: 'We were so happy to get away with it because it meant everything to us. There was no way we were going to leave that field without the Cup. I am just so proud of all the guys, and couldn't be happier. I will struggle a lot next year watching. I am content in my mind because the body is telling me it is time. But I still want to be involved on the coaching side, because I want to put something back into the game.'

MICHAEL FOLEY: 'It is hard to put into words how we feel... but I am absolutely thrilled, it's the most exciting moment in my rugby career. Everything else pales in comparison. It hasn't really sunk in to be quite honest. I know it is a cliche. But you finish the game and you won and you think well that's it. Before the game you think about the possibilities of losing, and you are terrified of those things. I am thankful we came away with the victory.'

RICHARD HARRY: 'There is never enough hoopla as far as I'm concerned. That's the greatest rugby moment in my life. Absolutely fantastic. I just enjoyed the occasion. Working with this team has been a fabulous part of my life. There were a number of penalties involved in the scrums. Maybe they couldn't handle the pressure and had to bail out.'

RESERVES:

OWEN FINEGAN: 'I ran 30 metres for that try, but it will probably be 100 metres by the end of a night of celebrating. I said to all my family that I was going to score a try in the World Cup final with five minutes to go, and I never really gave myself a chance. In the end, I got there.'

DAN CROWLEY: 'Both World Cup victories were fantastic. I am very, very happy. I was remembering back to 1991, and I was more nervous now because this one means so much more to me. It was my last game for Australia.'

NATHAN GREY: 'Unf.....believable. All the boys put in so much hard work and it has paid off. We came over here with a mission and the guys who played the whole game... well they were unbelievable. Australia are deserved world champions.'

JEREMY PAUL: 'I am just so glad to be here. These guys have been a big part of my life. I can't describe how I feel, there's not a word for how I feel about these guys. It is just an amazing feeling to be part of this whole campaign with these bunch of blokes. My voice is really croaky, because I was yelling to so many people in the crowd during the victory lap. You find friends in the crowd, and you start screaming. I am so excited I saw so many Australians in the crowd.'

JASON LITTLE: 'It will probably be the same as 1991 and it will not impact on us until we get home, and get the reception there. It is fantastic for me personally after losing in 1995. It means so much more to me now after losing one World Cup. Two years with everyone, you can imagine how closely knitted we are. It was a great thrill for me to finish with Timmy Horan in the centres, and see him win the player of the tournament. I'll wait and see about next year, because I'm getting married in a couple of weeks. If that is the way to end your career, what a way to finish.'

MARK CONNORS: 'It was just great to have the opportunity to be out there. To win a World Cup is every player's dream. It's been a fantastic year for me and this is the ultimate achievement.'

CHRIS WHITAKER: 'I was on the field all up for 29 seconds. It was worth it, yeah. I am not complaining. I am off to the bar to buy the coach a beer for putting me on.'

MATTHEW BURKE
Position: Fullback
Age: 26
Tests: 44
Test debut: 1993 v South Africa
Height: 1.85m
Weight: 98kg

CHRIS LATHAM
Position: Fullback
Age: 23
Tests: 6
Test debut: 1998 v France
Height: 1.92m
Weight: 93kg

BEN TUNE
Position: Winger
Age: 22
Tests: 36
Test debut: 1996 v Wales
Height: 1.85m
Weight: 92kg

JASON LITTLE
Position: Winger
Age: 29
Tests: 68
Test debut: 1989 v France
Height: 1.83m
Weight: 100kg

JOE ROFF
Position: Winger
Age: 23
Tests: 51
Test debut: 1995 v Canada
Height: 1.91m
Weight: 100kg

SCOTT STANIFORTH
Position: Winger
Age: 21
Tests: 1
Test debut: 1999 v USA
Height: 1.86m
Weight: 92kg

DANIEL HERBERT
Position: Centre
Age: 25
Tests: 38
Test debut: 1994 v Ireland
Height: 1.88m
Weight: 100kg

TIM HORAN
Position: Centre
Age: 29
Tests: 79
Test debut: 1989 v New Zealand
Height: 1.81m
Weight: 90kg

NATHAN GREY
Position: Centre
Age: 24
Tests: 18
Test debut: 1998 v Scotland
Height: 1.83m
Weight: 95kg

STEPHEN LARKHAM
Position: Five-eighth
Age: 25
Tests: 30
Test debut: 1996 v Wales
Height: 1.88m
Weight: 86kg

World Cup biographies

ROD KAFER
Position: Five-eighth
Age: 28
Tests: 3
Test debut: 1999 v New Zealand
Height: 1.76m
Weight: 96kg

GEORGE GREGAN
Position: Halfback
Age: 26
Tests: 54
Test debut: 1994 v Italy
Height: 1.71m
Weight: 80kg

CHRIS WHITAKER
Position: Halfback
Age: 24
Tests: 7
Test debut: 1998 v South Africa
Height: 1.79m
Weight: 79kg

TOUTAI KEFU
Position: Number eight
Age: 25
Tests: 25
Test debut: 1997 v South Africa
Height: 1.91m
Weight: 106kg

TIAAN STRAUSS
Position: Number eight
Age: 33
Tests: 11 Australia, 15 South Africa
Test debut: 1992 v France (for South
Africa) 1999 v Ireland (for Australia)
Height: 1.89m
Weight: 104kg

JIM WILLIAMS
Position: Number eight
Age: 30
Tests: 4
Test debut: 1999 v Ireland
Height: 1.93m
Weight: 103kg

DAVID WILSON
Position: Flanker
Age: 32
Tests: 72
Test debut: 1992 v Scotland
Height: 1.87m
Weight: 96kg

MATT COCKBAIN
Position: Flanker
Age: 26
Tests: 30
Test debut: 1997 v France
Height: 1.97m
Weight: 112kg

OWEN FINEGAN
Position: Flanker
Age: 27
Tests: 33
Test debut: 1996 v Wales
Height: 1.98m
Weight: 114kg

JOHN EALES
Position: Second rower
Age: 29
Tests: 69
Test debut: 1991 v Wales
Height: 2.00m
Weight: 115kg

DAVID GIFFIN

Position: Second rower
Age: 25
Tests: 16
Test debut: 1996 v Wales
Height: 1.98m
Weight: 113kg

MARK CONNORS

Position: Second rower
Age: 28
Tests: 10
Test debut: 1999 v South Africa
Height: 1.96m
Weight: 104kg

TOM BOWMAN

Position: Second rower
Age: 23
Tests: 16
Test debut: 1998 v England
Height: 2.01m
Weight: 118kg

ANDREW BLADES

Position: Prop
Age: 32
Tests: 32
Test debut: 1996 v Scotland
Height: 1.78m
Weight: 109kg

PATRICIO NORIEGA

Position: Prop
Age: 27
Tests: 9 Australia, 22 Argentina
Test debut: 1993 (for Argentina) 1998
v France (for Australia)
Height: 1.85m
Weight: 124kg

RICHARD HARRY

Position: Prop
Age: 31
Tests: 30
Test debut: 1996 v Wales
Height: 1.84m
Weight: 120kg

DAN CROWLEY

Position: Prop
Age: 34
Tests: 38
Test debut: 1989 v British Lions
Height: 1.73m
Weight: 105kg

ROD MOORE

Position: Prop
Age: 27
Tests: 1
Test debut: 1999 v USA
Height: 1.86m
Weight: 118kg

GLENN PANOHO

Position: Prop
Age: 28
Tests: 8
Test debut: 1998 v South Africa
Height: 1.86m
Weight: 120kg

PHIL KEARNS

Position: Hooker
Age: 32
Tests: 67
Test debut: 1989 v New Zealand
Height: 1.83m
Weight: 108kg

WorldCup biographies

JEREMY PAUL
Position: Hooker
Age: 22
Tests: 14
Test debut: 1998 v Scotland
Height: 1.86m
Weight: 108kg

MICHAEL FOLEY
Position: Hooker
Age: 32
Tests: 29
Test debut: 1995 v Canada
Height: 1.81m
Weight: 106kg

ROD MACQUEEN
Position: Head coach
Age: 49

TIM LANE
Position: Assistant coach
Age: 40

JEFF MILLER
Position: Assistant coach
Age: 37

JOHN McKAY
Position: Team manager
Age: 41

ALEX EVANS
Position: Technical adviser
Age: 60

JOHN MUGGLETON
Position: Defence coach
Age: 40

STEVE NANCE
Position: Trainer
Age: 45

JOHN BEST
Position: Team doctor
Age: 37

GREG CRAIG
Position: Physiotherapist
Age: 44

CAMERON LILLICRAP
Position: Physiotherapist
Age: 36

SCOTT HARRISON
Position: Video analyst
Age: 26

BEN SPINDLER
Position: Gear steward
Age: 24

DAVID PEMBROKE
Position: Media officer
Age: 36

October 1
POOL D MATCH

WALES v ARGENTINA
at Millennium Stadium, Cardiff

WALES: Shane Howarth, Gareth Thomas, Mark Taylor, Scott Gibbs, Dafydd James, Neil Jenkins, Rob Howley (c), Scott Quinnell, Brett Sinkinson, Colin Charvis, Chris Wyatt, Craig Quinnell, David Young, Garin Jenkins, Peter Rogers.
Reserves: Jason Jones-Hughes, Stephen Jones, David Llewellyn, Michael Voyle, Ben Evans, Andrew Lewis, Jonathan Humphreys.

ARGENTINA: Manuel Contepomi, Octavio Bartolucci, Eduardo Simone, Lisandro Arbizu (c), Diego Albanese, Gonzalo Quesada, Augustin Pichot, Gonzalo Longo, Lucas Ostiglia, Santiago Phelan, Alejandro Allub, Igancio Fernandez Lobbe, Mauricio Reggiardo, Mario Ledesma, Roberto Grau.
Reserves: Gonzalo Camardon, Felipe Contepomi, Nicolas Fernandez Miranda, Raul Perez, Rolando Martin, Omar Hasan, Agustin Canalda.

WALES 23 (Colin Charvis, Mark Taylor tries; Neil Jenkins 2 conversions, 3 penalty goals) def **ARGENTINA 18** (Gonzalo Quesada 6 penalty goals).

World Cup
statistics

October 1
POOL C MATCH

FIJI v NAMIBIA
at Stade Meditarranee, Beziers

FIJI: Alfred Uluinayau, Fero Lasagavibau, Viliame Satala, Waisake Sototu, Imanueli Tikomaimakogai, Waisale Serevi, Jacob Rauluni, Alifereti Mocelutu, Setareki Tawake, Apinesa Naevo, Emori Katalau, Simon Raiwalui, Joeli Veityaki, Greg Smith (c), Daniel Rouse. *Reserves:* Mosese Rauluni, Nicky Little, Meli Nakauta, Kolinio Sewabu, Ifereimi Tawake, Isaia Rasila.

NAMIBIA: Leandre van Dyk, Dirk Farmer, Arthur Samuelson, Schalk van der Merwe, Deon Mouton, Johan Zaayman, Riaan Jantjies, Sean Furter, Jaco Olivier, Quin Hough (c), Pieter Steyn, Heino Senekal, Gerhard Opperman, Hugo Horn, Mario Jacobs. *Reserves:* Glovin van Wyk, Sarel Janse van Rensburg, Herman Lintvelt, Johannes Theron, Andries Blaauw, Eben Smith.

FIJI 67 (Fero Lasagavibau 2, Viliame Satala, Imanueli Tikomaimakogai, Emori Katalau, Ifereimi Tawake, Alefereti Mocelutu, Greg Smith, Jacob Rauluni tries; Waisale Serevi 8 conversions, 2 penalty goals) def **NAMIBIA 18** (Heino Senekal, Mario Jacobs tries; Leandre van Dyk conversion 2 penalty goals).

October 2
POOL C MATCH

FRANCE v CANADA
at Stade Mediterranee, Beziers

FRANCE: Ugo Mola, Xavier Garbajosa, Richard Dourthe,
Stephane Glas, Christophe Dominici, Thomas Castaignede,
Pierre Mignoni, Christophe Juillet, Olivier Magne, Marc Lievremont,
Fabien Pelous, Abdel Benazzi, Franck Tournaire, Raphael Ibanez (c),
Christian Califano. *Reserves:* Emile N'Tamack, Christophe Lamaison,
Stephane Castaignede, Lionel Mallier, Olivier Brouzet,
Cedric Soulette, Marc Dal Maso.

CANADA: Scott Stewart, Winston Stanley, David Lougheed,
Scott Bryan, Courtney Smith, Gareth Rees (c), Morgan Williams,
Al Charron, Dan Baugh, John Hutchinson, Michael James, John Tait,
Jon Thiel, Pat Dunkley, Rod Snow. *Reserves:* Kyle Nichols,
Bobby Ross, John Graf, Mike Schmid, Ryan Banks, Richard Bice,
Mark Cardinal.

FRANCE 33 (Richard Dourthe, Olivier Magne,
Thomas Castaignede, Emile N'Tamack tries; Richard Dourthe
2 conversions, 3 penalty goals) def **CANADA 20** (Morgan Williams
2 tries; Gareth Rees conversion, penalty goal, Bobby Ross
conversion, penalty goal).

October 2
POOL A MATCH

SPAIN v URUGUAY
at Netherdale, Galashiels

SPAIN: Miguel Angel Frechilla, Oriol Ripol, Alvar Encisco, Sebastian Loubsens, Rafael Bastide, Andrei Kovalenco, Jaime Alonso, Alberto Malo (c), Carlos Souto, Jose Diaz, Sergio Souto, Jose Miguel Villau, Jose Ignacio Zapatero, Fernando de la Calle, Jordi Camps. *Reserves:* Francisco Puertas, Aitor Etxeberria, Aratz Gallastegui, Alfonso Mata, Oskar Astarloa, Victor Torres, Diego Zarzosa.

URUGUAY: Alfonso Cardoso, Martin Ferres, Pedro Vecino, Martin Mendaro, Pablo Costabile, Diego Aguirre, Federico Sciarra, Diego Ormaechea (c), Martin Panizza, Nicholas Brignoni, Mario Lame, Juan Carlos Bado, Pablo Lemoine, Diego Lamelas, Rodrigo Sanchez. *Reserves:* Juan Menchaca, Fernando Sosa Diaz, Augustin Ponce de Leon, Nicholas Grille, Juan Alzueta, Guillermo Storace, Francisco de Los Santos.

URUGUAY 27 (Diego Ormaechea, Alfonso Cardoso, Juan Menchaca tries; penalty try, Diego Aguirre conversion, penalty goal, Federico Sciarra conversion) def **SPAIN 15** (Andrei Kovalenco 5 penalty goals).

October 2
POOL B MATCH

—➤

ENGLAND v ITALY
at Twickenham, London

ENGLAND: Matt Perry, Dan Luger, Will Greenwood,
Phil de Glanville, Austin Healey, Jonny Wilkinson, Matt Dawson,
Lawrence Dallaglio, Neil Back, Richard Hill, Danny Grewcock,
Martin Johnson (c), Phil Vickery, Richard Cockerill, Jason Leonard.
Reserves: Nick Beal, Jeremy Guscott, Paul Grayson, Martin Corry,
Graham Rowntree, Darren Garforth, Phil Greening.

ITALY: Matt Pini, Paolo Vacari, Christian Stoica, Luca Martin,
Nicholas Zisti, Diego Dominguez, Alessandro Troncon,
Orazio Arancio, Mauro Bergamasco, Massimo Giovanelli (c),
Mark Giacheri, Valter Cristofoletto, Franco Properzi-Curti,
Alessandro Moscardi, Federico Pucciarello.
Reserves: Nicola Mazzucato, Francesco Mazzariol, Giampiero Mazzi,
Andrea de Rossi, Carlo Checchinato, Andrea Castellani,
Andrea Moretti.

ENGLAND 67 (Matt Dawson, Richard Hill, Phil de Glanville,
Matt Perry, Jonny Wilkinson, Dan Luger, Neil Back, Martin Corry
tries; Wilkinson 6 conversions, 5 penalty goals) def **ITALY 7**
(Diego Dominguez try, conversion).

October 2
POOL E MATCH

—————

IRELAND v UNITED STATES
at Lansdowne Road, Dublin

IRELAND: Conor O'Shea, Justin Bishop, Brian O'Driscoll, Kevin Maggs, Matt Mostyn, David Humphreys, Tom Tierney, Dion O'Cuinneagain (c), Andy Ward, Trevor Brennan, Jeremy Davidson, Paddy Johns, Paul Wallace, Keith Wood, Peter Clohessy. *Reserves:* Jonathan Bell, Eric Ellwood, Brian O'Meara, Eric Miller, Malcolm O'Kelly, Justin Fitzpatrick, Ross Nesdale.

USA: Kurt Shuman, Vaea Anitoni, Juan Grobler, Tomasi Takau, Brian Hightower, Mark Williams, Kevin Dalzell, Dan Lyle (c), Richard Tardits, Dave Hodges, Alec Parker, Luke Gross, Ray Lehner, Tom Billups, George Sucher. *Reserves:* Mark Scharrenberg, David Niu, Jesse Coulson, Fafita Mo'unga, Shaun Paga, Joe Clayton, Kirk Khasigian.

IRELAND 53 (Keith Wood 4, Justin Bishop, Brian O'Driscoll tries; penalty try; David Humphreys 4 conversions, 2 penalty goals, Eric Ellwood 2 conversions) def **USA 8** (Kevin Dalzell try, penalty goal).

October 3
POOL D MATCH

SAMOA v JAPAN
at Racecourse Ground, Wrexham

SAMOA: Silao Leaega, Afato So'oala, To'o Vaega, Va'aiga Tuigamala, Brian Lima, Stephen Bachop, Stephen So'oialo, Pat Lam (c), Craig Glendinning, Junior Paramore, Lama Tone, Sene Ta'ala, Robbie Ale, Trevor Leota, Brendan Reidy.
Reserves: George Leaupepe, Earl Va'a, Jon Clarke, Semo Sititi, Opeta Palepoi, Michael Mika, Onehunga Esau.

JAPAN: Tsutomu Matsada, Daisuke Ohata, Andrew McCormick (c), Yukio Motoki, Terunori Masuho, Keiji Hirose, Graeme Bachop, Jamie Joseph, Greg Smith, Yasunori Watanabe, Naoya Okubo, Rob Gordon, Kohei Oguchi, Masahiro Kunda, Shin Hasegawa.
Reserves: Pat Tuidrake, Akira Yoshida, Waturu Murata, Takeomi Ito, Hiroyuki Tanuma, Toshikazu Nakamichi, Masaaki Sakata.

SAMOA 43 (Brian Lima 2, Afato So'oalo 2, Silao Leaega tries; Leaega 3 conversions, 4 penalty goals) def **JAPAN 9** (Keiji Hirose 3 penalty goals).

October 3
POOL B MATCH

NEW ZEALAND v TONGA
at Ashton Gate, Bristol

NEW ZEALAND: Jeff Wilson, Tana Umaga, Christian Cullen, Alama Ieremia, Jonah Lomu, Andrew Mehrtens, Justin Marshall, Taine Randell (c), Josh Kronfeld, Reuben Thorne, Robin Brooke, Norm Maxwell, Kees Meeuws, Anton Oliver, Carl Hoeft. *Reserves:* Daryl Gibson, Carlos Spencer, Byron Kelleher, Andrew Blowers, Royce Willis, Craig Dowd, Mark Hammett.

TONGA: Siua Taumalolo, Fepikou Tatafu, Tevita Tiueti, Semi Taupeaafe, Taunaholo Taufahema, Elisi Vunipola (c), Sililo Martens, Va'a Toloke, Sonatane Koloi, Vaohingano Fakatou, Benhur Kivalu, Isileli Fatani, Tevita Taumoepeau, Fe'ao Vunipola, Ta'u Fainga'anuku. *Reserves:* Sione Tuipulotu, Isileli Tapueluelu, Falamani Mafi, David Edwards, Matt Te Pou, Ngalu Taufo'ou, Latiume Maka.

NEW ZEALAND 45 (Jonah Lomu 2, Josh Kronfeld, Norm Maxwell, Byron Kelleher tries; Andrew Mehrtens 4 conversions, 4 penalty goals) def **TONGA 9** (Siua Taumalolo 3 penalty goals).

October 3
POOL A MATCH

SCOTLAND v SOUTH AFRICA
at Murrayfield, Edinburgh

SCOTLAND: Glenn Metcalfe, Cameron Murray, Alan Tait,
John Leslie, Kenny Logan, Gregor Townsend, Gary Armstrong (c),
Gordon Simpson, Budge Pountney, Martin Leslie, Stuart Grimes,
Scott Murray, George Graham, Gordon Bulloch, Tom Smith.
Reserves: Jamie Mayer, Duncan Hodge, Bryan Redpath, Peter Walton,
Doddie Weir, David Hilton, Robert Russell.

SOUTH AFRICA: Percy Montgomery, Deon Kayser,
Robbie Fleck, Brendan Venter, Pieter Rossouw, Jannie de Beer,
Joost van der Westhuizen (c), Bob Skinstad, Andre Venter,
Johan Erasmus, Mark Andrews, Albert van den Berg, Cobus Visagie,
Naka Drotske, Os du Randt. *Reserves:* Chris Rossouw, Ollie le Roux,
Krynauw Otto, Andre Vos, Werner Swanepoel, Pieter Muller,
Breyton Paulse.

SOUTH AFRICA 46 (Brendan Venter, Robbie Fleck,
Ollie le Roux, Deon Kayser, Andre Venter, Joost van der Westhuizen
tries; Jannie de Beer 5 conversions, 2 penalty goals)
def **SCOTLAND 29** (Martin Leslie, Alan Tait tries; Kenny Logan
2 conversions, 4 penalty goals, Gregor Townsend dropped goal).

October 3
POOL MATCH

AUSTRALIA v ROMANIA
at Ravenhill Park, Belfast

AUSTRALIA: Matthew Burke, Ben Tune, Daniel Herbert, Tim Horan, Jason Little, Rod Kafer, George Gregan, Toutai Kefu, David Wilson, Owen Finegan, John Eales (c), David Giffin, Andrew Blades, Phil Kearns, Richard Harry. *Reserves:* Joe Roff, Nathan Grey, Chris Whitaker, Tiaan Strauss, Mark Connors, Dan Crowley, Jeremy Paul.

ROMANIA: Mihai Vioreanu, Cristian Sauan, Gabriel Brezoianu, Romeo Gontineac (c), Gheorghe Solomie, Lucien Vusec, Petre Mitu, Catalin Draguceanu, Erdinci Septar, Alin Petrache, Ovidiu Slusariuc, Tiberiu Brinza, Laurentiu Rotaru, Petru Balan, Constantin Stan. *Reserves:* Marius Iacob, Ionut Tofan, Radu Fugigi, Florin Corodeanu, Daniel Chiriac, Nicolae Dima, Razvan Mavrodin.

AUSTRALIA 57 (Toutai Kefu 3, Joe Roff 2, Tim Horan, Jason Little, Matthew Burke, Jeremy Paul tries; Burke 5 conversions, John Eales conversion) def **ROMANIA 9** (Petre Mitu 3 penalty goals).
Halftime: Australia 24–3.

October 8
POOL A MATCH

➤

SCOTLAND v URUGUAY
at Murrayfield, Edinburgh

SCOTLAND: Glenn Metcalfe, Cameron Murray, Alan Tait, Jamie Mayer, Kenny Logan, Gregor Townsend, Gary Armstrong (c), Gordon Simpson, Budge Pountney, Martin Leslie, Stuart Grimes, Scott Murray, George Graham, Gordon Bulloch, Tom Smith. *Reserves:* Shaun Longstaff, Duncan Hodge, Bryan Redpath, Peter Walton, Doddie Weir, David Hilton, Robert Russell.

URUGUAY: Alfonso Cardoso, Juan Menchaca,, Pedro Vecino, Martin Mendaro, Pablo Costabile, Diego Aguirre, Federico Sciarra, Diego Ormaechea (c), Martin Panizza, Nicholas Brignoni, Mario Lame, Juan Carlos Bado, Pablo Lemoine, Diego Lamelas, Rodrigo Sanchez. *Reserves:* Jose Viana, Fernando Sosa Diaz, Augustin Ponce de Leon, Nicholas Grille, Eduardo Berutti, Guillermo Storace, Francisco de Los Santos.

SCOTLAND 43 (Martin Leslie, Gary Armstrong, Gordon Simpson, Glenn Metcalfe, Gregor Townsend, Robert Russell tries; Kenny Logan 5 conversions, penalty goal) def **URUGUAY 12** (Diego Aguirre 3 penalty goals, Federico Sciarra penalty goal).

October 8
POOL C MATCH

___

FRANCE v NAMIBIA
at Stade Lescure, Bordeaux

FRANCE: Ugo Mola, Philippe Bernat-Salles, Richard Dourthe, Stephane Glas, Emile N'Tamack, Christophe Lamaison, Pierre Mignoni, Thomas Lievremont, Olivier Magne, Marc Lievremont, Fabien Pelous, Olivier Brouzet, Franck Tournaire, Raphael Ibanez (c), Christian Califano. *Reserves:* Cedric Desbrosse, Xavier Garbajosa, Stephane Castaignede, Arnaud Costes, Abdel Benazzi, Cedric Soulette, Marc Dal Maso.

NAMIBIA: Glovin van Wyk, Leandre van Dyk, Arthur Samuelson, Schalk van der Merwe, Deon Mouton, Johan Zaayman, Riaan Jantjies, Sean Furter, Mathys van Rooyen, Quin Hough (c), Pieter Steyn, Heino Senekal, Gerhard Opperman, Hugo Horn, Mario Jacobs. *Reserves:* Rock Loubser, Lukas Holtzhausen, Sarel Janse van Rensburg, Herman Lintvelt, Johannes Theron, Andries Blaauw, Eben Smith.

FRANCE 47 (Ugo Mola 3, Pierre Mignoni, Philippe Bernat-Salles, Emile N'Tamack tries; Richard Dourthe 4 conversions, 3 penalty goals) def **NAMIBIA 13** (Arthur Samuelson try; Leandre van Dyk conversion, 2 penalty goals).

October 9
POOL C MATCH

FIJI v CANADA
at Stade Lescure, Bordeaux

FIJI: Alfred Uluinayau, Fero Lasagavibau, Viliame Satala, Waisake Sototu, Marika Vunibaka, Nicky Little, Jacob Rauluni, Alifereti Mocelutu, Setareki Tawake, Ilie Tabua, Emori Katalau, Simon Raiwalui, Joeli Veityaki, Greg Smith, Daniel Rouse. *Reserves:* Mosese Rauluni, Waisale Serevi, Meli Nakauta, Kolinio Sewabu, Apenisa Naevo, Niki Qoro, Isaia Rasila.

CANADA: Scott Stewart, Winston Stanley, Kyle Nichols, Scott Bryan, David Lougheed, Gareth Rees (c), Morgan Williams, Mike Schmid, Dan Baugh, Al Charron, Michael James, John Tait, Jon Thiel, Pat Dunkley, Rod Snow. *Reserves:* Joe Pagano, Bobby Ross, John Graf, Ryan Banks, John Hutchinson, Duane Major, Mark Cardinal.

FIJI 38 (Viliame Satala 2, Marika Vunibaka tries; penalty try; Nicky Litle 3 conversions, 3 penalty goals, dropped goal) def **CANADA 22** (Mike James try; Gareth Rees conversion, 4 penalty goals, dropped goal).

October 9
POOL D MATCH

WALES v JAPAN
at Millennium Stadium, Cardiff

WALES: Shane Howarth, Jason Jones-Hughes, Mark Taylor, Scott Gibbs, Allan Bateman, Neil Jenkins, Rob Howley (c), Geraint Lewis, Brett Sinkinson, Martyn Williams, Michael Voyle, Craig Quinnell, David Young, Garin Jenkins, Peter Rogers. *Reserves:* Stephen Jones, Gareth Thomas, David Llewellyn, Chris Wyatt, Ben Evans, Andrew Lewis, Jonathan Humphreys.

JAPAN: Tsuyoshi Hirao, Daisuke Ohata, Andrew McCormick (c), Yukio Motoki, Pat Tuidrake, Keiji Hirose, Graeme Bachop, Jamie Joseph, Greg Smith, Naoya Okubo, Hiroyuki Tanuma, Rob Gordon, Naoto Nakamura, Masahiro Kunda, Shin Hasegawa. *Reserves:* Terunori Masuho, Akira Yoshida, Waturu Murata, Takeomi Ito, Yoshihiko Sakuraba, Toshikazu Nakamichi, Masaaki Sakata.

WALES 64 (Mark Taylor 2, Allan Bateman, Rob Howley, Scott Gibbs, Shane Howarth, David Llewellyn, Gareth Thomas tries; penalty try; Neil Jenkins 8 conversions, penalty goal) def **JAPAN 15** (Daisuke Ohata, Pat Tuidrake tries; Keiji Hirose conversion, penalty goal).

October 9
POOL B MATCH

➤

ENGLAND v NEW ZEALAND
at Twickenham, London

ENGLAND: Matt Perry, Dan Luger, Phil de Glanville, Jeremy Guscott, Austin Healey, Jonny Wilkinson, Matt Dawson, Lawrence Dallaglio, Neil Back, Richard Hill, Danny Grewcock, Martin Johnson (c), Phil Vickery, Richard Cockerill, Jason Leonard. *Reserves:* Nick Beal, Will Greenwood, Paul Grayson, Martin Corry, Graham Rowntree, Darren Garforth, Phil Greening.

NEW ZEALAND: Jeff Wilson, Tana Umaga, Christian Cullen, Alama Ieremia, Jonah Lomu, Andrew Mehrtens, Justin Marshall, Taine Randell (c), Josh Kronfeld, Reuben Thorne, Robin Brooke, Norm Maxwell, Craig Dowd, Anton Oliver, Carl Hoeft. *Reserves:* Daryl Gibson, Tony Brown, Byron Kelleher, Andrew Blowers, Royce Willis, Greg Feek, Mark Hammett.

NEW ZEALAND 30 (Jeff Wilson, Jonah Lomu, Byron Kelleher tries; Andrew Mehrtens 3 conversions, 3 penalty goals) def **ENGLAND 16** (Phil de Glanville try; Jonny Wilkinson conversion, 3 penalty goals).

October 9
POOL E MATCH

—•

UNITED STATES v ROMANIA
at Lansdowne Road, Dublin

USA: Kurt Shuman, Vaea Anitoni, Juan Grobler, Mark Scharrenberg, Brian Hightower, David Niu, Kevin Dalzell (c), Rob Lumkong, Fafita Mo'unga, Dan Lyle, Alec Parker, Luke Gross, Ray Lehner, Tom Billups, George Sucher. *Reserves:* Joe Clayton, Tomasi Takau, David Stroble, Shaun Paga, Dave Hodges, Richard Tardits, Kirk Khasigian.

ROMANIA: Mihai Vioreanu, Cristian Sauan, Gabriel Brezoianu, Romeo Gontineac, Gheorghe Solomie, Lucien Vusec, Petre Mitu, Catalin Draguceanu, Erdinci Septar, Alin Petrache, Tudor Constantin (c), Tiberiu Brinza, Constantin Stan, Petru Balan, Razvan Mavrodin. *Reserves:* Marius Iacob, Ionut Tofan, Radu Fugigi, Florin Corodeanu, Daniel Chiriac, Nicolae Dima, Laurentin Rotaru.

ROMANIA 27 (Gheorghe Solomie 2, Tiberiu Brinza, Adrian Petrache tries; Petre Mitu 2 conversions, penalty goal) def **USA 25** (Dan Lyle, Brian Hightower, Kurt Shuman tries; Kevin Dalzell 2 conversions, 2 penalty goals).

October 10
POOL D MATCH

SAMOA v ARGENTINA
at Stradey Park, Llanelli

SAMOA: Silao Leaega, Afato So'oala, George Leaupepe,
Va'aiga Tuigamala, Brian Lima, Stephen Bachop, Stephen So'oialo,
Pat Lam (c), Junior Paramore, Sene Ta'ala, Lama Tone, Opeta Palepoi,
Robbie Ale, Trevor Leota, Brendan Reidy. *Reserves:* To'o Vaega,
Tanner Vili, Jon Clarke, Kalolo Toleafoa, Michael Mika,
Onehunga Esau.

ARGENTINA: Manuel Contepomi, Octavio Bartolucci,
Eduardo Simone, Lisandro Arbizu (c), Diego Albanese,
Gonzalo Quesada, Augustin Pichot, Gonzalo Longo,
Rolando Martin, Santiago Phelan, Alejandro Allub,
Igancio Fernandez Lobbe, Omar Hasan. Mario Ledesma,
Mauricio Reggiardo. *Reserves:* Gonzalo Camardon,
Felipe Contepomi, Nicolas Fernandez Miranda, Miguel Ruiz,
Lucas Ostiglia, Martin Scelzo, Agustin Canalda.

ARGENTINA 32 (Alejandro Allub try; Gonzalo Quesada 8 penalty
goals, dropped goal) def **SAMOA 16** (Junior Paramore try;
Silao Leaega conversion, 3 penalty goals).

October 10
POOL MATCH

AUSTRALIA v IRELAND
at Lansdowne Road, Dublin

AUSTRALIA: Matthew Burke, Ben Tune, Daniel Herbert, Tim Horan, Joe Roff, Stephen Larkham, George Gregan, Toutai Kefu, David Wilson, Mark Connors, John Eales (c), David Giffin, Andrew Blades, Phil Kearns, Richard Harry. *Reserves:* Jason Little, Nathan Grey, Chris Whitaker, Tiaan Strauss, Owen Finegan, Dan Crowley, Jeremy Paul.

IRELAND: Conor O'Shea, Justin Bishop, Brian O'Driscoll, Kevin Maggs, Matt Mostyn, David Humphreys, Tom Tierney, Dion O'Cuinneagain (c), Andy Ward, Trevor Brennan, Malcolm O'Kelly, Paddy Johns, Paul Wallace, Keith Wood, Justin Fitzpatrick. *Reserves:* Jonathon Bell, Eric Elwood, Brian O'Meara, Eric Miller, Robert Casey, Peter Clohessy, Ross Nesdale.

AUSTRALIA 23 (Tim Horan, Ben Tune tries; Matthew Burke 2 conversions, 2 penalty goals, John Eales penalty goal) def **IRELAND 3** (David Humphreys penalty goal). *Halftime:* Australia 6–0.

October 10
POOL A MATCH

SOUTH AFRICA v SPAIN
at Murrayfield, Edinburgh

SOUTH AFRICA: Breyton Paulse, Kaya Molotana, Wayne Julies, Pieter Muller, Stefan Terblanche, Jannie de Beer, Werner Swanepoel, Andre Vos (c), Anton Leonard, Ruben Kruger, Fritz van Heerden, Krynauw Otto, Adrian Garvey, Chris Rossouw, Ollie le Rouz. *Reserves:* Deon Kayser, Percy Montgomery, Joost van der Westhuizen, Bob Skinstad, Mark Andrewqs, Os du Randt, Naka Drotske.

SPAIN: Francisco Puertas, Jose Ignacio Inchausti, Alberto Socias, Fernando Diez, Migual Angel Frechilla, Aitor Etxeberria, Aratz vGallastegui, Alberto Malo, Carlos Souto, Jose Diaz, Oskar Astarloa, Jose Miguel Villau, Jose Ignacio Zapatero, Diego Zarzosa, Jordi Camps. *Reserves:* Ferran Velasco, Antonio Socias, Jaime Alonso, Alfonso Mata, Luis Javier Martinez, Victor Torres, Fernando de la Calle.

SOUTH AFRICA 47 (Andre Vos 2, Werner Swanepoel, Anton Leonard, Pieter Muller, Bob Skinstad tries; Jannie de Beer 6 conversions) def **SPAIN 3** (Ferran Velazco penalty goal).

October 10
POOL B MATCH

———➤

ITALY v TONGA
at Welford Road, Leicester

ITALY: Matt Pini, Paolo Vacari, Christian Stoica,
Aleesandro Ceppolino, Fabio Roselli, Diego Dominguez,
Alessandro Troncon, Carlo Caione, Stefano Saviozzi,
Massimo Giovanelli (c), Mark Giacheri, Carlo Chechhinato,
Andrea Castellani, Alessandro Moscardi, Alesandro Moreno.
Reserves: Nicola Mazzucato, Francesco Mazzariol, Giampiero Mazzi,
Orazio Arancio, Valter Cristofoletto, Franco Properzi-Curti,
Andrea Moretti.

TONGA: Sateki Tuipulotu, Taunaholo Taufahema, Semi Taupeaafe,
Elisi Vunipola (c), Epeli Taione, Brian Woolley, Sililo Martens,
Katilimoni Tuipulotu, Sonatane Koloi, David Edwards,
Benhur Kivalu, Falamani Mafi, Ngalu Taufo'ou, Latiume Maka,
Ta'u Fainga'anuku. *Reserves:* Fifita Faletau, Tevita Tiueti,
Isileli Tapueluelu, Matt Te Pou, Isileli Fatani, Damien Penisini,
Sione Tuipulotu.

TONGA 28 (Taunaholo Taufahema, Sateki Tuipulotu, Isi Fatani
tries; Sateki Tuipulotu 2 conversions, 2 penalty goals, dropped goal)
def **ITALY 25** (Alessandro Moscardi try; Diego Dominguez
conversion, 6 penalty goals).

October 14
POOL B MATCH

NEW ZEALAND v ITALY
at McAlpine Stadium, Huddersfield

NEW ZEALAND: Jeff Wilson, Glen Osborne, Pita Alatini, Daryl Gibson, Jonah Lomu, Tony Brown, Byron Kelleher, Taine Randell (c), Andrew Blowers, Dylan Mika, Royce Willis, Ian Jones, Craig Dowd, Mark Hammett, Greg Feek.
Reserves: Christian Cullen, Andrew Mehrtens, Rhys Duggan, Scott Robertson, Robin Brooke, Carl Hoeft, Anton Oliver.

ITALY: Matt Pini, Paolo Vacari, Christian Stoica, Aleesandro Ceppolino, Nicholas Zisti, Diego Dominguez, Alessandro Troncon, Carlo Caione, Stefano Saviozzi, Massimo Giovanelli (c), Mark Giacheri, Carlo Chechhinato, Andrea Castellani, Andrea Moretti, Alesandro Moreno.
Reserves: Nicola Mazzucato, Francesco Mazzariol, Giampiero Mazzi, Orazio Arancio, Valter Cristofoletto, Franco Properzi-Curti, Alessandro Moscardi.

NEW ZEALAND 101 (Jeff Wilson 3, Jonah Lomu 2, Glen Osborne 2, Tony Brown, Dylan Mika, Taine Randell, Daryl Gibson, Scott Robertson, Christian Cullen, Mark Hammett tries; Tony Brown 11 conversions, 3 penalty goals; def **ITALY 3** (Diego Dominguez penalty goal).

October 14
POOL D MATCH

WALES v SAMOA
at Millennium Stadium, Cardiff

WALES: Shane Howarth, Gareth Thomas, Mark Taylor, Scott Gibbs, Dafydd James, Neil Jenkins, Rob Howley (c), Scott Quinnell, Brett Sinkinson, Martyn Williams, Chris Wyatt, Gareth Llewellyn, David Young, Garin Jenkins, Peter Rogers.
Reserves: Jason Jones-Hughes, Stephen Jones, David Llewellyn, Geraint Lewis, Michael Voyle, Ben Evans, Andrew Lewis.

SAMOA: Silao Leaega, Brian Lime, To'o Vaega, George Leaupepe, Va'aiga Tuigamala, Stephen Bachop, Stephen So'oialo, Craig Glendinning, Isaac Feaunati, Junior Paramore, Lama Tone, Lio Falaniko, Robbie Ale, Trevor Leota, Brendan Reidy.
Reserves: Terry Fanolua, Earl Va'a, Jon Clarke, Semo Sititi, Sene Ta'ala, Michael Mika, Onehunga Esau.

SAMOA 38 (Stephen Bachop 2, Lio Falaniko, Pat Lam, Silao Leaega tries; Leaega 5 conversions, penalty goal)
def **WALES 31** (Gareth Thomas try; 2 penalty tries; Neil Jenkins 2 conversions, 4 penalty goals).

October 14
POOL MATCH

AUSTRALIA v USA
at Thomond Park, Limerick

AUSTRALIA: Chris Latham Scott Staniforth, Jason Little (c), Nathan Grey, Matthew Burke, Stephen Larkham, Chris Whitaker, Jim Williams, Tiaan Strauss, Owen Finegan, Mark Connors, Tom Bowman, Rod Moore, Michael Foley, Dan Crowley. *Reserves:* Joe Roff, Rod Kafer, George Gregan, Matt Cockbain, David Giffin, Richard Harry, Jeremy Paul.

USA: Kurt Shuman, Vaea Anitoni, Juan Grobler, Mark Scharrenberg, Brian Hightower, David Niu, Kevin Dalzell (c), Rob Lumkong, Fifita Mo'unga, Dave Hodges, Alec Parker, Luke Gross, George Sucher, Tim Billups, Joe Clayton. *Reserves:* Tomasi Takau, Alatini Saulala, Jesse Coulson, Shaun aga, Eric Reed, Marc L'Huillier, Kirk Khasigian.

AUSTRALIA 55 (Scott Staniforth 2, Chris Latham, Matthew Burke, Stephen Larkham, Tiaan Strauss, Michael Foley, Chris Whitaker tries; Burke 5 conversions, penalty goal, Joe Roff conversion) def **USA 19** (Juan Grobler try, Kevin Dalzell conversion, 3 penalty goals, David Niu field goal).
Halftime: Australia 22–10.

October 14
POOL C MATCH

CANADA v NAMIBIA
at Stade Municipal, Toulouse

CANADA: Scott Stewart, Winston Stanley, David Lougheed, Kyle Nichols, Joe Pagano, Gareth Rees (c), Morgan Williams, Al Charron, Dan Baugh, John Hutchinson, Michael James, John Tait, Jon Thiel, Mark Cardinal, Rod Snow. *Reserves:* Scott Bryan, Bobby Ross, John Graf, Mike Schmid, Ryan Banks, Duane Major, Pat Dunkley.

NAMIBIA: Glovin van Wyk, Leandre van Dyk, Francois van Rensburg, Schalk van der Merwe, Arthur Samuelson, Johan Zaayman, Riaan Jantjies, Sean Furter, Mathys van Rooyen, Quin Hough (c), Pieter Steyn, Heino Senekal, Gerhard Opperman, Hugo Horn, Eben Smith. *Reserves:* Dirk Farmer, Lukas Holtzhausen, Ronaldo Pedro, Herman Lintvelt, Johannes Theron, Andries Blaauw, Frans Fisch.

CANADA 72 (Kyle Nichols 2, Winston Stanley 2, Rod Snow 2, Morgan Williams, Al Charron, Bobby Ross tries; Gareth Rees 9 conversions, 3 penalty goals) def **NAMIBIA 11** (Quin Hough try, Leandre van Dyk 2 penalty goals).

October 15
POOL B MATCH

➤

ENGLAND v TONGA
at Twickenham, London

ENGLAND: Matt Perry, Dan Luger, Will Greenwood,
Jeremy Guscott, Austin Healey, Paul Grayson, Matt Dawson,
Lawrence Dallaglio, Richard Hill, Joe Worsley, Garath Archer,
Martin Johnson (c), Phil Vickery, Phil Greening, Graham Rowntree.
Reserves: Nick Beal, Mike Catt, Jonny Wilkinson, Neil Back,
Danny Grewcock, Jason Leonard, Richard Cockerill.

TONGA: Sateki Tuipulotu, Tevita Tiueti, Fepikou Tatafu,
Salesi Finau, Semi Taupeaafe, Elisi Vunipola (c), Sililo Martens,
Katilimoni Tuipulotu, Sonatane Koloi, David Edwards,
Benhur Kivalu, Isileli Fatani, Tevita Taumoepeau, Fe'ao Vunipola,
Ngalu Taufo'ou. *Reserves:* Sione Tuipulotu, Isileli Taupueluelu,
Epeli Taione, Falamani Mafi, Va'a Toloke, Ta'u Fa'inga'anuku,
Latiume Maka.

ENGLAND 101 (Jeremy Guscott 2, Phil Greening 2, Dan Luger 2,
Will Greenwood 2, Austin Healey 2, Matt Dawson, Matt Perry,
Richrd Hill tries; Paul Grayson 12 conversions, 4 penalty goals)
def **TONGA 10** (Tevita Tiueti try, Sateki Tuipulotu conversion,
penalty goal).

October 15
POOL A MATCH

SOUTH AFRICA v URUGUAY
at Hampden Park, Glasgow

SOUTH AFRICA: Percy Montgomery, Deon Kayser, Robbie Fleck, Brendan Venter, Pieter Rossouw, Jannie de Beer, Joost van der Westhuizen (c), Bob Skinstad, Andre Venter, Johan Erasmus, Mark Andrews, Krynauw Otto, Cobus Visagie, Naka Drotske, Os du Randt. *Reserves:* Stefan Terblanche, Pieter Muller, Werner Swanepoel, Andre Vos, Albert van den Berg, Ollie le Roux, Chris Rossouw.

URUGUAY: Alfonso Cardoso, Juan Menchaca,, Pedro Vecino, Fernando Paullier, Pablo Costabile, Diego Aguirre, Fernando Sosa Diaz, Diego Ormaechea (c), Martin Panizza, Nicholas Grille, Mario Lame, Juan Carlos Bado, Pablo Lemoine, Diego Lamelas, Rodrigo Sanchez. *Reserves:* Jose Viana, Sebastian Aguirre, Nicholas Brignone, Eduardo Berutti, Juan Alzueta, Guillermo Storace, Francisco de Los Santos.

SOUTH AFRICA 39 (Albert van den Berg 2, Robbie Fleck, Joost van der Westhuizen, Deon Kayser tries; Jannie de Beer 4 conversions, 2 penalty goals) def **URUGUAY 3** (Diego Aguirre penalty goal).

October 15
POOL E MATCH

IRELAND v ROMANIA
at Lansdowne Road, Dublin

IRELAND: Conor O'Shea, James Topping, Jonathan Bell, Michael Mullins, Matt Mostyn, Eric Ellwood, Tom Tierney, Dion O'Cuinneagain (c), Kieron Dawson, Andy Ward, Malcolm O'Kelly, Paddy Johns, Paul Wallace, Ross Nesdale, Justin Fitzpatrick. *Reserves:* Gordon D'Arcy, Brian O'Driscoll, Brian O'Meara, Alan Quinlan, Jeremy Davidson, Angus McKeen, Keith Wood.

ROMANIA: Mihai Vioreanu, Cristian Sauan, Gabriel Brezoianu, Romeo Gontineac, Gheorghe Solomie, Lucien Vusec, Petre Mitu, Catalin Draguceanu, Erdinci Septar, Alin Petrache, Tiberiu Brinza, Tudor Constantin (c), Constantin Stan, Petru Balan, Razvan Mazrodin. *Reserves:* Marius Iacob, Ionut Tofan, Radu Fugigi, Florin Corodeanu, Daniel Chiriac, Nicolae Dima, Laurentin Rotaru.

IRELAND 44 (Conor O'Shea 2, Dion O'Cuinneagain, Tom Tierney, Andy Ward tries; Eric Ellwood 5 conversions, 2 penalty goals, Brian O'Driscoll dropped goal) def **ROMANIA 14** (Cristian Sauan try, Petre Mitu 3 penalty goals).

October 16
POOL C MATCH

FRANCE v FIJI
at Stade Municipal, Toulouse

FRANCE: Ugo Mola, Philippe Bernat-Salles, Richard Dourthe, Emile N'Tamack, Christophe Dominici, Christophe Lamaison, Stephane Castaignede, Christophe Juillet, Olivier Magne, Marc Lievremont, Fabien Pelous, Abdel Benazzi, Franck Tournaire, Raphael Ibanez (c), Christian Califano. *Reserves:* Cedric Desbrosse, Xavier Garbajosa, Fabien Galthie, Arnaud Costes, Olivier Brouzet, Pieter de Villiers, Marc Dal Maso.

FIJI: Alfred Uluinayau, Fero Lasagavibau, Viliame Satala, Waisake Sototu, Manasa Bari, Nicky Little, Jacob Rauluni, Alifereti Mocelutu, Setareki Tawake, Ilie Tabua, Emori Katalau, Simon Raiwalui, Joeli Veityaki, Greg Smith, Daniel Rouse. *Reserves:* Mosese Rauluni, Waisale Serevi, Meli Nakauta, Kolinio Sewabu, Ifereimi Tawake, Epeli Naituivau, Isaia Rasila.

FRANCE 28 (Christophe Juillet, Christophe Dominici tries; penalty try; Richard Dourthe 2 convrsions, 2 penalty goals, Christophe Lamaison penalty goal) def **FIJI 19** (Alfred Uluinayau try, Nicky Little conversion, 4 penalty goals).

October 16
POOL A MATCH

———➤

SCOTLAND v SPAIN
at Murrayfield, Edinburgh

SCOTLAND: Chris Paterson, Cameron Murray, Jamie Mayer, James McLaren, Shaun Longstaff, Duncan Hodge, Bryan Redpath (c), Stuart Reid, Cameron Mather, Peter Walton, Andrew Reed, Doddie Weir, Paul Burnell, Robert Russell, David Hilton. *Reserves:* Glenn Metcalfe, Gregor Townsend, Iain Fairley, Martin Leslie, Stuart Grimes, George Graham, Gordon Bulloch.

SPAIN: Francisco Puertas, Jose Ignacio Inchausti, Alvar Encisco (c), Sebastian Loubsens, Miguel Angel Frechilla, Andrei Kovalenco, Aratz Gallastegui, Alfonso Mata, Carlos Souto, Jose Diaz, Oskar Astarloa, Jose Miguel Villau, Jose Ignacio Zapatero, Diego Zarzosa, Victor Torres. *Reserves:* Ferran Velasco, Alberto Socias, Jaime Alonso, Agustin Malet, Steve Yiuneau, Luis Javier Martinez, Fernando de la Calle.

SCOTLAND 48 (Cameron Mather 2, Shaun Longstaff, James McLaren, Cameron Murray, Duncan Hodge tries; penalty try; Hodge 5 conversions, penalty goal) def **SPAIN 0**.

October 16
POOL D MATCH

——————

ARGENTINA v JAPAN
at Millennium Stadium, Cardiff

ARGENTINA: Ignacio Corletto, Gonzalo Camardon,
Eduardo Simone, Lisandro Arbizu (c), Diego Albanese,
Gonzalo Quesada, Augustin Pichot, Ignacio Fernando Lobbe,
Rolando Martin, Santiago Phelan, Alejandro Allub, Pedro Sporleder,
Omar Hasan. Mario Ledesma, Mauricio Reggiardo.
Reserves: Jose Orengo, Felipe Contepomi,
Nicolas Fernandez Miranda, Miguel Ruiz, Lucas Ostiglia,
Martin Scelzo, Agustin Canalda.

JAPAN: Tsutomu Matsuda, Daisuke Ohata,
Andrew McCormick (c), Yukio Motoki, Pat Tuidrake, Keiji Hirose,
Graeme Bachop, Jamie Joseph, Greg Smith, Naoya Okubo,
Hiroyuki Tanuma, Rob Gordon, Koehi Oguchi, Masahiro Kunda,
Toshikazu Nakamichi. *Reserves:* Terunori Masuho, Takeomi Ito,
Waturu Murata, Yoshihiko Sakuraba, Naoto Nakamura,
Shin Hasegawa, Masaaki Sakata.

ARGENTINA 33 (Augustin Pichot, Diego Albanese tries;
Felipe Contepomi conversion, Gonzalo Quesada 7 penalty goals)
def **JAPAN 12** (Keiji Hirose 4 penalty goals).

October 20
QUARTER FINAL PLAYOFF

ENGLAND v FIJI
at Twickenham, London

ENGLAND: Matt Perry, Dan Luger, Will Greenwood, Mike Catt, Nick Beal, Jonny Wilkinson, Austin Healey, Lawrence Dallaglio, Neil Back, Joe Worsley, Garath Archer, Martin Johnson (c), Darren Garforth, Phil Greening, Jason Leonard.
Reserves: Phil de Glanville, Paul Grayson, Matt Dawson, Richard Hill, Tim Rodber, Graham Rowntree, Richard Cockerill.

FIJI: Alfred Uluinayau, Marika Vunibaka, Viliame Satala, Meli Nakauta, Imanueli Tikomaimakogai, Waisale Serevi, Mosese Rauluni, Ifereimi Tawake, Kolinio Sewabu, Emori Katalau, Simon Raiwalui, Joeli Veityaki, Greg Smith, Daniel Rouse.
Reserves: Jacob Rauluni, Nicky Little, Waisake Sotutu, Inoke Male, Ratu Doviverata, Epeli Naituivau, Isaia Rasila.

ENGLAND 45 (Dan Luger, Neil Back, Nick Beal, Phil Greening tries; Jonny Wilkinson conversion, 7 penalty goals, Matt Dawson conversion) def **FIJI 24** (Viliame Satala, Imanueli Tikomaimakogai, Meli Nakauta tries; Nicky Little 3 conversions, Waisale Serevi penalty goal).

October 20
QUARTER FINAL PLAYOFF

SCOTLAND v SAMOA
at Murrayfield, Edinburgh

SCOTLAND: Glenn Metcalfe, Cameron Murray, Jamie Mayer, James McLaren, Kenny Logan, Gregor Townsend, Gary Armstrong (c), Gordon Simpson, Budge Pountney, Martin Leslie, Doddie Weir, Scott Murray, George Graham, Gordon Bulloch, Tom Smith. *Reserves:* Alan Tait, Duncan Hodge, Bryan Redpath, Cameron Mather, Stuart Grimes, Paul Burnell, Robert Russell.

SAMOA: Silao Leaega, Brian Lime, To'o Vaega, Terry Fanolua, Va'aiga Tuigamala, Stephen Bachop, Stephen So'oialo, Pat Lam (c), Craig Glendinning, Semo Sititi, Lama Tone, Lio Falaniko, Samuela Asi, Trevor Leota, Brendan Reidy. *Reserves:* Filipo Toala, Earl Va'a, Jon Clarke, Isaac Feaunati, Sene Ta'ala, Robbie Ale, Onehunga Esau.

SCOTLAND 35 (Martin Leslie, Cameron Murray tries; penalty try; Kenny Logan conversion, 5 penalty goals, Gregor Townsend dropped goal) def **SAMOA 20** (Semo Sititi, Brian Lima tries; Silao Leaega 2 conversions, 2 penalty goals).

October 20
QUARTER FINAL PLAYOFF

IRELAND v ARGENTINA
at Stade Felix Ballaert, Lens

IRELAND: Conor O'Shea, Justin Bishop, Brian O'Driscoll, Kevin Maggs, Matt Mostyn, David Humphreys, Tom Tierney, Dion O'Cuinneagain (c), Kieron Dawson, Andy Ward, Malcolm O'Kelly, Jeremy Davidson, Paul Wallace, Keith Wood, Reggie Corrigan. *Reserves:* Jonathon Bell, Eric Elwood, Brian O'Meara, Eric Miller, Robert Casey, Justin Fitzpatrick, Ross Nesdale.

ARGENTINA: Ignacio Corletto, Gonzalo Camardon, Eduardo Simone, Lisandro Arbizu (c), Diego Albanese, Gonzalo Quesada, Augustin Pichot, Gonzalo Longo, Rolando Martin, Santiago Phelan, Alejandro Allub, Ignacio Fernandez Lobbe, Omar Hasan. Mario Ledesma, Mauricio Reggiardo. *Reserves:* Manuel Contepomi, Felipe Contepomi, Nicolas Fernandez Miranda, Miguel Ruiz, Lucas Ostiglia, Martin Scelzo, Agustin Canalda.

ARGENTINA 28 (Diego Albanese try, Gonzalo Quesada conversion, 7 penalty goals) def **IRELAND 24** (David Humphreys 7 penalty goals, dropped goal).

October 23
QUARTER FINAL

AUSTRALIA v WALES
at Millennium Stadium, Cardiff

AUSTRALIA: Matthew Burke, Ben Tune, Daniel Herbert,
Tim Horan, Joe Roff, Stephen Larkham, George Gregan,
Tiaan Strauss, David Wilson, Matt Cockbain, John Eales (c),
David Giffin, Andrew Blades, Michael Foley, Richard Harry.
Reserves: Jason Little, Nathan Grey, Chris Whitaker, Mark Connors,
Owen Finegan, Dan Crowley, Jeremy Paul.

WALES: Shane Howarth, Gareth Thomas, Mark Taylor, Scott Gibbs,
Dafydd James, Neil Jenkins, Rob Howley (c), Scott Quinnell,
Brett Sinkinson, Colin Charvis, Chris Wyat, Craig Quinnell,
David Young, Garin Jenkins, Peter Rogers. *Reserves:* Stephen Jones,
Allan Bateman, David Llewellyn, Mike Voyle, Ben Evans,
Andrew Lewis, Jonathan Humphreys.

AUSTRALIA 24 (George Gregan 2, Ben Tune tries;
Matthew Burke 3 conversions, penalty goal) def **WALES 9**
(Neil Jenkins 3 penalty goals).
Halftime: Australia 10–9.

October 24
QUARTER FINAL

SOUTH AFRICA v ENGLAND
at Stade de France, Paris

SOUTH AFRICA: Percy Montgomery, Deon Kayser, Robbie Fleck, Pieter Muller, Pieter Rossouw, Jannie de Beer, Joost van der Westhuizen (c), Bob Skinstad, Andre Venter, Johan Erasmus, Mark Andrews, Krynauw Otto, Cobus Visagie, Naka Drotske, Os du Randt. *Reserves:* Stefan Terblanche, Henry Honiball, Werner Swanepoel, Andre Vos, Albert van den Berg, Ollie le Roux, Chris Rossouw.

ENGLAND: Matt Perry, Dan Luger, Will Greenwood, Phil de Glanville, Nick Beal, Paul Grayson, Matt Dawson, Lawrence Dallaglio, Neil Back, Richard Hill, Danny Grewcock, Martin Johnson (c), Phil Vickery, Phil Greening, Jason Leonard. *Reserves:* Austin Healey, Mike Catt, Jonny Wilkinson, Tim Rodber, Martin Corry, Darren Garforth, Richard Cockerill.

SOUTH AFRICA 44 (Joost van der Westhuizen, Pieter Rossouw tries; Jannie de Beer 2 conversions, 5 penalty goals, 5 dropped goals) def **ENGLAND 21** (Paul Grayson 6 penalty goals, Jonny Wilkinson penalty goal).
Halftime: South Africa 16–12.

October 24
QUARTER FINAL

➤

FRANCE v ARGENTINA
at Lansdowne Road, Dublin

FRANCE: Xavier Garbajosa, Philippe Bernat-Salles,
Richard Dourthe, Emile N'Tamack, Christophe Dominici,
Christophe Lamaison, Fabien Galthie, Christophe Juillet,
Olivier Magne, Marc Lievremont, Olivier Brouzet, Abdel Benazzi,
Franck Tournaire, Raphael Ibanez (c), Cedric Soulette.
Reserves: Ugo Mola, Stephane Glas, Stephane Castaignede,
Arnaud Costes, David Auradou, Pieter de Villiers, Marc Dal Maso.

ARGENTINA: Ignacio Corletto, Gonzalo Camardon,
Eduardo Simone, Lisandro Arbizu (c), Diego Albanese,
Gonzalo Quesada, Augustin Pichot, Gonzalo Longo,
Rolando Martin, Santiago Phelan, Alejandro Allub, Ignacio
Fernandez Lobbe, Mauricio Reggiardo, Mario Ledesma,
Roberto Grau. *Reserves:* Manuel Contepomi, Felipe Contepomi,
Nicolas Fernandez Miranda, Miguel Ruiz, Lucas Ostiglia,
Martin Scelzo, Agustin Canalda.

FRANCE 47 (Philippe Bernat-Salles 2, Xavier Garbajosa 2,
Emile N'Tamack tries; Christophe Lamaison 5 conversions,
4 penalty goals) def **ARGENTINA 26** (Augustin Pichot, Lisandro
Arbizu tries; Gonzalo Quesada 2 conversions, 3 penalty goals,
Felipe Contepomi penalty goal).
Halftime: France 27-20.

October 24
QUARTER FINAL

NEW ZEALAND v SCOTLAND
at Murrayfield, Edinburgh

NEW ZEALAND: Jeff Wilson, Tana Umaga, Christian Cullen, Alama Ieremia, Jonah Lomu, Andrew Mehrtens, Justin Marshall, Taine Randell (c), Josh Kronfeld, Reuben Thorne, Robin Brooke, Norm Maxwell, Craig Dowd, Anton Oliver, Carl Hoeft.
Reserves: Daryl Gibson, Tony Brown, Byron Kelleher, Andrew Blowers, Ian Jones, Kees Meeuws, Mark Hammett.

SCOTLAND: Glenn Metcalfe, Cameron Murray, Alan Tait, Jamie Mayer, Kenny Logan, Gregor Townsend, Gary Armstrong (c), Gordon Simpson, Budge Pountney, Martin Leslie, Doddie Weir, Scott Murray, Paul Burnell, Gordon Bulloch, Tom Smith.
Reserves: James McLaren, Duncan Hodge, Bryan Redpath, Cameron Mather, Stuart Grimes, George Graham, Robert Russell.

NEW ZEALAND 30 (Tana Umaga 2, Jeff Wilson, Jonah Lomu tries; Andrew Mehrtens 2 conversions, 2 penalty goals)
def **SCOTLAND 18** (Budge Pountney, Cameron Murray tries; Kenny Logan conversion, penalty goal, Gregor Townsend dropped goal).
Halftime: New Zealand 25–3.

October 30
SEMI FINAL

AUSTRALIA v SOUTH AFRICA
at Twickenham, London

AUSTRALIA: Matthew Burke, Ben Tune, Daniel Herbert,
Tim Horan, Joe Roff, Stephen Larkham, George Gregan,
Toutai Kefu, David Wilson, Matt Cockbain, John Eales (c),
David Giffin, Andrew Blades, Michael Foley, Richard Harry.
Reserves: Jason Little, Nathan Grey, Chris Whitaker, Mark Connors,
Owen Finegan, Rod Moore, Jeremy Paul.

SOUTH AFRICA: Percy Montgomery, Deon Kayser,
Robbie Fleck, Pieter Muller, Pieter Rossouw, Jannie de Beer,
Joost van der Westhuizen (c), Bobby Skinstad, Andre Venter,
Johan Erasmus, Mark Andrews, Krynauw Otto, Cobus Visagie,
Naka Drotske, Os du Randt. *Reserves:* Stefan Terblanche,
Henry Honiball, Werner Swanepoel, Andre Vos, Albert van den Berg,
Ollie le Roux, Chris Rossouw.

AUSTRALIA 27 (Matthew Burke 8 penalty goals,
Stephen Larkham field goal) def **SOUTH AFRICA 21**
(Jannie de Beer 6 penalty goals, field goal).
Halftime: Australia 12–6. Fulltime: 18–all.

October 31
SEMI FINAL

FRANCE v NEW ZEALAND
at Twickenham, London

FRANCE: Xavier Garbajosa, Philippe Bernat-Salles, Richard Dourthe, Emile N'Tamack, Christophe Dominici, Christophe Lamaison, Fabien Galthie, Christophe Juillet, Olivier Magne, Marc Lievremont, Fabien Pelous, Abdel Benazzi, Franck Tournaire, Raphael Ibanez (c), Cedric Soulette.
Reserves: Ugo Mola, Stephane Glas, Stephane Castaignede, Arnaud Costes, Olivier Brouzet, Pieter de Villiers, Marc Dal Maso.

NEW ZEALAND: Jeff Wilson, Tana Umaga, Christian Cullen, Alama Ieremia, Jonah Lomu, Andrew Mehrtens, Byron Kelleher, Taine Randell (c), Josh Kronfeld, Reuben Thorne, Robin Brooke, Norm Maxwell, Craig Dowd, Anton Oliver, Carl Hoeft.
Reserves: Daryl Gibson, Tony Brown, Justin Marshall, Andrew Blowers, Royce Willis, Kees Meeuws, Mark Hammett.

FRANCE 43 (Christophe Lamaison, Christophe Dominici, Richard Dourthe, Philippe Bernat-Salles tries; Lamaison 4 conversions, 3 penalty goals, 2 dropped goals)
def **NEW ZEALAND 31** (Jonah Lomu 2, Jeff Wilson tries; Andrew Mehrtens 2 conversions, 4 penalty goals).
Halftime: New Zealand 17-10.

November 4
THIRD PLACE PLAYOFF

SOUTH AFRICA v NEW ZEALAND
at Millennium Stadium, Cardiff

SOUTH AFRICA: Percy Montgomery, Breyton Paulse, Robbie Fleck, Pieter Muller, Stefan Terblanche, Henry Honiball, Joost van der Westhuizen (c), Andre Vos, Andre Venter, Johan Erasmus, Mark Andrews, Krynauw Otto, Cobus Visagie, Naka Drotske, Os du Randt. *Reserves:* Wayne Julies, Jannie de Beer, Werner Swanepoel, Ruben Kruger, Albert van den Berg, Ollie le Roux, Chris Rossouw.

NEW ZEALAND: Jeff Wilson, Tana Umaga, Christian Cullen, Alama Ieremia, Jonah Lomu, Andrew Mehrtens, Justin Marshall, Taine Randell (c), Josh Kronfeld, Reuben Thorne, Royce Willis, Norm Maxwell, Kees Meeuws, Mark Hammett, Craig Dowd. *Reserves:* Pita Alatini, Tony Brown, Rhys Duggan, Dylan Mika, Ian Jones, Carl Hoeft, Anton Oliver.

SOUTH AFRICA 22 (Breyton Paulse try, Henry Honiball conversion, 3 penalty goals, Percy Montgomery 2 dropped goals) def **NEW ZEALAND 18** (Andrew Mehrtens 6 penalty goals). *Halftime:* South Africa 16-12.

November 6
FINAL

AUSTRALIA v FRANCE
at Millennium Stadium, Cardiff

AUSTRALIA: Matthew Burke, Ben Tune, Daniel Herbert, Tim Horan, Joe Roff, Stephen Larkham, George Gregan, Toutai Kefu, David Wilson, Matt Cockbain, John Eales (c), David Giffin, Andrew Blades, Michael Foley, Richard Harry. *Reserves:* Jason Little, Nathan Grey, Chris Whitaker, Mark Connors, Owen Finegan, Dan Crowley, Jeremy Paul.

FRANCE: Xavier Garbajosa, Philippe Bernat-Salles, Richard Dourthe, Emile N'Tamack, Christophe Dominici, Christophe Lamaison, Fabien Galthie, Christophe Juillet, Olivier Magne, Marc Lievremont, Fabien Pelous, Abdel Benazzi, Franck Tournaire, Raphael Ibanez (c), Cedric Soulette. *Reserves:* Ugo Mola, Stephane Glas, Stephane Castaignede, Arnaud Costes, Olivier Brouzet, Pieter de Villiers, Marc Dal Maso.

AUSTRALIA 35 (Ben Tune, Owen Finegan tries; Matthew Burke 2 conversions, 7 penalty goals) def **FRANCE 12** (Christophe Lamaison 4 penalty goals). *Halftime:* Australia 12–6.

AUSTRALIA

Played:	6
Won:	6
Points For:	221
Points Against:	73
Tries Scored:	24
Tries Conceded:	1

FINAL POOL STANDINGS
(Played, Won, Drawn, Lost, Points For, Points Against, Total)

Pool A

	P	W	D	L	PF	PA	T
South Africa	3	3	—	—	132	35	9
Scotland	3	2	—	1	120	58	7
Uruguay	3	1	—	2	42	97	5
Spain	3	—	—	3	18	122	3

Pool B

	P	W	D	L	PF	PA	T
New Zealand	3	3	—	—	176	28	9
England	3	2	—	1	184	47	7
Tonga	3	1	—	2	47	171	5
Italy	3	—	—	3	35	196	3

Pool C

	P	W	D	L	PF	PA	T
France	3	3	—	—	108	52	9
Fiji	3	2	—	1	124	68	7
Canada	3	1	—	2	114	82	5
Namibia	3	—	—	3	42	186	3

Pool D

	P	W	D	L	PF	PA	T
Wales	3	2	—	1	118	71	7
Samoa	3	2	—	1	97	72	7
Argentina	3	2	—	1	83	51	7
Japan	3	—	—	3	36	140	3

Pool E

	P	W	D	L	PF	PA	T
Australia	3	3	—	—	135	31	9
Ireland	3	2	—	1	100	45	7
Romania	3	1	—	2	50	126	5
USA	3	—	—	3	52	135	3

AUSTRALIAN POINTS SCORERS
(Tries, Conversions, Penalty Goals, Dropped Goals, Total)

	T	C	PG	DG	T
Matt Burke	2	17	19	—	101
Toutai Kefu	3	—	—	—	15
Ben Tune	3	—	—	—	15
Joe Roff	2	1	—	—	12
Tim Horan	2	—	—	—	10
George Gregan	2	—	—	—	10
Scott Staniforth	2	—	—	—	10
Stephen Larkham	1	—	—	1	8
Jason Little	1	—	—	—	5
Chris Latham	1	—	—	—	5
Tiaan Strauss	1	—	—	—	5
Michael Foley	1	—	—	—	5
Owen Finegan	1	—	—	—	5
Chris Whitaker	1	—	—	—	5
Jeremy Paul	1	—	—	—	5
John Eales	—	1	1	—	5

LEADING TOURNAMENT POINTS SCORERS

Gonzalo Quesada (Argentina) 102; Matt Burke (Australia) 101; Jannie de Beer (South Africa) 97; Andrew Mehrtens (New Zealand) 79; Christophe Lamaison (France) 65; Neil Jenkins (Wales) 57; Paul Grayson (England) 54; Kenny Logan (Scotland) 51; Gareth Rees (Canada) 49; Richard Dourthe (France) 45

WorldCup **statistics**

LEADING TRY SCORERS

Jonah Lomu (New Zealand) 8; Jeff Wilson (New Zealand) 6; Keith Wood (Ireland) 4;
Dan Lugar (England) 4; Viliame Satala (Fiji) 4; Philippe Bernat-Salles (France) 4;
Toutai Kefu (Australia) 3; Joe Roff (Australia) 3; Ben Tune (Australia) 3;
Joost van der Westhuizen (South Africa) 3.

TOURNAMENT HIGHS

Highest score: 101 New Zealand v Italy, 101 England v Tonga
Most points in a match: 36 Tony Brown (NZ v Italy),
         36 Paul Grayson (England v Tonga)
Most tries in a match: 14 New Zealand v Italy
Most tries by individual in a match: 4 Keith Wood (Ireland v USA)
Most conversions in a match: 12 Paul Grayson (England v Tonga)
Most conversions in tournament: 17 Matt Burke (Australia)
Most penalties in a match: 8 Matt Burke (Australia v South Africa)
Most penalties in tournament: 31 Gonzalo Quesada (Argentina)

PLAYERS PLAYER AWARD 1999
(Voted by the Wallabies on a 5-4-3-2-1 basis)

Tim Horan 409pts; Toutai Kefu 320; Daniel Herbert 216; Joe Roff 209;
David Giffin 204; George Gregan 195; David Wilson 192; Matt Cockbain 188; Matt
Burke 159; Andrew Blades 141; Ben Tune 138.

Man of the match awards on player votes: v Ireland (1st Test) Daniel Herbert; v Ireland
2nd Test) Tim Horan; v England (Centenary Test) Joe Roff; v South Africa (Brisbane)
Tim Horan ; v New Zealand (Auckland) Daniel Herbert; v South Africa (Cape Town)
Matt Cockbain; v New Zealand (Sydney) Toutai Kefu; v; Romania (World Cup)
Toutai Kefu; v Ireland (World Cup) Toutai Kefu ; v USA (World Cup) Scott Staniforth;
v Wales (World Cup) Andrew Blades; v South Africa; (World Cup) Tim Horan; v France
(World Cup) Tim Horan.